This is a book about some of the basic concepts of metaphysics: universals, particulars, causality, and possibility. Its aim is to give an account of the real constituents of the world.

The author defends a realistic view of universals, characterizing the notion of universal by considering language and logic, possibility, hierarchies of universals, and causation. On the other hand, he argues that logic and language are not reliable guides to the nature of reality. All assertions and predications about the natural world are ultimately founded on "basic universals", which are the fundamental type of universal and central to causation. A distinction is drawn between unified particulars (which have a natural principle of unity) and arbitrary particulars (which lack such a principle); unified particulars are the terms of causal relations and thus real constituents of the world. Arbitrary particulars such as events, states of affairs, and sets have no ontological significance.

CAMBRIDGE STUDIES IN PHILOSOPHY

The physical basis of predication

CAMBRIDGE STUDIES IN PHILOSOPHY

General editor ERNEST SOSA

Advisory editors J. E. J. ALTHAM, SIMON BLACKBURN,
GILBERT HARMAN, MARTIN HOLLIS, FRANK JACKSON,
WILLIAM G. LYCAN, JOHN PERRY,
SYDNEY SHOEMAKER, BARRY STROUD

RECENT TITLES

FLINT SCHIER Deeper into pictures
ANTHONY APPIAH Assertion and conditionals
ROBERT BROWN Analyzing love
ROBERT M. GORDON The structure of emotions
FRANÇOIS RECANTI Meaning and force
WILLIAM G. LYCAN Judgement and justification
GERALD DWORKIN The theory and practice of autonomy
MICHAEL TYE The metaphysics of mind
DAVID O. BRINK Moral realism and the foundations of ethics
W. D. HART Engines of the soul
PAUL K. MOSER Knowledge and evidence
D. M. ARMSTRONG A Combinatorial theory of possibility
JOHN BISHOP Natural agency
CHRISTOPHER J. MALONEY The mundane matter of the mental language
MARK RICHARD Propositional attitudes
GERALD F. GAUS Value and justification
MARK HELLER The ontology of physical objects
JOHN BIGELOW AND ROBERT PARGETTER Science and necessity
FRANCIS SNARE Morals, motivation and convention
CHRISTOPHER S. HILL Sensations
JOHN HEIL The nature of true minds

The physical basis of predication

Andrew Newman

University of Nebraska at Omaha

CAMBRIDGE
UNIVERSITY PRESS

Published by the Press Syndicate of the University of Cambridge
The Pitt Building, Trumpington Street, Cambridge CB2 1RP
40 West 20th Street, New York, NY 10011-4211, USA
10 Stamford Road, Oakleigh, Victoria 3166, Australia

First published 1992

Printed in the United States of America

Library of Congress Cataloging-in-Publication Data
Newman, Andrew.
The physical basis of predication / Andrew Newman.
p. cm. – (Cambridge studies in philosophy)
Includes bibliographical references and index.
ISBN 0-521-41131-9
1. Universals (Philosophy) 2. Individuation (Philosophy)
3. Causation. I. Title. II. Series.
B105.U5N49 1992
111'.2 – dc20 92-3118
CIP

A catalogue record for this book is available from the British Library.

ISBN 0-521-41131-9 hardback

Contents

Acknowledgements   *page* vii
Introduction   ix

Chapter 1   "Real constituents of the world"   1
            1. A basis for predication   1
            2. The notion of particular and the notion
               of universal   5

Chapter 2   What can logic and language tell us
            about reality?   12
            1. The syntactic priority thesis   12
            2. Interpretations of logic   14
            3. Quine and quantification   26
            4. Quantification from another point of view   35
            5. Ontology and language   37
            6. Abstract things   39

Chapter 3   The "existence" of universals and the notion
            of possibility   41
            1. Universals and possibility   41
            2. Armstrong's instantiation requirement   43
            3. Arguments against the instantiation
               requirement   46
            4. Combinatorial theories of possibility   52
            5. Wittgenstein's theory of possibility   59
            6. Possible worlds   69

Chapter 4   The causal significance of basic attributes   73
            1. Basic universals   73
            2. Ontological determinacy   74
            3. Causality and basic attributes   82

v

4. Structural universals 87
5. Natural kind universals 93

Chapter 5 Hierarchies of universals 100
1. Determinates and determinables 100
2. Geach's function theory of hierarchies 102
3. The hierarchy of colour concepts 110
4. Essential subordination 113
5. Mass universals 121
6. The basis of higher-level attributes 127
7. What is a concept? 134

Chapter 6 Causal relations 136
1. Real relations 136
2. Spatial relations 143
3. Causal relations 147
4. Types of causal relation 149

Chapter 7 Arbitrary particulars and unified particulars 165
1. The distinction 165
2. Events 168
3. Arguments against events 170
4. Causality and continuity 178
5. Summary of why events are not terms
of causal relations 183

Chapter 8 Further considerations concerning the
causal relation 185
1. The logical form of sentences about causality 185
2. The ontology of causality 189
3. Causal relations and natural laws 195
4. Causality and counterfactual conditionals 200

Chapter 9 Arbitrary particulars and physical objects 208
1. Sets as arbitrary particulars 208
2. Parcels of matter 218
3. Physical objects 226
4. Supervenience 234
5. The construction of particulars 239

Bibliography 257
Index 265

vi

Acknowledgements

I should like to express my gratitude to John Watling for his help and support during the years I was developing these ideas and particularly for reading and commenting on part of this work. David Armstrong read an earlier version, and I benefited a great deal from his criticisms. I am also grateful to Travis Burton Copeland and Edward Becker for a number of helpful discussions and to the anonymous reader for Cambridge University Press for his or her extensive criticism. My revision of the book during the summer of 1991 was supported by a summer fellowship awarded by the University Committee on Research of the University of Nebraska at Omaha. Finally I should like to thank Elizabeth, Zack, Sarah and Annie for their support and encouragement.

Introduction

The aim of this book is to give an account of which things are the "real constituents of the world". The account is based, to begin with, on a characterization of the notion of universal. It also attempts to decide which particulars are real constituents of the world, and in doing so argues against events, and things like events, in a number of different ways. The focus is on causality, particularly the notion of causal relation, as a guide to what is real.

The central theme is that the natural world is a world of particulars and universals as understood by immanent realism. In order to make that more precise, I argue that it is special sorts of universals – namely, basic universals – and special sorts of particulars – namely, unified particulars – which are the real constituents of the world. It is not part of my intention to show that immanent realism is the correct theory of universals, since there are other works that do that, notably Armstrong's. In the course of the discussion, however, arguments will be given that will show the superiority of that theory. The work should be regarded as being in the area of metaphysics or general ontology; epistemology and semantics will, on the whole, be avoided. My interest is in how things are, not in how we come to know how they are. I hope the conclusions can serve as metaphysical foundations for scientific realism, while avoiding attachment to any particular scientific theory.

The discussion of universals has two aims, the first of which is to give an account of the nature of universals. The notion of universal is conceptually difficult, controversial, and in need of explanation. The sort of explanation offered is really a characterization: It is given in terms of such things as the multiple occurrence of universals, the structure of logic and language, the notion of possibility, hierarchies of universals, and causality. In the course of the discussion of language and logic, I argue that neither is a reliable guide to the nature of reality, despite the fact that they can be used to give a partial characterization of the notion of universal.

The second aim is to introduce the notion of "basic universal" as the fundamental type of universal. In the language of determinates and determinables, they are perfectly determinate, non-conjunctive universals. They determine how a particular is in a certain respect without any possibility for further details to be given about how the particular is in that respect. They are not general universals, since they do not classify other universals. I suggest that all assertions and predications about the natural world are ultimately based on these basic universals; they are the physical basis of predication of the title. In this sense – that is, with respect to universals – my theory is a form of metaphysical atomism.

In my discussion of which things are real, my starting point is the notion of basic attribute, where a basic attribute is monadic, attributive basic universal. Not all predicates correspond to universals, and among universals only some are what I call basic attributes. The notion of a basic attribute can be given a fairly general characterization that does provide motivation for regarding basic attributes as being of primary ontological significance. Which things are in fact examples of basic attributes, however, has to be agreed *a posteriori*. This is explained in Chapter 4. I argue that things such as the simple shapes and the simple properties of physics (e.g. mass and charge) satisfy the account just given of basic attributes. It is also generally accepted that these attributes are causally significant, if anything is, so they can be taken as real constituents of the world.

In the same way that their significance in causality is one of the reasons for singling out basic attributes as being of primary importance, it is causality that motivates my preference for unified particulars. I suggest that particulars can be divided into two sorts: arbitrary particulars and unified particulars. Unified particulars are particulars that have a natural principle of unity, such as our familiar material objects. Arbitrary particulars, on the other hand, do not have a natural principle of unity: What makes them units is the choices of human beings. The examples of arbitrary particulars that I consider are sets, events, and parcels of matter. I argue that only unified particulars are the terms of causal relations, so it is unified particulars that are real constituents of the world. Our world then is a world of unified particulars and basic universals – monadic, dyadic, and so on. The ontology developed in this work differs, therefore, from Armstrong's in that it is sparser and more economical: We do without such things as events, facts, and states of affairs.

Particulars such as events do not possess basic attributes; for example, it seems fairly clear that they do not possess mass or energy, and consequently do not enter into causal relations. This is not the only reason for thinking that events are not the terms of causal relations, and in fact in the course of this work I shall give a number of different reasons that fall into five main groups (summarized at the end of Chapter 7).

In the end, I single out three types of thing as having primary ontological significance: unified particulars, basic attributes and relations, and causal relations. Causal relations are a type of basic universal that has a special place in my ontology. Each of these three types of thing figures in a causal situation in a different way.

In our description of the natural world, we do not always use predicates that signify basic universals. And the more complicated forms that we do use do not always represent an arbitrary way of thinking about basic universals. Basic universals have an ontologically significant structure, and there are relations between them that are also ontologically significant. So it is not true that only predications involving basic universals are ontologically significant.

I consider only two examples of these predications that have a more complex basis. Firstly, I consider natural kind terms, suggest that they refer to universals, and discuss briefly the basis natural kinds have in basic universals. Secondly, I consider higher-level universals, which raises the old problem of determinates and determinables. Higher-level universals are universals that are more general than basic universals and can be said to classify them. My position is that higher-level universals are properties of particulars, not of lower-level universals, and that the relation between a lower-level universal and the corresponding higher-level universal is an internal relation, which I call 'essential subordination'.

The final picture I present of the world shows it as primarily a world of basic universals and unified particulars, which are rightly called real constituents of the world, but it includes other things such as natural kind universals, higher-level universals, and relations between universals, which are also ontologically significant. This is a two-tier ontology: There are the real constituents of the world, basic universals and unified particulars, which are in a sense isolable, and then there are structural features of those real constituents, which are ontologically significant in a secondary way.

1

"Real constituents of the world"

1. A BASIS FOR PREDICATION

Although the notion of particular is in need of some refinement, it can perhaps be accepted that the basic idea of a particular is familiar and not controversial. Certainly anyone today who wished to deny that there are particulars would have a lot of explaining to do. It is different with universals. The immanent realists' notion of universal is a metaphysician's idea, which not everyone regards as intuitively acceptable. But if, with Russell and Moore, we regard universals as "real constituents of the world", along with particulars, we shall have to give an account of the notion of universal. It will have to be an account that brings out the way in which a universal is a real thing, something ontologically significant.

Frege notes that fundamental notions such as "concept", and we may add "universal", cannot have proper definitions. With such fundamental notions, "there is nothing for it but to lead the reader or hearer, by means of hints, to understand the words as intended".[1] What can be said about fundamental notions Frege calls an 'explanation'; alternatively, it could be called a 'characterization'. Our first aim, then, is to discuss a number of ways of characterizing the notion of universal that bring out the way in which a universal is a real constituent of the world.

It is not the aim of this book to show directly that the immanent realist theory of universals is correct. It will be assumed that others, such as Armstrong, have done that.[2] We shall, however, in the course of our discussion have occasion to compare it with its most

1 Frege, "On Concept and Object", p. 183.
2 D. M. Armstrong, *Universals and Scientific Realism*, Volumes I & II, and *Universals, An Opinionated Introduction*; see also James Porter Moreland, *Universals, Qualities and Quality-Instances: A Defence of Realism*.

serious rivals such as Platonism, particularism, and extreme nominalism, and we shall take the occasion to show the merits of immanent realism.

In order to explain the fact that there are statements that contain relational terms, which are true and can be understood by us, Russell suggested that there really are such things as relations.[3] Russell's thought is that there must be some basis in reality for predication:

> Russell's argument requires only a narrower principle, which I shall henceforth call 'the Realist Principle'; namely, that primitive predicates occurring non-redundantly in the propositions denote real things, or, as Moore liked to say, 'real constituents of the world'. It is plain why Russell and Moore adhered to this principle. They could not conceive of how otherwise propositions containing primitive predicates could state facts about the world.[4]

As Donagan notes, it is not necessary to hold that all relational terms or all predicates correspond to universals. It is possible that a statement containing a certain predicate be true, not in virtue of a single universal corresponding directly to the predicate, but in virtue of the particular possessing a number of universals, none of which corresponds directly to the predicate. Donagan uses the term 'primitive predicate' for the predicates that do correspond directly to universals, while Russell calls predicates that do not, 'defined predicates'.

There are also predicates that are logical connectives, and predicates that signify what Wittgenstein called 'formal concepts'. The logical connectives could be understood in a truth-functional way, following Wittgenstein, which avoids regarding them as corresponding to something real. But however it is that formal concepts such as "individual", "particular", or "universal" are to be understood, it seems very difficult to regard them as elements of reality.

The doctrine that some predicates correspond to universals that are real constituents of the world is a version of realism. It is a form of immanent realism if it understands a universal as existing in a particular (i.e. as "inhering" in it), as opposed to transcendent realism, or Platonism, which understands a universal as having a singular, object-like existence in another realm.

It also seems intuitively plausible that there must be some basis in a particular for saying that a predicate is true of it. So the plausibility of realism derives partly from the problems associated with denying

3 Russell, *The Problems of Philosophy*, pp. 89–90.
4 Alan Donagan, "Universals and Metaphysical Realism", p. 133.

2

it: "If the ultimate non-logical and non-formal constituents of true propositions refer to nothing in the world, in what can the truth of such propositions consist?"[5] It is not possible to form sentences by joining together the names of particulars. There must always be some element in a sentence that is predicative and general. Therefore if there is to be some basis in the world (that is, in reality) for a sentence being true, there must be features of reality to which some predicates correspond.[6] Of course we never do regard particulars as devoid of features that make sentences true. They really do have shape and mass and so on. If there is anything unusual in drawing attention to these features, it is in making a metaphysical issue out of it.

Immanent realism also gains plausibility by contrast with its main rivals, extreme nominalism and transcendent realism. Extreme nominalists can hardly deny that particulars have features – that would sound too bizarre. What they have to deny is that those features have any ontological significance; they have to deny that such features are in any sense real constituents of the world. In order to do this extreme nominalists have to insist that it is only particulars that have any ontological significance. They have to say that there is only one way of being ontologically significant, and that is to be real in the way a particular is real. This position gains such plausibility as it has by focussing on the difficulties associated with the idea of a universal as an element of reality, since it is indeed difficult to conceive of something that can occur in many places at the same time.

Nominalism itself seems implausible, however, when we realize that what is being said is that there are no ontologically significant features of a particular in virtue of which sentences about the particular are true. It also seems implausible when we think about causality, for the nominalist is saying that particulars do not have ontologically significant features in virtue of which they interact causally with other particulars. Nominalism also has the related problem of explaining measurement. If objects do not have objective, ontologically significant features, then there is no explanation for measurements being objective.[7]

<hr>

5 Ibid.
6 This argument does not imply that every element of a sentence corresponds to a feature of reality, or that some predicate in every sentence corresponds to a feature of reality. Cf. Peter Geach, *Mental Acts*, p. 39.
7 Cf. Chris Swoyer, "The Metaphysics of Measurement".

The Platonist, or transcendent realist, is apparently impressed by the fact that a universal is independent of whether any particular exemplifies it or not. The existence of any particular is a contingent matter, and therefore whether a universal is instanced by it, or instanced at all, is also a contingent matter. On the other hand, it seems that whether there is a certain universal or not is an issue of a different order from whether it is exemplified or not. The Platonist is also impressed by the way a universal appears to be something singular and unique. Indeed, in language, terms that signify universals very often behave exactly like proper names. And it may be that it is linguistic considerations that really underlie Platonism.[8]

Nevertheless, there remains for the Platonist the same problem of what it is about a particular that makes it right to assert a certain predicate of it. If universals are singular and unique in the way that particulars are singular and unique, they cannot be inhabitants of this world. If it is also the case that to say that there is a certain universal is to make an ontologically significant statement, then we must "locate" universals in a world other than this one. But "locating" universals in another world leads to a very odd view of particulars. A particular would be merely "a meeting place of a variety of insubstantial, ghostly projections of other objects"[9] – the other objects being what the Platonist calls Forms. A Platonist, therefore, needs to give some account of how it is that a Form "projects into" a particular, since particular and Form must be related in some way. There must be some basis in the particular for saying that it participates in the Form.

Interpreters of Plato understand him as believing that the properties that exist in particulars are themselves particulars – in other words, that as far as the actual features of particulars go he holds to the doctrine Armstrong calls 'particularism':[10] "As a logical consequence of such participation a sensible particular thereby possesses (comes to have 'in it') an immanent character that is one particularization out of many of the Form participated in, and whose existence depends on that particular so participating (*Phaedo* 102a10–103a2)."[11] It seems that a Platonist needs a second theory of univer-

---

8 Cf. M. J. Loux, *Substance and Attribute*.
9 Mark L. McPherran, "Plato's Particulars", p. 528.
10 See Armstrong, Volume I, Chapter 8.
11 McPherran, "Plato's Particulars", p. 534.

sals to account for the actual features of particulars! Besides this difficulty there are the well-known problems associated with explaining the connection between the transcendent Forms and the immanent characters. These are the problems traditionally dealt with under the headings 'Separation' and 'Participation'.[12]

Particularism without Platonism is itself one of the main rivals of immanent realism. Like Platonism it also needs a second theory of universals to go with it. If the instances of universals are themselves particulars, then what is it about those secondary particulars, or "tropes", that makes us group them together in classes each corresponding to a predicate? "It seems that the full range of answers to this problem is open to the Particularist. Predicate, Concept, Class, Mereological and Resemblance Nominalism, Transcendent Forms and Aristotelian (Immanent) Realism, all seem to be *prima facie* answers."[13] The original problem was to explain what it was about ordinary particulars that makes it right to assert the same predicate of them. Particularists displace this problem without any real gain. They have to explain what it is about tropes that makes it right to assert the same predicate of the particulars that possess them.

It seems that the motivation behind particularism is essentially nominalist. Particularists seem to think the only way something can be ontologically significant is if it is a particular. They therefore face serious difficulties explaining what it is about a trope that makes a predicate apply to the particular it belongs to. If a trope is itself a particular, does it have features, and if it does have features, are those features ontologically significant? Whichever route is taken there are difficulties.[14]

2. THE NOTION OF PARTICULAR AND THE NOTION OF UNIVERSAL

So far our discussion has focussed on the notion of reality. The terms 'element of reality' and 'ontological significance' have been used,

---

12 For criticism of Platonism see Armstrong, Volume I, Chapter 7.
13 Armstrong, Volume I, p. 83.
14 For further criticism of particularism see Chapter 4, Section 4, Chapter 5, Section 2, Chapter 6, Section 1, and Chapter 9, Section 5. See also Armstrong, Volume I, Chapter 8; G. E. Moore, "Are the Characteristics of Particular Things Universal or Particular?"; and Moreland, *Universals, Qualities and Quality-Instances*. For a recent defence of particularism see Keith Campbell, *Abstract Particulars*, and for recent sympathy, Armstrong, *Universals, an Opinionated Introduction*.

perhaps inevitably, without any detailed explanation of what they mean. In order to explain what it is about particulars that makes sentences true, it has been argued that they possess features that are ontologically significant, but not in the way a particular itself is ontologically significant. It is sufficient for the present, however, that those arguments show there are other things besides particulars that are ontologically significant. They show, for example, that the nominalists' naive conception of reality needs to be replaced by something more sophisticated.

Unlike particulars, universals can be ontologically significant in two different ways. A universal can be ontologically significant if it is exemplified by some particular, and a universal can be ontologically significant if it is true to say that there is such a universal. It should be clear that each of these modes is of ontological significance and that each must be understood on its own terms. Unfortunately, ordinary language is of little help to someone who wants to talk about universals. Sometimes it seems best suited to the nominalist, though I do not think that fact is evidence for nominalism. Throughout this book I shall try to stick to certain locutions. I shall mainly talk about a universal as occurring, and sometimes as being instanced or exemplified; and I shall usually say that "there is a certain universal", rather than that a universal "subsists" or "has being", as Russell put it.[15]

The reason for separating these two ways in which a universal can be ontologically significant is the possibility of unexemplified universals. It is possible for a sentence to be true even though it contains a predicate which signifies an unexemplified universal. It is possible, for example, that there is a relation, $R,$ such that $-(\exists x)(\exists y)xRy$.[16] Not only is it possible for such sentences to be true, but it is possible for us to understand them, even if the universal never has been and never will be instanced. For example, we know what is being said when it is denied that a certain particular is regular chiliagon-shaped, even though that shape probably never has been instanced and probably never will be. There is such a universal as regular chiliagon-shaped; it is merely that it is not in-

15 See Russell, *The Problems of Philosophy,* p. 100, where he sometimes appears to be a Platonist.
16 For a discussion of Russell's attempt to escape from this problem using the principle of acquaintance, see Donagan, "Universals and Metaphysical Realism", pp. 134–5.

6

stanced. The issue of what it is to say that there is a certain universal will be taken up in Chapter 3.

Although there may be some difficulty in explaining what is meant by saying that there is a certain universal, it seems, at first sight, that there are no such difficulties associated with saying there is a certain particular. This is probably true if we confine ourselves to material objects. Everyone is supposed to know what it is for a material object to exist, since material objects are the paradigm case of existence: "Material bodies must be the basic particulars", as Strawson put it in a somewhat different context.[17] Material objects are not, however, the only things that are particulars. Sets, events, and parcels of matter are also particulars, though the ontological status of these sorts of particulars is not clear. A consideration of the ontological status of these different sorts of particulars will help us make a start on the notion of ontological significance in general.

Although the criterion of identity for sets is clear, it is not clear what a set is. A set of material objects can be formed by choosing material objects at random. The principle of unity of such a randomly chosen set is whatever it is that makes those randomly chosen things to be a single thing – namely, a set. It seems clear that such a set has an arbitrary principle of unity. Even if the members of a set are all the individuals that fall under a certain concept, the set as a set still has an arbitrary principle of unity, since the principle of unity must be the same for all sets. We may understand what it is for a material object to exist, but it is not at all clear what sort of ontological commitment is involved in saying that a set of material objects exists. And the matter becomes even more difficult when we consider sets whose numbers are not material objects.[18]

An event is something that happens, and sometimes the state of something at a certain time is also taken to be an event. To specify a point event we have to specify an object, a time, and the properties of the object that we have chosen to highlight. To specify an event that is a change of properties we have to specify an object, an interval of time, and the initial and final properties that are related to the change we are interested in. If we follow Strawson in thinking there are bare events (that is, events without an object that possesses

17 P. F. Strawson, *Individuals*, p. 39.
18 For further discussion of sets see Chapter 9, Section 1. If you think sets are abstract objects and not particulars, think of collections or aggregates of material objects.

the properties concerned), then we need to specify a space–time region and the properties which we are interested in.[19] There are many who think events are ontologically significant, on account of their supposed involvement in causality, for example, but whatever sort of ontological significance they may possess it is not the same as that of material objects.[20]

If a gold coin is melted down and the gold from the coin made into a gold ring, then the matter, which remains the same matter throughout the transformation, is called a parcel of matter. The identity of a material object through time involves its maintaining something like the same shape. But the identity of a parcel of matter through time is independent of any shape it might assume. It merely depends on whether it is the same matter or not, so that matter itself is seen as having a type of identity through time.

The notion of parcel of matter leads to a fairly obvious difficulty. Where we thought we had one particular it now seems that we have two particulars with different identity conditions, a material object and a parcel of matter.[21] Whatever solutions to this problem we come up with, or whatever form of words we adopt to describe this situation, it cannot be the case that the material object and the parcel of matter have the same ontological significance.[22]

We have, then, three different sorts of particulars in addition to material objects, namely, sets, events, and parcels of matter. They differ from each other in ontological status, and they all differ from material objects in ontological status. Therefore to say that something is a particular does not carry with it a great deal of ontological commitment. What they share with material objects is a certain sort of uniqueness. Sets, events, and parcels of matter are like material objects in that they can occur only once for a given instant of time. Although none of these has the same ontological status as material objects, they do have the same sort of uniqueness that material objects have.

To say that a particular can occur only once is not a definition of a particular, since definitions are ruled out, but it is an important part of the characterization of the notion of particular. The word 'occur' does not mean "exist" in the sense in which a material object

19 Cf. Strawson, *Individuals*, p. 46.
20 For further discussion of events see Chapter 7, Sections 1–3.
21 Cf. Locke, *An Essay concerning Human Understanding*, II, xxvii, 3.
22 For further discussion of parcels of matter see Chapter 9, Section 2.

8

exists. Something occurs if it is to be found in the familiar spatio-temporal world. The word 'occur' is a primitive term that covers the modes of occurrence of all the sorts of particulars we have considered.

We can now turn to universals and say that a universal can occur many times for a given instant of time. This likewise is not a definition of a universal, since definitions are ruled out, but it is a central part of the characterization of the notion of universal. As with particulars the use of the word 'occur' does not by itself carry a great deal of ontological commitment.

The phenomenon of the multiple occurrence of universals is a familiar one. The shape one object possesses can be possessed by another object, or indeed any number of objects. We are only too happy to say that they all have the same shape, or that the same shape is to be found in many places. This is really all there is to something occurring many times.

Two objects are qualitatively identical if they are the same in a certain respect. The notion of qualitative identity is merely another way of looking at the notion of multiple occurrence; it is the reverse side of the coin. For nominalists the notion of qualitative identity is incoherent, since for them the only sort of identity that makes any sense is numerical identity. On the other hand, it is true that qualitative identity is "literally inexplicable, in the sense that it cannot be further explained. But that does not make it incoherent. Identity in nature entails that the universe is unified in a way that the Nominalist finds unintuitive. But I take that to be simply the fault of the Nominalists' intuitions."[23] To show that the notion of qualitative identity is incoherent it would have to be shown that it led to a contradiction. The most obvious way of doing this would be to try to show that there was something contradictory in the very notion of something, that is one thing, that can occur many times. The point would be that a universal is a unity and at the same time not a unity. For this argument to work it would have to be maintained that the immanent realist is trying to say that a universal can occur only once and also can occur many times. In this way it could perhaps be argued that there is a strict contradiction.

One answer to this objection would be to say that a universal occurs once in one way, and many times in another way, and since the

23 Armstrong, Volume I, p. 109.

two modes of occurrence are different there is no contradiction. It is difficult to assess this answer without knowing something about the ontological significance of the two modes of occurrence proposed. On the surface, however, it looks like a form of Platonism where the universal occurs once as a Form, and occurs many times as instances of that Form.[24] There would indeed be something very odd about a universal occurring once as a unity, in the same world as, and alongside, its multiple occurrences, so Platonists suggest that a universal occurs once as a unity in a world totally different and separate from this one. But this move itself suggests that there is something wrong with the notion of two sorts of occurrence.

The immanent realist, however, does not believe that a universal occurs in two different ways. A universal occurs in only one way and that is the way in which it is found in particulars. In this way the immanent realist avoids Platonism and contradictions. A universal may be a unity in a sense, but it is not a unity in the sense that it occurs once in the way a particular does. What an immanent realist is maintaining is that a universal is *one thing that can occur many times,* and that there is nothing contradictory or incoherent about such a notion. Like the notion of qualitative identity it cannot be explained any further.

It is true that there are predicates that can only apply to one individual, but whether universals correspond to them is another issue altogether. For instance, the predicate 'is identical with Socrates' seems to correspond to something predicative, which by its very nature can occur only once. It is not at all clear, however, that the predicate does in fact correspond to a universal, or real constituent of the world. In fact, Morris and Armstrong argue strongly that it does not.[25]

Predicates such as the 'being the smallest planet' are complicated, involving a kind term and an adjective, quite apart from the supposition of uniqueness that has to be built into the logical form. My strategy, however, will be to start with simple attributes that will function as a base. In the first place the characterization of *can occur only once* applies to them. If it could be shown that these unique application predicates correspond to universals, then I would have to

---

24 See McPherran, "Plato's Particulars".
25 Cf. Thomas V. Morris, *Understanding Identity Statements,* Chapter 1, and Armstrong, Volume II, p. 11.

restrict my characterization to simple attributes. I do not think, however, that it can be shown that they do correspond to universals.[26]

The notion of a thing that can occur only once and the notion of a thing that can occur many times are basic metaphysical notions, if fairly thin ones.[27] It is conceivable that there are things that can occur only twice, but as far as I can tell there are no such things, and it seems that the idea of something that can occur only twice is of no ontological significance. So for all practical purposes, the distinction between things that can occur only once and things that can occur many times is an exhaustive distinction. A thing is either one or the other.[28]

26 Cf. Armstrong's discussion of relational properties, Volume II, pp. 78ff.
27 Cf. Russell, "On the Relations of Universals and Particulars", pp. 106–7, and A. J. Ayer, "Individuals", pp. 8–11. Unlike Russell I am not considering things that are not in any place, and I think that some relations do exist in space.
28 If our ontology were closely tied to language it could be argued that there are things that are sometimes particulars and sometimes universals, since there are terms that are sometimes subjects and sometimes predicates. But metaphysically, no sense can be made of a protean thing that on some occasions "can occur only once" and other occasions "can occur more than once". Such a metamorphosis is not consistent with identity through time.

2

What can logic and language tell us about reality?

1. THE SYNTACTIC PRIORITY THESIS

Some philosophers have held that language, which is taken to include logic, is the only guide we have to the nature of the world. Russell divided philosophers into three classes on the issue of the relation of language to the world. The second and third classes are not very promising, but the first consists of "those who infer properties of the world from properties of language", "a very distinguished party" Russell called them. He then says: "If, therefore, we are confined to the above three alternatives, we must make the best of the first."[1]

Presumably it is for such reasons that Russell concluded that facts are objects we come across in the world, and that Wittgenstein concluded the world is composed primarily of facts.[2] Facts are things in the world that correspond to sentences in language. The reason for thinking that facts are ontologically significant is, presumably, that sentences are linguistically significant.[3]

Later the principle that Russell understood as characterizing the first class of philosophers became known as the syntactic priority thesis. It arises in the discussion of Frege's philosophy, and it is regarded as how Frege characterized, and presumably justified, the concept–object distinction, and also, at a lower level, how he determined which classes of things were classes of objects. It can therefore have two roles.

According to Crispin Wright, "The really fundamental aspect of Frege's notions of object and concept is that they are notions whose

---

1 Russell, *An Inquiry into Meaning and Truth*, Chapter 25.
2 Russell, "The Philosophy of Logical Atomism", cf. p. 182, and Wittgenstein, *Tractatus* 1.1.
3 Cf. D. W. Hamlyn, *Metaphysics*, p. 42.

12

proper explanation proceeds *through linguistic notions.*"[4] And Dummett is adamant that this is the only way of proceeding; for him it is the only way of doing ontology: "An object is, as has been stated, the objective correlate of a proper name: it is that which we use a proper name to talk about. No other general characterization of an object, save via the linguistic notion of a proper name, is possible."[5] If the direction of inference is from language to the world, then the structure of language must be clear. It must be possible to determine whether a term is a proper name or not on purely linguistic grounds, in other words, from syntactic considerations alone. Indeed, the notion of proper name itself must be an entirely syntactic notion devoid of metaphysics:

> The lynch-pin of Frege's platonism, according to our interpretation, is the syntactic priority thesis: the category of objects in particular, is to be explained as comprising everything which might be referred to by a singular term, where it is understood that possession of reference is imposed on a singular term by its occurrence in true statements of an appropriate type. Evidently this conception will fall completely flat unless it proves possible to explain the notion of singular term in, broadly speaking, syntactic terms; that is, by appeal to characteristics of the behaviour of the relevant terms, and without involving the notions of object or reference. Can this really be done?[6]

After much discussion Wright seems doubtful that this can be done with sufficient generality, though he admits that his discussion is incomplete because there are certain difficult issues he does not deal with.[7] It does seem unlikely that syntactic categories can be explained without reference to semantics or metaphysics.

For example, when students of logic are given instructions about how to convert sentences into quantifier notation, they are told first to convert the sentences into ones about properties employing predicate letters, and then to introduce variables.[8] Before a sentence can be put into logical form it has to be determined which things are properties. Either someone has to know independently which things are properties, or certain things have to be taken to be properties for the purposes of the exercise.

4 Crispin Wright, *Frege's Conception of Numbers as Objects*, p. 13.
5 Michael Dummett, "Frege", in *The Encyclopedia of Philosophy*, vol. 3, p. 229, cf. Dummett, *Frege: Philosophy of Language*, Chapters 4 and 16.
6 Wright, *Frege's Conception of Numbers as Objects*, p. 53.
7 Ibid., p. 64.
8 Cf. E. J. Lemmon, *Beginning Logic*, p. 97.

When we talk about language in this context, logic is never far away. Although some of the forms of ordinary language, such as definite descriptions, are held to be significant, it is language as revised by logic that is usually considered. The point about modern logic is that it is supposed to have discovered the true logical form that lies behind the sentences of ordinary language. The significance of the quantifiers and the associated variables is that they represent the true structure of language. Perhaps there is at work here a stronger principle than the syntactic priority thesis. Perhaps the thought is that the forms language has to be put into for the purposes of deductive argument are a guide to the structure of reality.

2. INTERPRETATIONS OF LOGIC

Consider a form of predicate calculus that has only proper names, monadic predicates, and the logical connectives, but no quantifiers. We shall call this language 'fragment 1'. Let us say that "objects" are what proper names refer to, and "concepts" are what predicates refer to. What then does fragment 1 tell us about the nature of objects and concepts?

The rules of combination of fragment 1 presumably include a syntactic rule that proper names and predicates form two separate classes of terms. The rule that proper names only refer to objects and predicates only refer to concepts is a semantic rule that does not follow from the syntactic rule. It is only from the syntactic rule taken in conjunction with the semantic rule that it follows that no concept is an object, and no object is a concept, in other words that the distinction between concept and object is an exclusive one. It may be a valid inference, but it is scarcely a sensible reason for believing the conclusion, since the semantic rule does not make any sense unless concepts and objects form disjoint classes.

The relationship between concepts and objects in fragment 1 can be represented by the accompanying diagram.

The arrows represent the asymmetric relation "applies to". A concept applies to an object, and conversely an object falls under a concept. The diagram represents the fact that one object can fall under many concepts, and that one concept can apply to many objects. For fragment 1 an atomic sentence is always a pair of terms joined together, a proper name and a predicate. Syntactically, therefore, the asymmetry of the relationship "applies to" arises entirely from the fact that proper names and predicates are taken to form separate classes of terms. Otherwise, inasmuch as fragment 1 characterizes the notions of concept and object, it characterizes them in the same way.

Suppose for some reason it was assumed that fragment 1 was the most complete or most significant language, so that it was the language from which the properties of the world could be inferred. What then could we conclude about the world? All that we could conclude was that there were two and only two separate classes of things, and even this comes from a semantic rule that is tainted with metaphysics. We could conclude nothing about the ontological status of those two classes of things.

But even this conclusion is not without its problems. Why should we assume that a language is complete, or sufficiently comprehensive, so that we can safely draw the conclusion that there are two, and only two, classes of things? Why should anyone trust linguistic considerations on such an issue? Suppose we did have a world with only two ontologically significant classes of things, what difference would it make to fragment 1 if proper names were sometimes used for concepts and predicates for objects? It seems that it would make no difference at all.

Consider now a form of predicate calculus that has proper names, predicates of all types, and the logical connectives, but still no quantifiers. We shall call this language fragment 2. The sorts of symbols it uses can be displayed by the accompanying diagram.

$$
\begin{array}{lll}
a & b & c \ldots \\
F(\ ) & G(\ ) & H(\ ) \ldots \\
R(\ )(\ ) & S(\ )(\ ) & T(\ )(\ ) \ldots \\
\vdots & & \\
\end{array}
$$

There are now different types of predicates. Some predicates require one proper name to form a complete sentence, some require two or three, and so on. The language is now quite asymmetrical in the way that predicates and proper names behave. The brackets are a way of displaying the rules of combination.

As before we have two separate classes of terms, proper names and predicates, but now the fact that they are separate classes of

15

terms is required by the way in which the predicates are divided into subclasses, monadic, dyadic, and so on. It is only proper names that will combine with all the various types of predicates to produce sentences. The bracket notation expresses these rules of combination very nicely. It would therefore be natural to use the syntactic terms 'complete' and 'incomplete' to describe proper names and predicates, respectively. Even so, the rule that proper names refer only to objects and predicates refer only to concepts is still a semantic rule and not a syntactic rule.

If, then, we were persuaded that fragment 2 was the most complete, or the most significant language, we might infer that the objects and concepts that existed in the world possessed some corresponding property. We could say, as it is usually said, that corresponding to proper names, which are complete, are objects that are saturated, and corresponding to predicates, which are incomplete, are concepts that are unsaturated. It is clear that saturatedness and unsaturatedness have to do with the ontological significance of objects and concepts, but that is all that is clear. The only information we have about the nature of saturatedness and unsaturatedness comes from a syntactic characterization. It is difficult to see how that could be a starting point for an enquiry into the ontological significance of the constituents of the world. There are no grounds in this syntax for saying whether something is "subsistent" or not, for example, to use a term Frege uses in this context. It is one thing to claim to infer the properties of the world from the properties of language; it is another to do it without smuggling in metaphysical notions.

There is a fairly obvious interpretation of fragment 2. Proper names can be taken to refer only to particulars, and predicates can be taken to refer only to the universals of immanent realism, whether properties, relations or triadic relations, and so on. We can then give an interpretation of the terms 'saturated' and 'unsaturated'. That a particular is saturated does not mean that it is "subsistent", for there are several sorts of particulars and they vary in ontological status. It has to do with the fact that a particular can occur only once and that a universal needs a particular in order to occur at all. The unsaturatedness of a universal has to do with the fact that it can occur many times and that it only occurs exemplified by a particular. In other words, saturatedness and unsaturatedness have to do with some sort of asymmetric "relation" (formal relation, Wittgenstein;

non-relational tie, Strawson); though it would be better to talk about a way of fitting together rather than a relation, in fact the symbolism suggests this.[9] The immanent realist interprets that relation as being the relation of inherence, where a universal inheres in a particular, depending for its occurrence on the existence of the particular. The notion of inherence is related to the idea that a universal occurs *in* a particular.

The immanent realist interpretation of fragment 2 is just that, an interpretation. It is consistent with the syntax of fragment 2, but it is not dictated by it. If we already accept that there are only two classes of things, particulars (which can occur only once) and universals (which can occur more than once), and we have some sort of intuitive notion of inherence, then we can regard fragment 2 as helping to characterize the notions of universal and particular.

The reason fragment 2 does not dictate immanent realism is because there are other interpretations that are consistent with it. Platonism is also an interpretation of fragment 2. Proper names can be understood as referring only to objects in the world of appearances, and predicates can be understood as referring only to the Forms. On this interpretation there are no things that can occur more than once. Objects in the world of appearances occur only once in the way peculiar to them, and the Forms occur only once in the way peculiar to Forms.

In Platonism the order of ontological dependence is reversed: It is Forms that have an independent sort of existence, and objects in the world of appearance that are dependent.[10] Instead of the relation of inherence we have the relation of participation. What corresponds to the syntactic notion of incompleteness is the fact that for some Forms, monadic Forms, any object that participates in it does so independently of whether other objects participate in it. Whereas for other Forms, dyadic Forms, objects participate in them in pairs; if one object participates in a dyadic Form, then another object must participate in it in a way that complements the first object. Pairs of objects, considered as pairs, participate in the same dyadic Form independently of each other. Forms are unsaturated merely in the sense that a single object can participate at the same time in many different

9 Cf. *Tractatus*, 2.03 and 2.031.
10 An object in the world of appearances has a dependent sort of existence because it is "a meeting place of a variety of insubstantial, ghostly projections of other objects" (namely, the Forms). McPherran, "Plato's Particulars", p. 528.

monadic Forms, and conjointly with another object in many different dyadic Forms, and so on. The notion of unsaturatedness as applied to Forms carries with it no connotation of dependence, or of a "need" of the Forms for objects.

Like immanent realism, Platonism is consistent with fragment 2, but not dictated by it.[11] If metaphysical arguments have convinced you of the truth of Plato's ontology of a world of Forms and a world of appearances, then you could regard fragment 2 as helping to characterize that ontology.

Frege's version of Platonism provides another interpretation of fragment 2, since his objects and concepts differ in ontological status from the objects and the Forms of Plato. Frege acknowledges three realms of things. Things in the first realm are objects of the senses; they are public in that many people can sense them, and they have an independent mode of occurrence in that they do not need an owner. Things in the second realm are ideas understood as mental things. They are not sensed as such; they are private to one person, and they have a dependent sort of existence in that they need an owner. Things in the third realm are things that cannot be sensed but are public in that many people can "grasp" them; and they have an independent mode of occurrence in the sense that they, like the things in the first realm, also do not need an owner.[12] Objects – that is to say, Fregean objects – are to be found in the first realm and in the third realm; like Frege we shall ignore the second realm. Concepts, however, are to be found only in the third realm.[13]

Frege says that concepts have the property of being unsaturated, which corresponds to the incompleteness of predicates. And he explains the ontological significance of the unsaturatedness of concepts by saying that concepts are a type of function. If we understand the mathematical notion of function, then we understand something of the relationship between object and concept. Instead of the relation of inherence or participation, we have the relation of function to

11 Platonists, like immanent realists, need a second interpretation (see later) of fragment 2, or of the complete predicate calculus, so that they can talk about relations between Forms.
12 See Frege, "Thoughts", pp. 360–6.
13 But see *Foundations of Arithmetic*, Sections 26 and 53, where Frege speaks of objective qualities. What he says appears to be consistent with immanent realism or particularism. Like Plato, he needs another theory of universals to explain those features of objects in virtue of which concepts apply to them.

argument.[14] Whether a concept is rightly regarded as a type of function or not, it is quite a good analogy, since it shows a way of avoiding the regress arguments about relations that are usually associated with Bradley.[15] However we understand the "relation" between concept and object, or between universal and particular, that relation cannot be understood as a "real constituent of the world". The relation of function and argument gives us an intuitive notion of two things fitting together without the need of an intermediary.

It does seem that Frege is trying to make a comment about the ontological status of concepts, as well as make a point about semantics. His metaphysics is very thin metaphysics, and it is not entirely derived from syntax. The notion of unsaturatedness is supposed to tell us something about the nature of concepts, though what it tells us is very intuitive, if not metaphorical. It also shows how concepts can be objective. If we have no problem with mathematical functions being objective, then why should concepts present any difficulties? As a point about semantics it is supposed to explain how the combination of terms in a sentence pictures how the things signified by the terms are combined together.

Otherwise, Frege does not have a lot to say about the ontological status of things in the third realm. Part IV of the *Foundations of Arithmetic* has the subtitle "Every individual number is a self-subsistent object." But when he says what he means by numbers being self-subsistent, it is not what we would expect: "The self-subsistence which I am claiming for number is not to be taken to mean that a number word signifies something when removed from the context of a proposition, but only to preclude the use of such words as predicates or attributes, which appreciably alters their meaning."[16] It is likely that the context principle – namely, that only in the context of a sentence does a word have meaning – is

---

14 See "Function and Concept", "What Is a Function?", and "Foundations of Geometry: First Series", p. 281. Although the reference of a predicate, the concept properly so-called, is unsaturated, Frege thinks that the term 'unsaturated' seems more suited to the sense of the predicate; I am not clear, however, whether it is a function or not. *Posthumous Writings*, p. 119. For the notion of reference of a predicate see Montgomery Furth's introduction to his edition of Frege's *Basic Laws of Arithmetic*, p. xxxix.

15 F. H. Bradley, *Appearance and Reality*, Chapter 2; cf. Loux, *Substance and Attribute*, pp. 25–6.

16 *Foundations of Arithmetic*, Section 60; cf. Section 58.

designed to explain something of the status of numbers, and perhaps of other objects in the third realm. According to Frege, number terms function semantically in sentences only as object terms, and though the use of numbers in sentences is objective, numbers are not to be regarded as self-subsistent in the usual Platonist sense. Elsewhere Frege says that numbers are "objective" but not "real", [17] whereas a true Platonist would regard only abstract objects as truly real. If this interpretation is right, then we must not regard Frege's third realm as a separate Platonic heaven. The third realm is merely characterized by all that Frege has said about it and its members – given that all of what he has said is consistent.

Frege has given a subtle interpretation of what after all is his logic, though so far we are still only dealing with fragment 2. And it is Frege who insists that the terms 'object' and 'concept' cannot be defined but must be explained or characterized. Fragment 2 does contribute to a characterization of Frege's notions of concept and object, but as we have in effect shown, Frege does not give a purely syntactic characterization of these notions. His characterization also includes metaphysical notions of a sort, as well as semantical considerations.

Before we consider quantification, we must consider one more very important interpretation of fragment 2. Within an immanent realist ontology it is possible that there be relations between universals, for example, "The whale is a mammal" or "Scarlet is a kind of red". Frege called this type of relation 'subordination'. [18] Nothing in fragment 2 precludes interpreting proper names as referring to universals, and predicates as referring to properties of universals and relations between universals.

There is no syntactic reason why a proper name has to refer to something that can occur only once. It is true that in ordinary language and in ordinary thought there is a presupposition of uniqueness associated with proper names and definite descriptions used referentially, but there is no reason to suppose that it is uniqueness in the sense of occurring only once. Definite descriptions do not nec-

---

17 Frege, *The Basic Laws of Arithmetic*, p. 24. For Frege's distinction between "objective" and "real", see *Foundations of Arithmetic*, Sections 26, 61, 85, and 105.
18 Frege, *Foundations of Arithmetic*, Section 47. Both of the examples given in the text are of internal relations, which are relations that are necessary to their terms, though as we shall show, there are relations between universals that are not internal relations.

essarily refer to particulars, and if they did a lot of ordinary language would be illegitimate. A universal is in one sense a single thing; a universal is *one thing that can occur many times,* and that is enough. There is therefore no reason why a proper name, syntactically understood, should not refer to a universal.[19]

We therefore have two different interpretations within the immanent realist ontology; a statement belongs either to the first interpretation or to the second. In the first interpretation proper names refer to particulars and predicates refer to first-order universals, whereas in the second interpretation proper names refer to first-order universals and predicates to second-order universals. When quantification is introduced to convert fragment 2 to predicate calculus, quantification will be over particulars in the first interpretation, and over first-order universals in the second interpretation. Proper names that refer to particulars, or to variables that range over particulars, do not occur in the statements of the second interpretation. Statements such as '(F)(Fa & Fb)' are ill-formed; they belong to neither interpretation. In order to avoid confusion we need to be clear which interpretation is being used, and it seems that the best way of doing this is to keep the two interpretations separate. Statements in the second interpretation could look formally exactly like statements in the first interpretation; the distinction is, after all, only one of interpretation.

The alternative view that there is only one interpretation is based, perhaps, on the view that there is only one world and therefore there should only be one language to describe it. But there is very little reason to accept this view, quite apart from the difficulties it leads to. Suppose we take the world to be all the particulars that there are and all the universals that there are. Then we might assume that there is only one language, such as fragment 2, which describes the world – so that the proper names of fragment 2 refer to the particulars, and the predicates of fragment 2 refer to the universals. There will then be difficulties finding the correct logical form of sentences like 'The whale is a mammal' in our universal language. The best we can do is something like $(x)(Wx \rightarrow Mx)$, which can be shown to

19 Frege is happy to use definite descriptions to refer to shapes and to allow the terms that refer to shapes to function in identity sentences. He has a well-known method for moving from a sentence where a shape term occurs attributively to one where it occupies the subject position. See *Foundations of Arithmetic,* Section 64. Cf. E. J. Lowe, "What Is a Criterion of Identity?", p. 4.

be wrong (see Chapter 5). On the other hand, if we reject a universal language and assume that a language like fragment 2 can have more than one interpretation, we can avoid certain difficulties. We can avoid Frege's "concept horse" problem, and we can avoid some of the difficulties Wittgenstein had in the *Tractatus*.

There is also a problem associated with the fact that predicates and the corresponding property names cannot formally be substituted for each other in ordinary language. Examples of predicates and corresponding property names are '. . . is courageous' and 'courage', and '. . . is circular' and 'circularity'. The members of each pair do not function syntactically in the same way. There is an apparent violation of the Leibnizian principle of intersubstitutivity: " 'Redness' and '. . . is red' cannot be substituted *salva congruitate,* let alone *salva veritate.*"[20]

On account of these difficulties it is controversial whether a predicate refers to the same thing as the corresponding property name. I shall argue, however, that a predicate and the corresponding property name refer to the same universal, since there is only one ontologically significant thing available that could correspond to them – namely, the universal. This is, of course, an argument based on a particular metaphysical point of view, not a general argument aimed at all philosophers of language. But if ontology cannot be derived from language, as I have argued, then the question can only be settled by importing some ontology.

Suppose a predicate refers to a genuine universal, such as "spherical", which a physical object actually possesses. What then does the corresponding property name, 'sphericity', refer to, supposing that it refers to something different? There are two possibilities: It refers either to a particular or to a universal, that is, to something that can occur only once or to something that can occur more than once. If it refers to a universal, then we have a second universal. The second universal cannot occur in the object in which the original universal occurs, so it must occur somewhere else, either in Frege's second world or in his third world. If it occurs in the second world, it is something mental, and it seems clear that a universal like "sphericity" cannot be regarded as something mental. If it occurs in the third world, then it is subject to all the usual criticisms of Platon-

20 Roger Teichman, "Three Kinds of Realism about Universals", p. 145; see Loux, *Substance and Attribute,* pp. 27–33, for a detailed discussion of the problem.

ism. If, on the other hand, the property name refers to something that can occur only once, then that something does not occur in the first world; it too must inhabit the third world, with all the attendant difficulties.

There is no reason to think that the two sentences 'a is spherical' and 'a falls under the concept sphericity' do not have the same truth conditions. There is something about a, which is an object in the material world, that makes both sentences true, and it is the same something. For the immanent realist, that one thing is the universal inhering in the object, whereas for the Platonist that one thing is a Form participated in by the object. For the Fregean there are indeed multiple entities: There is the extension, there is the concept, which is the reference of the predicate, and there is also the sense of the predicate, if that is in fact another entity. Nevertheless, if the Fregean has an account of what it is about the object in virtue of which the sentences in question are true, then it must be that the object falls under the concept.[21] He could perhaps suggest that the property name refers to the extension and the predicate refers to the concept, though I cannot see any basis for this.

The problem about the references of predicates and property names cannot be considered apart from the theory of universals. Metaphysical theories that posit multiple entities are possible, such as Platonism combined with particularism, and presumably theories that posit two sorts of things from linguistic considerations are doing something like this, but it is simply not clear what sort of ontology is being put forward.

Those who regard predicates and property names as both referring to the same universal have sometimes called them different modes of signification – perhaps rather obscurely. But there is an explanation available to the immanent realist. The different forms that we find in ordinary language – namely, '. . . is red' and 'redness' – can be regarded as corresponding to the two different interpretations of predicate calculus. The form '. . . is red' corresponds to the interpretation where proper names refer to particulars and predicates refer to universals. The form 'redness' corresponds to the second interpretation where proper names refer to the ordinary universals that apply to particulars, and predicates refer to relations between universals, or to properties of universals. It is in this interpretation that

21 See note 13, this chapter.

23

we quantify over universals – second-order quantification. The failure of substitutivity could be explained in terms of the fact that the predicates of the first interpretation function syntactically in a different way from the proper names of the second interpretation, and in that ordinary language there is felt a need to keep apart what we regard as two interpretations.

There is also something of an ontological distinction between the two interpretations. We refer to universals or quantify over them only if there are such universals, where 'there are' is used in the sense appropriate to universals. When we predicate a universal of a particular, what is being asserted or denied is that the universal is instanced by the particular. Nevertheless there is only one universal involved.[22]

In fact, you cannot keep the two interpretations entirely apart. Here is an example of an argument in which the two interpretations are mixed, though each sentence is in one interpretation or the other:

$C'a$	a is claret
$C'\mathrm{sub}R$	claret is a shade of red
$\therefore (x)(C'x \to Rx)$	$\therefore (x)$(if x is claret x is red)
$\therefore Ra$	$\therefore a$ is red

To say that the universal "claret" is subordinate to the universal "red" is to make a statement in the second interpretation. But it is a statement that has consequences for the first interpretation; in other words, it has consequences for statements about particulars. In fact, this argument makes it very difficult to maintain the view that the property name and predicate do not refer to the same universal, since $C'\mathrm{sub}R$ and $(x)(C'x \to Rx)$, 'C'' must signify the same thing in both formulas, and so must 'R'.

It has been suggested to me that a systematic correlation short of identity will save the inference.[23] In other words, $C'^*\mathrm{sub}R^*$ could also entail $(x)(C'x \to Rx)$, where R^* and R are systematically correlated in that both correspond to the predicate R, and similarly for C'^* and C'. In fact, Wiggins does just this: He attempts to solve these problems about reference by constructing formal or abstract entities. He argues that what we quantify over in second-order quantification are concepts that are neither saturated nor unsaturated.

22 See Chapter 3 for more discussion of this distinction.
23 By the anonymous reader for Cambridge University Press.

A concept is converted into something saturated by the action of the copula. Wiggins thereby provides a linguistic explanation of how to construct the correlate of R, though it is important to note that immanent realists would not agree that the attachment or removal of the copula was ontologically significant. For Wiggins the copula functions as an operator that converts concepts into a certain type of unsaturated entity that can apply to Fregean objects. Such a procedure would appeal to mathematicians, who are generally happy with the construction of abstract entities. Ontologically it is obscure.[24]

Suppose that R is the attribute an object actually possesses when it is true to say that it is red, and C' is the attribute it possesses when it is true to say that it is claret. And suppose that there is an operator symbolized by * that creates correlates of attributes, where the correlates have a different metaphysical status from the attributes. For Wiggins * would be the operator that removes the copula. Then the attribute C' should be subordinate to the attribute R, and there should be some way of saying so. The alternative view is that it is only the correlates C'^* and R^* that are related to each other, so that R and C' are related only indirectly via C'^* and R^*.

If there is a relation between C' and R^*, why can't there be a relation between C' and R? If we are in the business of constructing correlates, why can't we construct a correlate relation between C' and R? The proponents of correlates need to show that the relation between C'^* and R^* is metaphysically more significant than a correlate relation between C' and R. Now it is true that $C'^*\mathrm{sub}R^*$ would entail $(x)(C'x \rightarrow Rx)$, but only because $C'\mathrm{sub}R$ does. '$C'^*\mathrm{sub}R^*$' is not about attributes; it says that correlates of attributes are subordinate to one another, whatever that means. The metaphysically important statements are about the subordination of attributes. All this of course relies on the point of view developed in the previous pages.

24 Cf. David Wiggins, "The Sense and Reference of Predicates: A Running Repair to Frege's Doctrine and a Plea for the Copula". See also P. F. Strawson, "Concepts and Properties or Predication and Copulation", who, though agreeing with Wiggins to some extent, argues that property names and predicates signify the same thing, despite verbal differences. Strawson's own argument is of use to us. Frege himself has a doctrine of abstract correlates. The concept that is the reference of a predicate is an unsaturated entity that is correlated with the extension, where the extension, being a set, is saturated. They are correlated in that they are individuated together. Cf. note 14, this chapter.

3. QUINE AND QUANTIFICATION

Our fragment 2, inasmuch as it deals with predicates, is really only a descriptive language. If we wish to engage in logical arguments that make use of the predicate structure of sentences, we have to add to fragment 2 the formalism of quantifiers and variables. We only considered fragment 2 in order to see what could be learnt from a language that only admitted proper names and predicates of various sorts. It is the quantifier formalism, of course, that enables considerable portions of natural language to be reduced to sentences with a simple logical form based ultimately on the distinction between predicates and proper names. It enables us to dispense with expressions such as 'all men' and 'some men' as logical subjects, and it enables us to deal with some negative existential statements. But does it go any further? Does it do any more to characterize the things proper names and predicates refer to, which it might do if there is an intrinsic connection between quantification and a certain ontological category? I answer that it does not.

According to Quine, what he calls the "canonical notation of quantification" is inevitably linked with objects. It is not that Quine believes in the syntactic priority thesis – that which things are objects is to be determined from the structure of logic or language. He describes his position as one of ontological relativity. It is by means of the notion of quantification that we express which things we take to be objects:

In our canonical notion of quantification, then, we find the restoration of law and order. Insofar as we adhere to this notation, the objects we are to be understood to admit are precisely the objects which we reckon to the universe of values over which the bound variables of quantification are considered to range. Such is simply the intended sense of the quantifiers '(x)' and '($\exists$x)': 'every object x is such that', 'there is an object such that'. The quantifiers are encapsulations of these specially selected, unequivocally referential idioms of ordinary language. To paraphrase a sentence into the canonical notation of quantification is, first and foremost, to make its ontic context explicit, quantification being a device for talking in general of objects.[25]

Quine cannot be saying that if we are interested in certain things that we take to be objects, and we have a theory about those things, then a formal rendering of that theory will inevitably quantify over those things. This may be true, but it is philosophically not very

25 Willard Van Orman Quine, *Word and Object*, p. 242.

interesting. Neither can he be merely observing that scientists in their theories only quantify over what they take to be objects – which can be shown to be false. He is saying that a properly formulated theory should only quantify over things that are taken to be objects, since there is something wrong about quantifying over things that are not taken to be objects. It must not be assumed that the theory has got it right, that there is in reality such a class of objects; all that is necessary is that the conception be a conception of a class of objects.

In practice it seems that it is possible to quantify in a theoretically useful way over things that are not objects. A scientist who is working on colours will inevitably quantify over shades of colour. And a scientist who is working on taxonomy will inevitably quantify over species of animal and their properties.[26] Even if the statements of their theories can be reduced to statements that quantify over objects, such as sets, it does not follow that it is a mistake to quantify over something else.

The strongest way for Quine to show that it is wrong to quantify over things that are not objects would be to show that there is an intrinsic connection between the syntax of quantification and the notion of object, and he would have to include an explanation of the notion of object. As far as I know his writings contain neither, despite the occurrence of the phrase "quantification being a device for talking in general of objects".

Quine is certain that physical objects are *bona fide* objects, and usually happy to include classes and numbers as well.[27] Although he does not use the term 'parcel', he also includes parcels of matter as objects.[28] What seems to emerge is that particulars in the familiar spatio-temporal world are at least good examples of Quine's "objects", though by the word 'object' Quine does not mean "particular" in our sense of something that can occur only once.

---

26 Cf. Elliot Sober, "Evolutionary Theory and the Ontological Significance of Properties".

27 See Quine, *Word and Object;* for physical objects, p. 238 and Section 55; for classes, p. 209 and Section 55; for numbers, p. 245.

28 For parcels of matter as the reference of mass terms used in the subject position, see Quine, *Word and Object*, p. 98. As a singular term 'water' refers to "the world's water as a total scattered object" (p. 98). "Scatter is in fact an inconsequential detail" (p. 99). He also seems to admit time slices of physical objects as objects. See "Identity, Ostension and Hypostasis", in *From a Logical Point of View*.

Besides recognizing concrete objects Quine follows Frege in re-garding classes[29] and numbers as abstract objects, but unlike Frege he has no distinction between saturated and unsaturated to separate things in the third realm into "objects" and concepts. According to Frege it is syntactic considerations that enable a distinction to be made between things that are saturated and things that are unsatu-rated; it is syntactic considerations, for example, that tell us numbers are objects. Now it may turn out that what is an object for Frege is also an object for Quine, and vice versa, but the approach is quite different. A Fregean might say that we know that numbers are ob-jects because we quantify over them; Quine must first discover which things are objects in order to justify quantifying over them. So far we have not discovered what Quine means by the term 'ob-ject', though we know that the explanation of what he means cannot be based on syntax. Quine's views about quantification have no room for the syntactic priority thesis; the structure of language doesnot tell us anything about the nature of objects, and it does not tell us which classes of things are classes of objects.

According to Quine, quantification over a type of thing is pos-sible or allowable only if there is associated with that type of thing a clear criterion of identity:

We cannot know what something is without knowing how it is marked off from other things. Identity is thus of a piece with ontology.[30]

But the big difference between "rabbit" and "sepia" is that whereas "sepia" is a mass term like "water," "rabbit" is a term of divided reference. As such it cannot be mastered without mastering its principles of individuation: where one rabbit leaves off and another begins. And this cannot be mastered by pure ostension, however persistent.[31]

Quine's reasons for this connection between quantification and cri-teria of identity are based on semantic considerations. It is only things that are sufficiently clearly marked off from each other that can be quantified over on account of the nature of quantification. Presumably, then, any kind of thing that is sufficiently clearly marked off from other things is a kind of object, though metaphys-ically this tells us nothing about the nature of objects. It seems to be a matter of accident that the things that are sufficiently clearly

---

29 W. V. Quine, *Ontological Relativity and Other Essays*, p. 21. For a criticism of the doctrine that classes or sets are abstract objects see Chapter 9, Section 1, of this book.
30 Quine, ibid., p. 55.   31 Ibid., p. 31.

marked off from each other are all examples of what many philosophers normally call objects.

Although Quine does not say what an object is, he seems clear that universals or attributes are not objects, though we should not assume from this that by 'object' he means "particular". As we remarked before, Quine must first discover which things qualify as "objects" in order to justify quantifying over them, where an object is something with a sufficiently clear criterion of identity. It is as though Quine takes some established view of what objects are and assumes that those things and only those things have adequate criteria of identity. He could, for example, take Frege's notion of object, which is supposed to be based on syntax, or he could take the notion of particular, which is a metaphysical notion, but neither is really consistent with his approach.

Things that can be quantified over can also be elements of sets, taken in groups they can be counted, and taken individually they can be the subject of singular reference – and all of this can be done without ambiguity. It is clear from the nature of the sorts of things that can be elements of sets, such as the numbers themselves, that objects need not be marked off from each other physically or spatially; physical objects merely provide a paradigm case of things that are clearly marked off from each other.

Quine's explanation, then, of why it appears possible in practice to quantify over shades of colour and biological species, which are not objects in any traditional sense, must be that it is possible only up to a point. The irreducible fuzziness of these things must lead to problems in the end. Perhaps, but in practice there appear to be no difficulties.

And theoretically there is no reason why some universals should not be the subjects of singular reference, or be members of sets, or, if taken in groups, be counted. For example, the fully determinate shape attributes such as "spherical with radius five inches" can be members of sets, they can be counted, and, taken individually they can be the subject of singular reference. If the determinable universal "spherical" is taken as a kind universal, then the universals that are subordinate to it, such as "spherical with radius five inches", can be put into one-to-one correspondence with the real numbers. These universals are indexed by the real numbers, and it therefore follows that if the real numbers can be quantified over, as Quine must admit, then so can these universals. If the real numbers have a criterion of identity, then so do the determinate spherical attributes.

Universals are marked off from each other in the manner relevant to universals, in the same way that numbers are marked off from each other in the manner relevant to numbers. All that is required is that the universals be sufficiently clearly marked off from each other; it is not necessary that they have an explicit criterion of identity. Lowe for one specifically denies that every sortal term that classifies particulars has a criterion of identity associated with it.[32] If this is true of some kinds of particulars, then it is very likely true of some kinds of universals.

Quine might reply that numbers can be reduced to sets, whereas any criterion of identity for universals will inevitably make an appeal to synonymy, and there is no clear criterion of identity for meanings. I argue, however, that whatever can be said about universals can also be said about numbers.

Criteria of identity apply to types of things. The shape attributes such as "spherical radius five inches" are determinate spherical attributes. The criterion of identity for determinate spherical attributes as follows: If x and y are determinate spherical attributes, then x is identical with y if and only if their characteristic radii are the same. This is not about the qualitative identity of particulars, it is about identity for universals considered as things in their own right.

The criterial condition part "if and only if the characteristic radii are the same" does not appear to appeal to synonymy; it merely appeals to the criterion of identity for real numbers. To use the criterion one also must be able to determine or to recognize that x and y are determinate spherical attributes, and personally I would not have thought that was very difficult, since they occur in the world of experience.

The criterion of identity for real numbers is as follows: If x and y are real numbers, then x is identical with y if and only if C_R. In general it is difficult to formulate the criterial condition, C_R, for real numbers. We could try something based on one of the set-theoretic representations of real numbers – I prefer the term 'representation', because 'reduction' seems to imply some sort of identity. C_R would then be "the set that represents x is the same set as the set that represents y", which merely depends on the criterion of identity for a set.

---

32 E. J. Lowe, *Kinds of Being*, p. 20.

With the criterion of identity for determinate spherical attributes one must be able to recognize or determine that x and y are indeed determinate spherical attributes; similarly with any criterion of identity for real numbers one has to be able to recognize or determine that x and y are indeed real numbers. This is in fact much more difficult because we are not sure what real numbers are. Appeal to sets here does not help, it only makes matters worse. Benacerraf has shown that a number is not the same as any of the sets that can be used to represent it; therefore, recognizing that x is a real number is not a matter of recognizing that something is a set that represents a number.[33] Not only are real numbers clearly marked off from each other, which is expressed by the criterion of identity, they are also clearly marked off from the various sets used to represent them, which is not expressed by the criterion of identity for real numbers. In fact, it is difficult to see how a criterion of identity could express how things of that kind were marked off from all other things.[34]

In the same way that a criterion of identity for real numbers can be phrased in terms of sets, so also can the criterion of identity for determinate spherical attributes, since they are indexed by the positive real numbers. Whatever applies to real numbers also applies to determinate spherical attributes. If we can quantify over one we can quantify over the other.

Quine may be thinking that if we consider universals in general they are not sufficiently clearly marked off from one another, even though universals of a certain type may be marked off from other universals of that type. This may be true, but if it is true, then it is equally true of particulars, most of which are recognized by Quine as "objects". Criteria of identity distinguish particulars of a certain kind from other members of that kind, not from all other particulars. For example, material objects, parcels of matter, events, and time slices of material objects are arguably all kinds of particulars and hopefully possess adequate criteria of identity that distinguish members of each kind from each other. But distinguishing members of the different kinds from each other is another matter. They need not represent distinct elements of reality. In a physical situation all of these types of particulars may be present with no obvious "real distinctions" between them. In fact, Quine does not make it clear

33 P. Benacerraf, "What Numbers Could Not Be". His arguments can be extended to real numbers.
34 Cf. Frege, *Foundations of Arithmetic*, Section 66.

whether he intends all his "objects" to be distinct elements of reality.

There is a problem of explaining what the ranges of second-order variables are,[35] but then there is also a similar problem of explaining what the ranges of first-order variables are. Perhaps the range of first-order variables would be all "objects" with adequate criteria of identity admitted as such by a certain theory. But it would be quite a mixed bag: There might be physical objects, classes, numbers, time slices of physical objects, and parcels of matter. Presumably they would all have the same ontological status in that they were all "objects".

Perhaps Quine intends that the objects admitted as such by a certain theory should be a basic type of object so that all other types of object can be reduced to them; for example, one theory could take time slices of material objects as basic objects. But there is no *a priori* reason why the same cannot be done for universals; indeed, there is no *a priori* reason why it *can* be done for particulars.

From the point of view of this book, the ranges of second-order variables are fully determinate universals such as "spherical with radius five inches", which we shall call 'basic universals'. All basic universals have the same ontological status, and they are all clearly distinct from each other as the example of "spherical with radius five inches" shows. In fact, from the point of view developed in this book the ranges of second-order variables are in better shape than the ranges of first-order variables.

It is only kinds of things that have a criterion of identity associated with them. This at least raises the problem of universals, because things that fall under a certain type must have something objective in common to explain why they are of that type, or at least some sort of ontological explanation is required. Understanding a criterion of identity for a type of particular, or "object", depends on grasping certain universals, not only sortals but other universals, and it therefore involves understanding how one universal is to be distinguished from another. Criteria of identity for "objects" depend on criteria of identity for universals.

Singular reference requires that the individual concerned be marked off clearly from all other things, and followers of Frege also argue that singular reference always involves understanding some

35 See Dummett, *Frege: Philosophy of Language*, pp. 521 and 539–41.

sortal. They will agree with Quine that we cannot know what something is without knowing how it is marked off from other things, but will add, perhaps partly by way of explanation, that we cannot know what something is without knowing what sort of thing it is. "In short, it is plausible to claim that reference to particulars is only ever secured through the application of general concepts of the sortal or substantival variety."[36]

The usual examples of counting or quantifying over require particulars that are all of one type; in other words, the particulars counted or quantified over must all have something in common: "While looking at one and the same external phenomenon, I can say with equal truth both 'It is a copse' and 'It is five trees', or both 'Here are four companies' and 'Here are 500 men'. "[37] Even if I insist on counting the members of a set with arbitrarily chosen members such as the Taj Mahal, the president of the United States, and the number 3, those particulars enter the set as individuals of a certain sort. If the five trees are individually members of the set, the copse is not thereby a member of the set. Frege might not be exactly right in saying that numbers apply to concepts, but a concept in the sense of a sortal universal is always involved.

My point is that quantification presupposes universals, because we quantify over particulars of a certain type. Moreover, first-order sets presuppose universals, because a particular is enrolled in a set only on account of being a particular of a certain type.

A criterion of identity is a principle we use to judge the truth or falsehood of an identity statement concerning individuals. It should tell us what it takes for x or y to be the same or different. "In other words it should specify – in an informative way, be it added – the *truth*-conditions of the statement 'x is identical with y'. "[38] This is consistent with Frege's original idea of recognizing something again as the same.

E. J. Lowe suggests the following as the general form of criteria of identity: "If x and y are fs, then x is identical with y if and only if x and y satisfy condition C_f."[39] The condition C_f may be different for different kinds, though it is also possible for two different kinds to have the same criterion of identity. Lowe says that the criterion

36 Lowe, "What Is a Criterion of Identity?", p. 11.
37 Frege, *Foundations of Arithmetic*, Section 46.
38 Lowe, *Kinds of Being*, p. 16.
39 Ibid., p. 13.

of identity for a given sort of thing partly gives the meaning of the corresponding sortal term,[40] but it does not exhaust that meaning. If you understand the nature of the sortal you should be able to formulate the corresponding criterion of identity for individuals of that sort, or at least recognize the criterion of identity as the appropriate one if it is presented to you. Understanding the criterion of identity is no substitute for understanding the nature of the sortal itself. In fact, to use the criterion of identity you will need to understand the nature of the sortal concerned sufficiently to be able to recognize which individuals are examples of the sortal. Quine says, "We cannot know what something is without knowing how it is marked off from other things",[41] but that is not all there is to knowing what that something is. The criterion of identity of a set is straightforward, but explaining the nature of a set is anything but straightforward.[42]

Lowe argues that a criterion of identity for individuals of a given sort will presuppose the criterion of identity for individuals of another sort. The criterion of identity for a set is that the members of the set should be the same, but when you get down to first-order sets the members are things that are not sets. Hence the criterion of identity for a set depends on the criteria of identity for individuals that are not sets and which therefore have different criteria of identity. Lowe then argues that since you cannot go on in this way indefinitely there must be "*some* 'basic' sorts for which we can give *no* informative criterion of identity".[43]

For Lowe the "basic sorts" will be sorts of individuals – in other words, objects or particulars. It is also possible, however, for a criterion of identity for particulars to depend on universals that must be recognized as the same again.[44] So instead of arguing that there must be some basic sorts of particulars without an informative criterion of identity, it could be argued that there are some basic universals without informative criteria of identity. This is possible if there are determinates that are all subordinate to the same determin-

40 Ibid., p. 17.
41 Quine, *Ontological Relativity and Other Essays,* p. 55.
42 See Max Black, "The Elusiveness of Sets", and Chapter 9, Section 1 of this book.
43 Lowe, *Kinds of Beings,* p. 20.
44 The criterion of identity that Lowe gives for ships, such as the famous one belonging to Theseus, will depend on recognizing the right type of material as the same again. Cf. "What Is a Criterion of Identity?", p. 20.

able but that differ from each other *simpliciter*. Although I shall give no examples, it is not a possibility that I would want to exclude.

I have already given an example of a criterion of identity for determinate spherical attributes, and a criterion of identity for species universals could easily be constructed based on their component properties that function as *differentiae*.[45] I shall also argue that universals such as determinate spherical attributes and determinate mass attributes do not differ *simpliciter,* but rather on account of internal relations, so that even for fairly fundamental universals there are still criteria of identity.[46]

4. QUANTIFICATION FROM ANOTHER POINT OF VIEW

In the first interpretation of predicate calculus, proper names refer to particulars and predicates refer to universals. When quantification is introduced, it is as a syntactically asymmetric device, which picks out particulars as the class of things to be quantified over. However, it can be shown that the reason it is asymmetric, that it is particulars and not universals we quantify over, is based on a previously understood metaphysical distinction, such as that between universal and particular.[47] In this case metaphysics is prior to syntax.

According to Max Black, it seems certain Wittgenstein wanted to understand quantification in terms of infinite conjunctions and infinite disjunctions of atomic sentences. The alternative, and more common view, is to regard quantification as something quite new and *sui generis,* though even if this alternative is taken, the corresponding infinite conjunctions and disjunctions are still a guide to understanding quantified formulas.

45 Criteria of identity are truth conditions for identity sentences, and some people have claimed that there are problems associated with identity sentences for universals. See Leonard Linsky, *Oblique Contexts*, p. 29. His point seems to be that different terms for the same universal cannot differ in cognitive value. It is true that universals have few, if any, real monadic properties, which are, of course, second-order properties. This is an important way in which universals differ from particulars, and though it is reflected in ordinary language it is essentially a metaphysical difference. There are many ways of referring to universals such as 'Hume's missing shade of blue' and 'Frege's favourite colour', which do allow identity sentences to have cognitive value.
46 Are there criteria for identity for these internal relations, which are second–order universals? Yes, and *ad infinitum!*
47 The distinction between Fregean concepts and objects would do equally well.

35

On Wittgenstein's view predicate calculus can be understood as a simple extension of fragment 2:

On this view, $(x).fx$ is assimilated to '$fa.fb.fc. \ldots$ ', i.e. to an indefinitely continued conjunction of all propositions having the form fx. But it is easy to see that the dots in the indefinite conjunction function just like a quantifier, though less perspicuously. . . . Hence, Wittgenstein links the essence of generality with the notion of a variable, rather than with that of a quantifier.[48]

Why in the infinite conjunctions and disjunctions is the variable introduced in the place of the proper names with the predicate repeated, rather than vice versa? The answer is based on metaphysical considerations concerning particulars and universals, or objects and concepts, or something similar. Wittgenstein himself does not make a distinction between universal and particular; his term 'object' probably covers both, as it does in Russell's logical atomism.[49] On the other hand, the objects that proper names and predicates refer to differ in their internal properties, as we shall see in the next chapter.

Consider what would happen if the predicate were made the variable; we would obtain:

$$(X)(Xa) = Fa \ \& \ Ga \ \& \ Ha \ \& \ \ldots$$
$$(\exists X)(Xa) = Fa \ v \ Ga \ v \ Ha \ v \ldots$$

The first says that a certain particular has all properties, which is necessarily false. The second says that a certain particular has at least one property, which is necessarily true and not worth saying. We only get interesting and useful formulas if we introduce the variable in the place of the proper names with the predicate repeated.

This argument shows why we quantify over particulars if we believe the world is a world of universals and particulars, and we have started by using a simple language, such as fragments 1 or 2, in which universals are asserted of particulars. Similarly, it shows why we quantify over objects if we believe the world is a world of concepts and objects. It shows that those reasons are metaphysical in nature. There is indeed an inevitable connection between quantification and particulars (or objects) in the first interpretation of predicate calculus, but it is not quantification as syntax that explains what particulars are. It is metaphysics that explains the syntax. Quantification does to a limited extent characterize the notion of

48 Max Black, *A Companion to Wittgenstein's Tractatus*, pp. 281–2.
49 Cf. ibid., p. 57.

particular, but only in that it reflects the metaphysical facts mentioned earlier, which dictate that quantification in the first interpretation should be over particulars.[50]

The inevitable connection does not, however, rule out quantification over universals. There is a second interpretation of predicate calculus that deals with properties of universals and relations between them – second-order universals.

5. ONTOLOGY AND LANGUAGE

We have argued that predicate calculus admits of a number of interpretations; the examples we considered were immanent realism, Platonism, Frege's version of Platonism, and properties and relations of universals. Which of the first three you choose depends on your assessment of certain metaphysical arguments. That choice cannot be based on the structure of logic or language. On the other hand, once the choice has been made, predicate calculus can be regarded as contributing to the characterization of the chosen ontology. Perhaps it is possible to construct ontologies that do not fit in easily with predicate calculus – for example, ones that do not keep the categories of object and concept separate. I am not certain that such ontologies are ruled out merely on the grounds that predicate calculus is the right way of doing logic. On the particular–universal ontology, however, it would not make any sense for there to be protean things that on some occasions "can occur only once" and on other occasions "can occur more than once".

In his chapter on ontology, Hamlyn discusses the relation of logic and language to various sorts of ontology:

It is often suggested that it was a discovery of fundamental importance that the predicate parts of propositions correspond to concepts, not objects, and that abstract objects are in general parasitical on concrete objects, in the sense that there would not be redness if it did not at least make sense to speak of things as red. And so in many ways it was. We are given thereby a pair of fundamental categories which are presented as basic to thought – those of concept and object . . . It might nevertheless be asked, by way of criticism, why, first, it should be accepted that thought must necessarily conform to this function/argument structure, and why, second, it should be accepted even so that the basic kind of object must be concrete. Why cannot thought have some other structure which is not parasitical on the function/

50 I think that the "Aristotelian criterion" discussed by Wright is based on similar metaphysical considerations. *Frege's Conception of Numbers as Objects*, p. 12.

argument structure, and what is the rationale, whether it can or not, for the belief that it is concrete objects that are fundamental among objects?[51]

By contrast our claim is not that the two categories, particular and universal, are basic to thought or language or logic. Our claim is a metaphysical claim that these two categories are basic to how reality is.

Hamlyn goes on to give examples of other ontologies. He mentions what he calls 'property location language' where basic statements locate a property at a space-time region. This is in fact an ontology of base events, which I mentioned in Chapter 1 and shall discuss in more detail in Chapter 7. He also mentions Bradley's view about judgements bringing reality under ideas. Apparently Bradley suggested that what are "supposed to be ordinary concrete objects are really 'concrete universals' – collections of ideas characterizing reality in a particular way when taken together".[52] This makes Bradley's theory sound like a mixture of Platonism and Russell's bundle theory of particulars.

Properties located at a space-time region are either universals instanced at a space-time region, or else they are particular property instances – in other words tropes. "Concrete universals" as collections of ideas are either bundles of universals instanced together as in Russell's bundle theory, or else they are bundles of tropes. Like all bundle theories it will have to face the question of whether a bundle of universals is itself a universal, and if so whether it can substitute for a particular.

Given that there are particulars, if it can also be shown that there are such things as universals, then we have a convenient interpretation of formal logic. In Chapter 1, I gave some reasons for thinking that there are such things as universals, and others such as Armstrong have given more elaborate and systematic reasons. But even so it does not follow that all true statements assert that a particular possesses a certain universal. Reality has structural features that have to be understood in ways other than in terms of particulars possessing properties, or relations holding between particulars, though the structural features have to do with properties and relations. Our interpretation does not rule out second-order quantification, nor does it rule out more complicated forms.

Neither have we claimed yet that concrete objects are the fundamental particulars, though we have come near to it in observing

---

51 Hamlyn, *Metaphysics*, p. 48.   52 Ibid., p. 49.

that material objects are paradigmatic particulars. Material objects, sets, events, and parcels of matter are all examples of particulars. Later we shall make a distinction between "unified particulars", of which material objects are a good example, and "arbitrary particulars", such as sets, events, and parcels of matter. We shall argue that arbitrary particulars are in some sense based on unified particulars, which are therefore more fundamental. But none of these arguments will have anything to do with the structure of language. If the alternative theories Hamlyn mentions are to be ruled out, then they are to be ruled out for metaphysical reasons, such as those given by the philosophers who write about universals and particulars.

6. ABSTRACT THINGS

So far the notions of particular and universal have been explained in terms of the primitive notion of occurrence; we have said that a particular can occur only once and a universal can occur many times. Something "occurs" if it is to be found in the familiar spatio-temporal world. To begin with, occurrence could be understood in terms of experience: Something occurs if it can be experienced. A more sophisticated approach will talk about causality rather than experience: Something occurs if it is significant for causality – though this needs to be made more precise. Occurrence is therefore linked to the familiar spatio-temporal world, or perhaps to some purely temporal world, and so provides no guide to a world of abstract things such as Frege's third realm.

Although I do not want to commit myself to a world of abstract things, it does look as though mathematics presupposes such a world, and it is very often useful to talk as though there were such a world. My hope is that the entities discussed by mathematics can be dealt with as universals, or as relations between universals, or as structural features of universals, perhaps in a way similar to John Bigelow's account of real numbers.[53]

The syntactic categories of proper name and predicate are from our point of view relative. In the first interpretation of predicate

---

53 John Bigelow, *The Reality of Numbers*. Cf. John Bigelow and Robert Pargetter, *Science and Necessity*, pp. 352–63. However, in Chapter 5, Section 5, I disagree with their theory of quantities and in Chapter 9, Section 1, with their account of the nature of sets. See also P. Forrest and D. M. Armstrong, "The Nature of Number".

calculus, proper names refer to particulars and predicates refer to universals; in the second interpretation, proper names refer to first-order universals and predicates refer to second-order universals, but there is no reason why there should not be a third and a fourth interpretation, and so on. Consequently, if we come across a piece of mathematics described in a formal language using proper names and predicates, the language itself is no guide as to which level of interpretation is the right one. The only way to come to any conclusions about the ontological status of the things discussed is to relate the theory to the spatio-temporal world.

Group theory as applied to rotations is a good example. In that theory rotations are referred to by proper names; they are quantified over and a rotation is represented by a matrix, which is a sort of set of numbers. From the point of view of group theory rotations are the basic type of individual; they are "objects". However, when we consider what a rotation is in the spatio-temporal world we discover that it cannot be a particular; it is something many physical objects can undergo.

This brief and rather schematic suggestion has a number of difficulties associated with it. Although it is difficult to explain what a set is, it is also difficult to regard a set as anything other than a particular; in fact, I will suggest later that a set of particulars should itself be regarded as a particular and not as something abstract.[54] Even a set of universals does not appear to be a repeatable feature of anything, though John Bigelow has argued, wrongly in my view, that a set is a non-repeatable relation between its elements.[55] At any level it seems that sets are referred to by proper names. On the other hand, it is difficult to take sets seriously ontologically; they are, if anything, formal entities.

There is another difficulty concerning sets. Mathematicians have a habit of ignoring the distinction between an entity and the set that merely represents it. Both functions and relations, for example, are often simply regarded as sets of ordered pairs. Only a few people like Frege insist on maintaining the distinction between a function and the set of ordered pairs that represents it. Perhaps, the way mathematics is done does not allow for an easy way of making ontological distinctions.

54 See Chapter 9, Section 1.
55 Bigelow, *The Reality of Numbers*, pp. 103–9; cf. Bigelow and Pargetter, *Science and Necessity*, pp. 366–76.

3

The "existence" of universals and the notion of possibility

1. UNIVERSALS AND POSSIBILITY

It is central to immanent realism to conceive of a universal as an ontologically significant feature that can occur in many places at the same time. If a universal can occur many times or just once, it is equally possible for it not to occur at all. Nevertheless a sentence containing a predicate says something irrespective of whether the universal corresponding to the predicate occurs or not. For example, a sentence that denies that a certain object is regular chiliagon-shaped says something, even though that shape probably never has occurred and probably never will occur. Such sentences can be true, and we can understand what is being said, even though no object instances the universal concerned.

It appears, then, that talking about and referring to a universal is just as possible whether it occurs many times or not at all. It seems that, in one sense, whether "there is a universal" is independent of whether it occurs, and it also seems that the meaning of the corresponding predicate is also independent of whether the universal occurs.

In his book on universals, Armstrong took the position that it is important to separate the theory of meaning and the theory of universals,[1] but later, in *What Is a Law of Nature?*, he took a slightly different view: "It may well be that it is impossible to explain the use of general words without postulating universals."[2] This seems to be right. If there are universals existing in the world, the meaning of a predicate that corresponds to a universal has at least some connection with that universal, even though there is no reason to suppose that each predicate corresponds to a universal existing in the world.

---

1 Armstrong, Volume II, pp. 11–12.
2 D. M. Armstrong, *What Is a Law of Nature?*, p. 83.

Consider the sentence, '*Sa*', which says that a certain object *a* has a certain shape *S*. In order to know what is being said by this sentence I need to know which object is referred to by '*a*' and which characteristic is being asserted of it;[3] in other words, I need to know which shape – that is, which universal – is involved. It does not follow that the meaning of this predicate is identical to the universal, as Russell appears to assume.[4] One could, for example, use a modification of Putnam's theory of meaning and say that using 'means' as a verb, a predicate "means" or refers to a universal, whereas the "meaning" as nominalization is only to be given in the context of "what it is to know the meaning of the predicate", which is described by a multi-component vector.[5]

When we say that there is such a universal as regular chiliagon-shaped we mean that there is such a shape. If we agree that there is such a shape, we are not agreeing that there has been at least one instance of a regular chiliagon. Our agreement, I suggest, has more to do with what is possible in the broadest sense of possibility.[6] After all, the characterization of a universal as something that "can" occur many times is essentially modal.

It is my claim in this chapter that to say "there is" a certain universal is much more like a statement about possibility than it is like a statement that asserts the existence of a particular. For this reason it is probably better to avoid talking about the "existence" of universals, though "existence" for universals could be understood on its own terms in the way that "mathematical existence" is understood on its own terms.

I shall argue that the notion of universal and the notion of possibility, and modality in general, are inevitably interrelated. On the one hand, that there is a universal has to be explained in terms of possibility, and on the other, what is possible has to be explained in terms of all the universals that there are. It is the nature of all the universals that there are that determines what is possible; conversely, the explanation of the nature of modality is to be found in the nature of all the universals that there are.

3 Cf. David Bell, *Frege's Theory of Judgement*, p. 116.
4 See Russell, "The Philosophy of Logical Atomism", p. 186.
5 See Hilary Putnam, "The Meaning of Meaning", pp. 224 and 269. I do not intend to endorse any other aspects of this theory of meaning.
6 It may be that, on account of the rough and imperfect nature of the world we live in, regular chiliagons are impossible. But this is a different sort of impossibility; it is even narrower than physical possibility, which does allow for such perfect shapes.

Since the notion of universal and the notion of possibility are fundamental metaphysical notions, we would not expect true definition. Instead, if they can be characterized at all it is in ways that relate them. There is some precedent for this in the way Frege characterized the notions of concept and object, or more formally, in the way Hilbert characterized the notions of point and line.

My plan is to start by discussing Armstrong's instantiation requirement and to show that its rejection leads to a different view of what it is to say that there is a universal. It shows that to say that there is a certain universal is a modal statement, and that the notion of universal itself is essentially modal. I then consider the various types of combination rules that a combinational theory of possibility would have to take account of, with the aim of using this analysis to discuss the nature of modality. The diversity of combination rules seems to imply a diversity of explanations of what is possible.

To begin with there are the rules of what I call 'naive combinatorialism', which are the combination rules corresponding to the syntactic rules of predicate calculus. These form a base theory that needs to be supplemented by certain rules and restricted by others. In the *Tractatus* Wittgenstein explained the rules of naive combinatorialism by what he called 'internal properties', showing the importance of these properties for the explanation of modality. Using Wittgenstein as my starting point I shall argue for the limited conclusion that the nature of all the universals that there are determines what is possible. Lastly, I criticize the possible-worlds approach, which purports to explain the modal in terms of the non-modal.

2. ARMSTRONG'S INSTANTIATION REQUIREMENT

According to Armstrong's version of the immanent realist theory of universals, to say that there is a certain universal entails that the universal is instanced at least once. This is Armstrong's instantiation requirement. Sometimes, indeed, he appears to reduce one to the other: To say that there is a certain universal is to say that it is instanced.[7] Perhaps part of his motivation for this approach is that

---

7 Armstrong, Volume II, pp. 9, 10; "The Nature of Possibility", p. 578; and cf. *A Combinatorial Theory of Possibility*, pp. 54–7. I am not sure how Armstrong would deal with his conjunctive universals. If the conjuncts have been instanced but the

he wants to avoid what he regards as peculiar existence claims, such as those involved in claiming that uninstantiated universals "exist". If it were said that a certain universal "existed" independently of whether it is instanced or not, then it might appear that universals exist in the way particulars exist.

Armstrong's instantiation requirement is related to his theory of possibility. That theory is a combinatorial theory based on the principle of combinatorialism, which is that the possible can be constructed out of the actual. And for Armstrong a universal is part of what is actual only if it instanced. Unfortunately it is not obvious what should be regarded as actual.

A plausible view would be that what is actual consists of all the particulars that "there are", and all the universals that "there are", where 'there are' is understood, firstly, in the way appropriate to particulars and, secondly, in the way appropriate to universals. So if you wish to explain what is actual you should have already settled the issue of what it is to say that "there is" a certain universal.

In "The Nature of Possibility" Armstrong simply rejects uninstantiated universals without explaining the relationship to time, whereas in his book on universals he says that "a universal exists if there was, is, or will be particulars having that property or relation".[8] Admittedly, if a universal is instanced at present, then it could be perceived; if it cannot be perceived, then it should in some way be accessible to investigation. In this way the instantiation requirement would appeal to an empiricist. Unfortunately any accessibility requirement is likely to be too restrictive, as a universal could be instanced and be inaccessible to present methods of investigation. It is also too restrictive to require that a universal be exemplified only in the present. Intuitively we may agree that the universals that are instanced at present are part of the actual, but to extend the instantiation requirement to past and future stretches that intuition out of shape. Something that only will exist, does not exist. It is not part of the actual.

The only way to make sense of Armstrong's instantiation requirement, which involves past, present, and future, is to see the world as a McTaggart B-series universe, where the four dimen-

---

conjunction has not, it is difficult to regard the conjunction as impossible. Armstrong tells me that his acceptance of an instantiation requirement preceded his coming to a combinatorial theory of possibility.

8 Armstrong, Volume II, pp. 9, 10.

sions, three of space and one of time, are imagined as laid out together in front of us. In effect, it is a way of looking at the space-time continuum as analogous to a timeless four-dimensional spatial continuum. It is the nearest you can get to making the instantiation of a universal look like the existence of a particular, though it is not the same as timeless mathematical existence, which is something Armstrong is trying to avoid. It is the view that lies behind Armstrong's instantiation requirement and makes it appear plausible to him. But the B-series view of time is not without its problems, and not every philosopher accepts it.

Any account of what it is to say that there is a universal seems to have implications for what is possible. It has been suggested to me, however, that the inference from "there is no such universal" to "certain things are not possible" follows only if the possible can be constructed out of the actual; in other words, it follows only if a combinatorial theory of possibility is true. Consider the instantiation account of what it is to say that there is a universal. Without the combinatorial requirement there would be existing universals, because instanced, and non-existing universals, which are not instanced. Hume's missing shade of blue considered as a universal would not exist, but it would be possible for it to exist. There would be no such shape as regular chiliagon-shaped in the sense that there is no such universal; but it would still be possible for there to be chiliagon-shaped objects. It is the combinatorial requirement, which constructs what is possible out of particulars and existing universals, that makes "non-existing universals" irrelevant to what is possible.

One of the difficulties with the view that "there are" both existing universals, which are actual, and non-existing universals, which are merely possible, has to do with reference. Both are required for the purposes of reference, since we can refer to a universal whether it is instanced or not – think of Hume's missing shade of blue. In fact, referring to a universal does not take into account any particular instance of that universal; referring to a certain instance of a universal is a quite different act. Consequently there is not much difference between referring to an existing and a non-existing universal. This distinction between existing (instanced) and non-existing (non-instanced) universals is irrelevant to explaining reference to universals.

If the distinction between existing and non-existing universals has implications for possibility only if combined with a combinatorial

45

theory of possibility, it follows that the distinction by itself has no implications for possibility. But to see the existence or non-existence of a universal as having no implications for reference or possibility is to make the distinction to be of no importance, and it turns the instantiation requirement into a mere modification of our way of speaking: To say that a universal exists is merely to say that it is instanced.

3. ARGUMENTS AGAINST THE INSTANTIATION REQUIREMENT

Consider first a naive version of the instantiation requirement, not held by anyone I know of, that there is a universal if and only if it is instanced in the present. Suppose that we have an object made of clay with a certain determinate shape, which we shall call S, and suppose that it is the only object with that shape. If one object has that shape, then it follows that another lump of clay could be given exactly that shape: Actuality establishes possibility.[9] Suppose now that we smash the object with a hammer so that S is no longer instanced anywhere. The naive version of the instantiation requirement implies that it is no longer possible for a potter to give another lump of clay the shape S. The lump of clay has the potentialities it has always had, and the potter has the abilities and capacities he has always had; nevertheless this version of the instantiation requirement implies that S is no longer possible. The conclusion seems absurd.

Consider then the more general version of the instantiation requirement, that there is a universal if and only if it is instanced at some time past, present, or future. Suppose that a potter has decided to make a pot with a shape, S, which has never been instanced before. And suppose that before he actually makes it he dies, so that

9 If a proposition is true, then it follows that it is possibly true. And if a certain situation obtains, then we may conclude that the situation considered as a particular situation is possible. A conclusion that has more significance is that situations of that general type are possible, since if we already know that situations of that type are possible, then we may infer that many different particular situations are possible. The inference depends on recognizing that the particular situation conforms sufficiently to the general type. We do this by focussing on the universal features of the situation (that is, upon the universals involved), since only considerations having to do with universals can justify propositions about a general situation (that is, a type of situation). Cf. Peter Long, "Possibility and Actuality": "The role of the actual in demonstrating a logical possibility is essentially one that can be taken over by a picture or drawing" (p. 193).

46

the shape is conceived of, but never once instanced in the history of the world. According to Armstrong's instantiation requirement the potter was contemplating something logically impossible. What made it logically impossible was an event that was not only contingent but future. If the potter had told another person that he was contemplating a shape that had never been thought of before, that person would have had it in his power to make what the potter was thinking of logically impossible, by shooting him for example.

It follows that a future contingent event determines whether what the potter was contemplating is logically possible or not, which is in some ways analogous to the future causing the past. We know, however, that which shapes are possible is in fact determined by more enduring and stable factors. Since we are only considering logical possibility, it is geometrical and topological considerations that determine which shapes are possible.

Of course it is quite possible for a potter to contemplate something logically impossible. He might think, for example, that he could make one of those Escher staircases with four sides that join up in the way a circle does but that nevertheless are ascending in every part. Such a structure can be imagined in the sense that we can picture it, but it is not a possibility.[10] Or he could, for example, think that he could make a Klein bottle without intersection, which is known to be impossible in three dimensions. We know that Escher staircases and Klein bottles without intersection are impossibilities,[11] and we know that certain other shapes are possible on very general grounds that have nothing to do with contingent events, future or otherwise. There are criteria for the possibility of shapes of pots that are based either on similarity to actual shapes or on general mathematical considerations. So it is quite possible for a well-informed potter to contemplate a shape and know that it is possible even if it never will be instanced.

Armstrong's instantiation requirement contradicts some of our strongest intuitions about what is possible. It also implies that

---

10 There is no continuous function from the circle to the real numbers that is increasing (monotonic) all the way round; cf. James Franklin, "Mathematical Necessity and Reality", who argues that some necessary mathematical statements determine necessary statements about the real world. W. D. Hart argues that imaginability implies possibility, and he mentions the Escher staircase but gives no explanation of how it could be possible. *The Engines of the Soul*, p. 17.

11 Mathematicians tell us that a Klein bottle without intersection is possible in four dimensions.

mathematical methods for determining which shapes are possible are sometimes irrelevant; it implies that certain shapes are not possible because they have not been and will not be instanced, whatever mathematics says.

In fact, the instantiation requirement makes elementary geometry to be about things that are logically impossible. Because the world is a rough and imperfect place, the perfect spheres and pyramids of elementary geometry are not, or perhaps in some sense cannot be instanced, though this form of impossibility is narrower even than physical impossibility. So according to the instantiation requirement those shapes are also logically impossible. To adopt the instantiation requirement seems to require that we have two notions of logical necessity, one for use in mathematics and one for use elsewhere.

Our rejection of the general version of the instantiation requirement is based partly on intuition and partly on the fact that it is mathematical considerations that determine which shapes are possible. However, the more general reason for rejecting the instantiation requirement is that necessities should not depend on contingencies. Any form of the instantiation requirement will make a contingent truth to entail a necessary truth. It would be nice if we could argue formally against this view, though unfortunately I do not think it can be done, however unacceptable the view may be.

That a necessity should depend on a contingency is allowed for by formal modal systems. Consider a certain shape, S. In some worlds this shape has been or will be instanced; in the other worlds it is never instanced. What Armstrong is saying is that relative to a world where S is not instanced only certain other worlds are possible worlds; they are said to be "accessible" from that world. Which worlds form the set of all possible worlds is relative to a world, so that the notion of necessity is relative to a world.[12] There is nothing formally wrong with Armstrong's instantiation requirement; it merely gives rise to an S4 modal logic as opposed to the usual S5 modal logic.

One might be forgiven for thinking that an S4 modal logic commits you to two notions of possibility. There is possibility as governed by all the possible worlds accessible from the actual world, and then there is whatever it is that makes the set of all worlds you start off with allowable. Those worlds have to be constructed ac-

12 Armstrong, "The Nature of Possibility", p. 585.

cording to some principles; something must make them allowable, so each is in a sense possible. If not, then that set of worlds would contain some strictly impossible worlds, ones containing real three-dimensional Escher staircases for example. These worlds should be accessible from no strictly possible worlds and so would be outside the system of worlds we normally deal with, though strictly speaking there are no such worlds. We would still be left, however, with a set of strictly possible worlds, in other words, the system of worlds we normally deal with. These would also fix a sense of possibility – the usual sense.

Now the existence of a formal system is not itself particularly significant. There are many formal systems and we have to make the judgement that a certain formal system adequately represents our intuitions. It is, for example, a significant judgement that our logical intuitions are adequately represented by the usual formal system of mathematical logic. And it is a significant judgement that the axioms of geometry adequately represent our intuitions about lines and points – that they are "the logical analysis of our intuitions about space", as Hilbert puts it. Similarly we have to make a judgement as to which formal system of modal logic best represents our intuitions about modality. The incident of the potter and what he can understand about possible shapes from mathematics shows that S4 modal logic as generated by the instantiation requirement does not adequately represent our intuitions about modality. Our judgement is of course based on more than intuition, since it is also based on what we know about possibility from mathematics.

Armstrong's instantiation requirement is in some ways a very reasonable one. He wants to construct the possible out of the actual, and a universal is clearly part of the actual if it is instanced. However reasonable this position may be, it is not tenable. The arguments against the instantiation requirement seem conclusive enough, so we are forced to consider some other account of what it is for a universal to be part of the actual. Russell once said that it was "the point of philosophy to start with something so simple as to not seem worth stating, and end with something so paradoxical that no one will believe it".[13] I do not think our situation is quite as bad as that, though we started with some fairly straightforward considerations – namely,

13 Russell, "The Philosophy of Logical Atomism", p. 193.

49

the rejection of the instantiation requirement – and and we find that they impel us towards some not so straightforward conclusions.

It seems that it is not the fact of some instantiation that is crucial to whether there is a certain universal or not; it is whether certain things are possible or not. In place of Armstrong's instantiation requirement a possibility requirement would be more reasonable: There is a universal if and only if certain things are possible. Certainly no one is going to say that there is a certain universal if what is purportedly described is logically impossible because it is logically contradictory,[14] though there may be other reasons for saying that there is no such universal.

The requirement that there is a universal if and only if certain things are possible is not very informative. There are statements that are possibly true and that appear to involve reference to negative universals, disjunctive universals, and conjunctive universals. But it does not follow from the fact that those statements are possibly true that there are such universals, though corresponding to those statements there will be possible situations involving some genuine universals. Which predicates correspond to genuine universals is determined by quite different considerations. If there is a certain universal, then it entails that certain situations are possible; if certain situations are possible, it is on account of there being certain universals. Possibility is only part, however, of the characterization of the notion of universal.

David Lewis also seems to have a form of the instantiation requirement: There is a certain property if and only if it is instanced in some possible world, in other words, if the class identified with the property (namely, the class of all actual and possible instances) is not the empty class.[15] Presumably some nominalistic explanation has to be given of what instantiation is in a possible world. Lewis's theory at least has the virtue that it brings out the connection between the existence of a property and the notion of possibility.

For a universal a predicate refers to the universal whether that universal occurs or not, since it is possible to speak of an unexemplified universal. But even if the universal is instanced, referring to the universal does not take into account that particular occurrence of the universal. Referring to an instance of a universal is a quite different

14 Cf. Wittgenstein, *Tractatus*, 3.031.
15 David Lewis, "New Work for a Theory of Universals".

act. A universal is always referred to considered as something general, or something abstract (i.e. something abstracted from its context).[16] It is referred to as some *one thing* that can occur exemplified by any number of objects. The notion of possibility is already built in to the notion of universal, as David Lewis has pointed out.

Initially Lewis was sympathetic to the notion of a universal as something that was wholly present at many different places. But when the issues of uninstantiated universals and once-instanced universals were raised he began to realize that the notion of universal was essentially modal:

> This means that the definition of a universal is modal. A universal is something that satisfies a certain *de re* modal condition; it has a certain potentiality, whether or not this is realized. So far, so good. But what makes it so that one thing has the potentiality for repeated presence and another thing lacks it when in fact neither thing is repeatedly present? Is that just a brute modal fact? I would hope not. For the most part things have their potentialities in virtue of their non-modal characteristics.[17]

A thing that is a universal and happens to occur just once has the potentiality for repeated presence, whereas a thing that is a particular and happens to occur just once lacks that potentiality. These do strike me as being brute facts. They are modal facts because if something is a universal, then necessarily it is a universal, and therefore necessarily it can occur many times, whereas if something is a particular, then necessarily it is a particular, and therefore necessarily it can occur only once. If these facts are based on properties of universals and particulars, then they are a special sort of property, which are called 'internal properties'. Lewis's view that "things have their potentialities in virtue of their non-modal characteristics" makes sense for particulars for normal sorts of potentialities such as causal potentialities. A particular possesses a potentiality because it possesses a certain property, and that it possesses a property that is responsible for a causal potentiality is in general a non-modal fact. These sorts of properties are what we normally think of when we use the term 'property'; they are external properties as opposed to internal properties – to use the language of the *Tractatus*.

I suggest that fundamental metaphysical notions are more likely to be modal than is generally recognized. The characterization of the notion of particular and the characterization of the notion of

---

16 Not in the North American or Quinean sense, as Armstrong would put it.
17 David Lewis, "Against Structural Universals", p. 44.

universal are equally modal. Ask David Lewis, or any nominalist, whether a particular can occur in more than one place at the same time, and I am sure that he will agree that it is impossible.

There are some things that can be defined. For example, it is possible to explain what is meant by the term 'momentum' by giving a definition. Once it has been explained that momentum is mass times velocity there is no more to be said; you understand what momentum is. But if you go on to try and explain what mass and velocity are, it gets more difficult. Eventually you will reach certain fundamental terms that cannot be defined, but for which it may be possible to provide a characterization. As Frege puts it, "One cannot require that everything shall be defined, any more than one can require that a chemist shall decompose every substance."[18]

It seems likely that the fundamental notions in a given area are to be characterized in a way that involves each other. For example, the notions of point and line are like this, since the notion of point and the notion of line have to be characterized in terms of one another. The problem with Euclid's "definitions" of point and line is that they do not bring out the way in which the two notions are dependent on each other, whereas the virtue of Hilbert's axioms is that they characterize the two notions in a way that does not try to provide separate definitions. If in some area there were true definitions of certain notions, then it is very likely that they would not be fundamental notions.

The notion of universal and the notion of possibility are fundamental metaphysical notions. A central characterization of the notion of universal involves the notion of possibility, and it seems that any account of what it is to say that *there is* a certain universal will involve the notion of possibility. It seems likely also that any account of the nature of possibility will in some way involve the notion of universal.

4. COMBINATORIAL THEORIES OF POSSIBILITY

Many situations that are possible but not actual are nevertheless conceivable, and they can be described by sentences that are possibly true.[19] There is then a correspondence between possible situations

---

18 Frege, "On Concept and Object", p. 182.
19 Perhaps there are situations that are possible but that are not conceivable by human beings and not describable by human language. Inevitably we shall ignore them.

and sentences that are possibly true. A sentence is formed by putting together linguistic elements, mainly proper names and predicates. For sentences that describe simple situations proper names correspond to particulars, and predicates correspond to universals, so the putting together of a sentence mirrors the putting together of a situation. It has to be assumed, of course, that logical connectives and quantifiers are functions or operators and do not correspond to anything of ontological significance.

In a combinatorial theory of possibility the possible is constructed out of the actual, so that what is possible is explained by the nature of what is actual. For any immanent realist what is actual consists of all the particulars that there are and all the universals that there are. Because of the correspondences between particulars and proper names, universals and predicates, and possible situations and sentences that are possibly true, it is natural to understand a combinatorial theory of possibility in terms of syntax.

If there are rules that govern the putting together of particulars and universals to form possible situations, then there are corresponding rules that govern the putting together of words to form sentences that are possibly true. We already have, in the syntax of the predicate calculus, rules that enable us to construct well-formed formulas that have to be understood as possibly true sentences. Providing that the terms correspond to actual particulars and universals and the rules of syntax have been obeyed, then as far as logic goes well-formed formulas are possibly true.[20]

We can call the theory that only uses the rules expressed by the syntax of predicate calculus the 'naive combinatorial theory of possibility'. It tells us that if '*a*' and '*b*' are proper names that refer to particulars, and '*R*' is a two-place predicate that corresponds to a relation, then '*aRb*' describes a possible situation. In many cases the naive theory works. But if '*a*' refers to the Taj Mahal, '*b*' to the Tower of London, and R is the relation "is the father of", then clearly '*aRb*' does not describe a possible situation. Unfortunately syntax cannot predict all the situations we know to be impossible, and we shall see that it also cannot predict all the situations we know to be possible.

---

20 "The notion of a possible state of affairs is introduced semantically, by means of the notion of atomic *statement*." Concerning a false atomic sentence Armstrong says: "While failing to correspond to an atomic state of affairs, it corresponds to the *form* of an atomic state of affairs." Armstrong, *A Combinatorial Theory of Possibility*, p. 45.

In the naive theory it is syntax that provides a way of predicting which situations are possible, but syntax does not by itself explain why the situations are possible. In a sense, syntax represents or pictures whatever it is about particulars and universals that explains which situations are possible. There is something about the particulars, *a* and *b,* and the universal, *R,* which makes the situation described by '*aRb*' at least *prima facie* possible. Wittgenstein called that something the internal properties of *a, b,* and *R.* A more sophisticated combinatorial theory designed to predict more of what is possible will improve on the naive theory by adding other rules that say more about the internal properties of particulars and universals, and it may introduce other factors. Presumably, combinatorial theories of this type, both naive and sophisticated, are possible for other interpretations of predicate calculus.

The naive theory can be regarded as a base theory that needs supplementing by additional rules. There need to be rules that *permit* certain situations not predicated by the naive theory, and there need to be rules that *forbid* situations that would otherwise be allowed.

One way in which the naive theory needs supplementing is by rules that govern the creation of new particulars, which Armstrong calls "alien individuals", since situations are possible that involve particulars other than the ones that currently exist. If a universal, for example, a sortal such as "mouse", is instanced, then that in itself establishes the possibility of further examples of mice.[21] Since we cannot regard the world as containing both actual particulars and possible particulars, alien individuals could be thought of as just that, further examples of mice, or further examples of horses. But in order to develop a combinatorial theory in the manner of the naive theory, it is of no use just to talk about further examples of mice; there need to be rules about alien individuals so that possible situations involving them can be described, and that involves giving them names. But this just introduces reference to *possibilia,* something combinatorialism is meant to avoid.

To avoid including *possibilia* as elements of the actual, Armstrong claims that alien individuals can be constructed out of the already given elements of the actual world, which unfortunately brings in metaphysical theories about the nature of particulars. "Haecceitism" is the doctrine that particulars have individual essences that cannot

21 Cf. Armstrong, "The Nature of Possibility", p. 582.

be constructed out of already given elements, thereby ruling out a combinatorial theory of alien individuals. At the other extreme is Russell's doctrine that particulars are nothing more than bundles of their properties. Somewhere in the middle is Armstrong's doctrine, which he calls weak anti-Haecceitism. On this view, particulars are "barely, numerically different from each other. They are *simply* other".[22] From his paper it seems that Armstrong only contemplates a particular's properties as its elements.

Nevertheless, referring to an alien individual, or indeed any individual, is not a matter of referring to the things the particular is constructed out of. Unless those elements are in fact assembled there is still no particular. As Armstrong himself says, an individual is simply different from other particulars, including the particulars and other things that are its components. Even if a particular is merely a bundle of properties, then those properties have to be instanced for the particular to exist and reference to be possible. So it still seems impossible to give a name to a possible particular. Possible situations with alien individuals can be dealt with only by describing them in general terms: It is possible that there be a mouse in my study in addition to the mice already in my study.

In the same way that we do not have names for further examples of mice, we do not have names for the particulars formed by dividing matter. Some parts of particulars (for example, organs of a body) can be regarded as particulars in their own right, but most acts of division would produce new particulars, corresponding to fairly arbitrary shapes. I suggest that this is true whether matter is infinitely divisible or atomic. These new particulars are also alien individuals, and likewise we do not have names for them.

The construction of new matter is a more fundamental problem for combinatorial theories of possibility. At its simplest, a parcel of matter is a parcel of one type of matter, such as bronze or water, which corresponds to a certain universal that we can call a mass universal. If there is such a mass universal, then it is possible that there be any number of parcels of matter of that type. It is certainly possible, however, that there be new, different parcels of matter. Neither Armstrong's combinatorialism nor any form of combinatorialism can account for this possibility. Armstrong can only construct his alien individuals out of already existing parcels of matter.

22 Ibid., p. 584.

The problem of parcels of matter is not a new or an isolated difficulty, since the bare, or numerical, difference between material objects arises at least in part from the bare, or numerical, difference between parcels of matter. Parcels of matter, therefore, present a difficulty for any form of combinatorialism. And it is an important difficulty, since a combinatorial theory of possibility should be able to account for the material objects of classical physics. These are not only possible objects, they are well-understood possible objects.

The naive combinatorial theory is one where possible situations can be described by sentences that are possibly true. The actual particulars and universals correspond to proper names and predicates from which possibly true sentences are constructed. In practice, of course, very few things have been given names, though in theory any element of the actual can be given a name. So in a sense such a theory appeals to possible names, which might provide a difficulty if this theory were regarded as an explanation of the nature of possibility.

A combinatorial theory supplemented with additional rules for the construction of alien individuals is still a combinatorial theory, since it constructs the possible out of the actual. But it is a different sort of theory from the naive theory and works in a different way, since in the naive theory all possible situations can be described by sentences that are possibly true. And it appears that no sort of combinatorial theory can account for new parcels of matter.

So far we have discussed the rules of naive combinatorialism, the factors that govern the construction of new particulars (i.e. "alien individuals"), and we have mentioned in passing the existence of rules that place restrictions on what is allowed by naive combinatorialism. We now give a systematic summary of those rules to help us draw general conclusions about what can be done with combinatorial theories of possibility.

Summary of the rules that govern possibility

1. Rules of naive combinatorialism. These are presented as syntactic rules that take all the particulars there are and all the universals there are and form sentences that are possibly true from the corresponding proper names and predicates. It is assumed that we have names for them – possible names?

There are possible situations that naive combinatorialism does not predict, namely, those involving particulars that do not exist but could. So it needs to be *supplemented* by:

2. Rules that govern the construction of new particulars, i.e. alien individuals. There are a number of ways to construct an alien individual:

a. By using an already existing parcel of matter.
b. By putting together actual particulars, which then become the proper parts of the new individual.
c. By physically dividing an existing material particular.
d. By using a newly created parcel of matter.

There are no names for the new particulars that can be made in any of these ways. In a, b, and c the new particulars are constructed out of already existing elements. In d something totally new is created, something no combinatorial theory can account for.

There are also certain combinations of universals and particulars that are formally permissible; they are allowed by the rules of naive combinatorialism, but are in fact impossible. So naive combinatorialism needs to be *restricted* by rules such as the following:

3. Rules that govern incompatible properties and relations.

a. Impossible situations described by '*Fa* & *Ga*'; e.g. 'Socrates has velocity three miles per hour and thirty miles per hour'.
b. Impossible situations described by '*Fa*'; e.g. 'Socrates is prime'.
c. Impossible situations described by '*aRb*'; e.g. 'The Taj Mahal is the father of the Tower of London'.

Nevertheless neither naive combinatorialism nor any of the rules just given tell us whether someone's description of a situation corresponds to a genuine universal or not. So there also need to be:

4. Methods for determining whether there is such a universal or not. Very often mathematical arguments can be used to tell us whether there is such a universal or not. For example, it can be shown that there is no such shape as the staircase imagined by Escher and those who look at his pictures, and that there is no such shape as a Klein bottle in three dimensions without intersection.[23]

These four classes of rules summarize a sophisticated combinatorial theory of possibility. The rules in class 1 form the base theory; they

23 See note 10, this chapter.

57

say which situations are formally allowable. The rules in classes 2, 3, and 4 add to those rules. Those of class 2 say that certain things not contemplated by class 1 are possible, whereas those of class 3 say that certain things allowed by class 1 are not possible. Despite the failure of the rules of naive combinatorialism as displayed by classes 2 and 3, we do need the rules of class 1 in order to predict which situations are possible; the other rules by themselves would not be enough. This brings out the importance of naive combinatorialism and shows that it is indeed a base theory.

If it were not for the problem of parcels of matter, which some people might be prepared to neglect, it could be maintained that the possible can be constructed out of the actual. Possible particulars can be constructed using rules 2a, 2b, and 2c, using the word 'construct' in a rather physical sense. Possible situations can then be constructed from universals and particulars according to the rules of 1, as restricted by 3 – using the word 'construct' in a rather different sense. A combinatorial theory of this sort "constructs" in two different ways: a physical sort of construction in rules 2a, 2b, and 2c and a rather different sort in rule 1 as restricted by 3.[24]

Rules 1 and 3 go together easily. Rule 1 as restricted by 3 allows us to form sentences that, though not true, are possibly true and so describe possible situations. It is the way we would have liked to have developed a sophisticated combinatorial theory. It is rule 2 with its lack of names that stands in the way. Whether the lack of names for alien individuals should be regarded as an insuperable difficulty or a mere awkwardness depends on what a combinatorial theory of possibility is meant to achieve.

But whatever the purpose of combinatorial theory, it cannot be used to explain the nature of possibility. Even if the rules of the naive theory were sufficient by themselves, they would not explain the nature of possibility. It is the internal properties of universals and particulars that explain why the situations predicted by naive combinatorialism are *prima facie* possible. And in the same way that the naive theory needs supplementing by additional rules, so also do those additional rules need explaining by further metaphysical considerations, perhaps including additional internal properties.

---

24 "Let us not conceal that this manoeuvre does involve a qualification of, a move away from, Combinatorialism. Our alien individuals are not reached combinatorially but, rather, conceptually, 'by analogy'." Armstrong, *A Combinatorial Theory of Possibility,* p. 60.

In contrast, the methods of class 4 have nothing to do with syntax or the combinations that syntax represents. They represent a quite different approach to establishing what is possible and explaining why it is possible. The other rules assume that there are certain universals and that they can be instanced by particulars, whereas the methods of rule 4 have to do with investigating whether a certain description or conception corresponds to a genuine universal. To say that "there is" a universal is to make a statement with modal content; the methods of rule 4 are methods for establishing whether "there is" a universal.

It can be seen from our investigations that there is no one factor or type of factor that explains the nature of modality. The diversity of combination rules seems to imply a diversity of explanations of what is possible.

5. WITTGENSTEIN'S THEORY OF POSSIBILITY

The theory of possibility that we find in Wittgenstein's *Tractatus* can be interpreted as a form of the naive combinatorial theory,[25] which makes certain assumptions about particulars in order to avoid alien individuals and which extends the notion of internal properties so that they are the basis for rule 3a as well as for naive combinatorialism. In this section we shall use his theory to investigate the notion of fact and the internal properties of particulars and universals that explain possibility.

Where up to now we have used the single term 'situation', Wittgenstein uses two terms: "fact" (*Tatsache*) and "state of affairs" (*Sachverhalt*), which correspond to fundamental categories in the *Tractatus*, as well as the more general term "situation" (*Sachlage*). For Wittgenstein the world is first a world of facts, with the objects that are components of facts having only a secondary status. Wittgenstein regards facts as the fundamental category, and what the world is ultimately made of, presumably because he regards sentences as the basic units of meaning.

Whatever states of affairs are, both facts and states of affairs consist of objects fitted together. Wittgenstein's objects are the things with internal properties that explain what is possible. On one

---

25 "If things can occur in states of affairs, this possibility must be in them from the beginning. (Nothing in the province of logic can be merely possible. Logic deals with every possibility and all possibilities are its facts.)" *Tractatus*, 2.0121.

interpretation, the one we shall adopt, 'object' is a generic term that covers both universals and particulars.

There is a dispute about the interpretation of the *Tractatus* concerning the ontological status of the two fundamental ontological categories: facts and states of affairs. The dispute is between Stenius and Black over what a state of affairs is. Black says that a state of affairs is simply an atomic fact, where all facts, atomic or otherwise, correspond to true sentences.[26] *Tractatus* 4.2211 seems to support him on this. But according to Stenius, states of affairs correspond to both true and false atomic sentences. For Stenius a state of affairs is an arrangement of objects where the word 'arrangement' maintains its customary ambiguity between actual arrangement and possible arrangement.[27]

In favour of Stenius we can point out that the *Tractatus* says that "a proposition is a description of a state of affairs" (4.023) and "a proposition shows how things stand if it is true. And it says that they do so stand" (4.022). Black, on the other hand, would have the *Tractatus* say that only true propositions describe states of affairs.[28] The *Tractatus* also characterizes states of affairs differently from the way it characterizes facts. There are existent and non-existent states of affairs, and actual and possible states of affairs.[29] It makes no sense to talk about a non-existent fact or a possible fact, as Black himself points out in his discussion of the relevant passages of the *Tractatus*.[30]

Wittgenstein really needs four categories: facts, atomic facts, situations, and atomic situations, where both true and false atomic sentences correspond to atomic situations, and only true atomic sentences correspond to atomic facts. Of course there is some awkward-

26 Max Black, *A Companion to Wittgenstein's Tractatus*, pp. 39–45; cf. G. E. M. Anscombe, *An Introduction to Wittgenstein's Tractatus*, p. 30. For a vigorous defence of Black's position see Donald Peterson, *Wittgenstein's Early Philosophy*, Appendix. An atomic fact corresponds to an atomic sentence or elementary proposition, which is a sentence that is directly connected with the world and does not derive its meaning from other propositions.
27 Erik Stenius, *Wittgenstein's Tractatus*.
28 "In a proposition a situation is constructed by way of experiment" (4.031); " 'A state of affairs is thinkable': what this means is that we can picture it to ourselves" (3.001); "What is thinkable is possible too" (3.02). But see Wittgenstein's letter to Russell of 19 August 1919 (*Letters to Russell, Keynes, and Moore*, p. 72), which is often quoted in favour of the Black interpretation. Neither Russell nor Frege could understand what a state of affairs was just from reading the *Tractatus*.
29 *Tractatus*, 2, 2.012, 2.0124, 2.04, 2.06, 3.11, 4.023, 4.1, 4.25, 4.27, 4.3.
30 Black, *A Companion to Wittgenstein's Tractatus*, p. 34.

60

ness here in regarding an atomic fact, which for Wittgenstein is an element of the world, as a kind of atomic situation, since many atomic situations are not part of the world. This awkwardness underlies the interpretational problem, which probably rests on unresolved philosophical problems.

We can talk about possible particulars in general terms; what we cannot do is talk about individual possible particulars. If there is no such particular it is not possible to refer to it, let alone understand *which* particular is being referred to. Situations, it seems, are not like particulars in this respect. If there is a particular *a* and a universal *F*, and '*Fa*' is a false sentence, then '*Fa*' can be taken as describing the merely possible situations of "*a* having *F*". It is not merely that we understand what sort of situation is meant; we understand *which* situations or *which* possible fact is meant. It seems that possible situations are not problematic in the way that possible particulars are problematic.

Although we may understand what is meant by the sentence '*Fa*' even if it is false, that does not imply that there is a something that is being referred to, a something that is a "possible situation". In fact, the lack of analogy with other particulars counts against reifying situations, even if they obtain. If being a particular were merely a matter of only being able to occur once, then a fact would count as a particular; but there is no reason to credit facts with any ontological significance, since they lack the sort of individuality or principle of unity associated with the more serious particulars. These considerations also count against regarding sentences as names that refer to situations or facts, a conclusion Wittgenstein agrees with (see *Tractatus* 3.144).

In *Tractatus* 3.11 and 3.12 Wittgenstein provides an alternative to reifying situations. He suggests that situations – it should be noted that he uses the more general term *Sachlage* – have a sort of projective or intentional status:

3.11 We use the perceptible sign of a proposition (spoken or written, etc.) as a projection of a possible situation. The method of projection is to think of the sense of the proposition.

3.12 I call the sign with which we express a thought a propositional sign. – And a proposition is a propositional sign in its projective relation to the world.[31]

31 3.12 shows that a proposition (*Satz*) is not just a sentence considered as an object.

There is no attempt here to reify situations; they are constructed in thought, in the sense that we know how things would stand if the proposition were true. It is similar to Leibniz's combinatorial approach to possible worlds, except that Leibniz appeals to ideas in the mind of God.[32] This approach is consistent with our desire not to include things like facts, states of affairs, or events, possible or actual, in our ontology. It is true that we have to make use of terms such as 'situation', but it is only a way of speaking.

Atomic sentences are composed of terms that refer to the 'objects' of the *Tractatus,* since there are no possible objects for Wittgenstein. And facts and states of affairs have no other components besides objects: Objects simply fit into each other in the appropriate ways to produce facts and states of affairs (2.03). It follows that both sorts of terms that are the components of sentences refer to objects.[33] And since we also know that objects differ in logical form from each other, it seems that Wittgenstein's term 'object' could cover what we normally call particulars and universals: "It would certainly be a mistake to identify objects with what we normally call 'individuals', or to suppose that they cannot be at all like what we commonly call relations."[34] And it is worth noting that Russell, in his version of logical atomism, uses the term 'object' to cover both particulars and universals.

The reason why Wittgenstein does not make an explicit distinction between universals and particulars is probably because he wants his account of the world to be based on the most general "logical" considerations. He may hold to something like the syntactic priority thesis, which would explain the priority he gives to facts. And he may think that the structure of logic is such that it does not dictate the usual distinction between universal and particular, or between concept and object; for as I argued in Chapter 2, logic has several different metaphysical interpretations. It also seems that for Wittgenstein quantification is not available as the basis for the dis-

---

32 Leibniz, "Meditations on Knowledge Truth and Ideas", pp. 26–7, and Hidé Ishiguro, *Leibniz's Philosophy of Logic and Language,* p. 124.

33 This inference is not uncontroversial. Wittgenstein seems to believe in properties in his pretractarian writings, in the *Tractatus* itself, and in "Some Remarks on Logical Form". See Edwin B. Allaire, "The *Tractatus:* Nominalistic or Realistic?". Allaire is arguing against the nominalistic interpretation of Anscombe, *An Introduction to Wittgenstein's Tractatus,* Chapter 7, which has recently been defended by Peter Carruthers, *The Metaphysics of the Tractatus,* p. 6.

34 Black, *A Companion to Wittgenstein's Tractatus,* p. 57.

tinction, since it seems that he understands quantified sentences in terms of infinite conjunctions and infinite disjunctions.[35]

The objects of the *Tractatus* differ in logical form from each other, so it seems that there are different kinds of objects. Some of these differences correspond to what Wittgenstein calls 'internal properties'. Since the symbols that refer to the objects of the *Tractatus* are the symbols dealt with by formal logic, those symbols may be written as follows:

$$a \qquad b \qquad c \ldots$$
$$F(\ ) \qquad G(\ ) \qquad H(\ ) \ldots$$
$$R(\ )(\ ) \qquad S(\ )(\ ) \qquad T(\ )(\ ) \ldots$$
$$\cdot$$
$$\cdot$$
$$\cdot$$

The first row presents proper names; the second row, one-place predicates; the third row, two-place predicates; and so on. Normally, predicates are not written with brackets, but the rules of combination, which the brackets represent, are at least always understood when the symbols of formal logic are written down. The brackets indicate how the corresponding objects fit into one another, in accordance with Wittgenstein's view that the internal properties of objects should be reflected in the symbols for them (see *Tractatus* 4.126).

If there were only two types of symbol, those of the first row and those of the second row, then although we would have two disjoint classes of symbol, both classes would be characterized in symmetrical ways as in fragment 1. There would be no reason to call the symbols of one class complete (bracket fillers) and the symbols of the other class incomplete (symbols with brackets that need filling). As it is, there are more types of symbol than just those of the first and the second row. There is therefore a basis in the formalism for calling one class of symbol complete and the other classes incomplete. This distinction for symbols represents, and in some way characterizes, a corresponding distinction among the objects of the *Tractatus*. Using Frege's metaphor we can say that there is a class of saturated objects and several classes of unsaturated objects: singly unsaturated objects, doubly unsaturated objects, and so on, as in

35 Ibid., p. 281.

fragment 2, although it should be understood that the metaphor adds nothing by way of explanation. As far as logical considerations go nothing further can be said to characterize this difference in logical form between objects.

It is metaphysical considerations, however, that would lead us to identify the saturated objects with the unique objects of our acquaintance (which we call particulars), and to identify the unsaturated objects with the repeatable things of our acquaintance (which we call universals). To make such an identification is not inconsistent with the system of the *Tractatus*. However, in order to bring out what is going on in the Tractarian theory of possibility we need to talk about universals and particulars, because only an interpretation will give us any insight into the nature of internal properties. This becomes clearer when we consider the second sort of internal properties mentioned in the *Tractatus*.

There are two sorts of properties mentioned in the *Tractatus* that are internal properties – that is, properties that are part of the logical form of objects. I have already described the first type. They are properties that we have already represented in the symbols for objects. They are the basis for the combination rules used in predicate calculus, and for this reason they can be called 'logical internal properties'. Examples of these properties are being saturated, being singly unsaturated, being doubly unsaturated, and so on; or, using our metaphysical interpretation, being a particular, being a property, being a relation, and so on.

The second type of internal property can be called 'categorial internal properties'. If an object has a determinate colour or a determinate shape or a determinate position, then it also falls under a certain higher-level universal such as being coloured or being shaped or being spatial, which we can call categories.[36] Categories are also called absolute determinables.[37] The determinate colour, the determinate shape, and the determinate position are examples of external properties, but higher-level universals, such as being coloured, are internal properties; they too are part of the logical form

---

36 Cf. *Tractatus*, 2.0131. Wittgenstein is here committed to the principle of ontological determinacy, which he later abandoned; see P. T. Geach, *Truth, Love and Immortality*, Chapter 4. The determinate shape is a fully determinate shape such that a more specific shape is not possible. Such universals are at the bottom of their hierarchies, since they do not classify other universals. See also Donald Peterson, *Wittgenstein's Early Philosophy*, p. 22, on *Tractatus* 2.013ff.

37 See John R. Searle, "Determinables and Determinates".

of the objects (*Tractatus* 2.0251). With colours and shapes there are also intermediate determinables, such as "red", which are not internal properties since there is a determinable above them. It is the highest determinables, which we have called categories, that are the internal properties. Black attempts to construct a formalism in which internal properties of this type are also reflected in the symbols.[38]

The notion of categorial internal properties has to be discussed in terms of particulars and universals, since it is universals that come in hierarchies. The notion of hierarchy of universals is needed to explain the relationship between a determinate shade of colour and a colour determinable. And it is particulars that have determinate properties, and particulars that fall under categories such as being coloured.

Universals also have internal properties that express the logical form of the type of universal (*Tractatus* 4.123). For example, the relationship between scarlet and red, which is one of subordination, is an example of an internal property, in this case an internal relation (see Chapter 5). There can be internal relations between universals; what is much less clear is whether there are internal relations between particulars.

Tractatus 6.3751 indicates how Wittgenstein has extended the notion of what is "logical" to cover everything that is included in his notion of logical form: "For example, the simultaneous presence of two colours at the same place in the visual field is impossible, in fact logically impossible, since it is ruled out by the logical structure of colour." Since colours are secondary qualities and phenomenologically complicated, Wittgenstein's point has given rise to a certain amount of controversy, so it is interesting that he should also give an example involving primary qualities: "A particle cannot have two different velocities at the same time." The phenomenon of colour exclusion should be regarded as an illustration of a general principle of determinate exclusion: If a particular falls under a category (absolute determinable), then it possesses only one perfectly determinate attribute subordinate to that category.[39]

---

38 See Black, *A Companion to Wittgenstein's Tractatus*, pp. 199–200.
39 See Searle, "Determinables and Determinates", p. 358; Edwin Allaire, "Tractatus 6.3751". Armstrong attempts an explanation of determinate exclusion based on his analysis of determinate quantities; see *A Combinatorial Theory of Possibility*, pp. 78–84; cf. Volume II, p. 126. In Chapter 5, Section 6, I criticize another version of his analysis. For colours, determinate exclusion can take three forms: (1) No point can be two perfectly determinate shades of colour at the same time; (2) no point that is red can be two perfectly determinate shades of red at the same

In 6.375 Wittgenstein says that "the only impossibility that exists is *logical* impossibility". And then in 6.3751 he says that the simultaneous presence of two colours is ruled out by the logical structure of colour. We must conclude that by 'logical impossibility' he means something broader than what is given by deductive logic, something like broadly logical impossibility.[40] Earlier in the *Tractatus* he had said, "Logic deals with every possibility and all possibilities are its facts" (2.0121c). This should be taken as a statement about Wittgenstein's view of the nature and province of logic; it deals with every sort of possibility.

What is possible is determined by the nature of objects (particulars and universals). Their nature, in this sense, is their internal properties (2.0124, 2.01231, 2.014). The rules of logic fall into two types: rules of valid inference and combination rules. The combination rules govern the formation of atomic sentences and the formation of compound sentences out of atomic sentences, though it is only the former that are related to the internal properties of objects. In order to construct well-formed sentences that correctly describe reality we have to sort out which things are particulars, which things are monadic universals, which things are dyadic universals, and so on, and where it is appropriate to introduce variables.[41] In other words, we have to take into account those properties of objects that we have called logical internal properties.

Wittgenstein can be interpreted as saying that, if we have to take into account the nature of objects as given by their logical internal properties, then we should equally take into account the categorial internal properties of objects. He thinks that both are equally part of the logical form of objects. Both dictate which sentences describe possible situations and which do not. In this way Wittgenstein has extended the notion of logic and its combination rules.[42]

The internal properties of a particular are that it is a particular and that it falls under certain categories, whether it is a coloured object,

time; (3) no point that is coloured can be two determinable colours at the same time, such as red and green. C. L. Hardin's discussion of incompatible colours seems confined to (3); see *Color for Philosophers,* pp. 121–7. In reality, colour determinables do not divide determinate colours into well-defined classes.

40 But compare the end of 6.3751 where he says: "The statement that a point in the visual field has two different colours at the same time is a contradiction."

41 Cf. Lemmon, *Beginning Logic,* p. 97.

42 Facts about categorial internal properties are brute facts, but then so are facts about logical internal properties.

a spatial object, and so on. The internal properties of a universal are that it is a universal and whether it is a monadic universal, or dyadic universal, and so on. The internal properties of universals can also be taken to include any category the universal may be subordinate to, and its position in that hierarchy of universals. For example, scarlet is subordinate to red, and consequently scarlet and red differ in their position in the hierarchy of colour universals.

How objects can fit together to form situations depends on the internal properties of objects, and properties we have just described, the internal properties of particulars and universals. Which situations are possible, therefore, depends to a large extent on the nature of universals. It depends generally on the fact that a universal is repeatable, and also on the fact that a particular is not repeatable. It also depends on the specific nature of the universals concerned, and on the specific nature of the particulars given by the higher-level universals (i.e. categories) they fall under.

Unfortunately Wittgenstein's world is different from any world that we can contemplate. His objects are simple and unalterable; they cannot be broken down any further, and they cannot come into or go out of existence.[43] Were this allowable, he would have a true combinatorial theory of possibility without alien individuals.

A combinatorial theory of possibility aims to construct the possible out of the actual. A successful theory would give rules that govern how that construction should proceed, such as the rules given in Section 4. The difficulties with those rules had to do with the creation of new particulars and the diverse nature of the rules; there were at least two different sorts of construction, and sometimes the rules involved the possibility of providing names for the components and sometimes names could not be provided. However, if we ignore these difficulties about particulars the rules do give us a sort of combinatorial theory. On the other hand, a combinatorial theory based on these rules is not an explanation of the nature of possibility. For that, following Wittgenstein, we have to look to the internal properties of particulars and universals.

Rules of type 1, those of naive combinatorialism, are explained by logical internal properties. Rules such as 3a are explained by

---

43 See *Tractatus*, 2.02, 2.027, 2.0271. At one point he justifies his metaphysical atomism by appealing to semantic reasons; 2.021, 2.0211.

categorial internal properties. This looks like the beginning of a programme, though it is not clear how all the rules typified by 3b and 3c could be explained in this way. These rules have to do with essences such as the sortal essence of a natural kind, and it could be argued that some of them at any rate are impossibilities in a sense other than broadly logical impossibility.[44] However successful a programme based on internal properties might be, it cannot explain which descriptions correspond to universals as in the methods of type 4; they are of a different sort altogether. It appears that a unified explanation of possibility is not available.

Nevertheless we can draw the very general conclusion that what is possible is determined by all the universals that there are and their natures – that is, their internal properties. Which particulars are possible is determined by all the sortal universals that there are. Which parcels of matter are possible is determined by all the matter universals that there are. And which situations are possible depends on the internal properties of universals and particulars. But the internal properties of a particular are not peculiar to that particular; they go with the sortal universal the particular falls under, and so can be regarded as components of the sortal universal. What determines whether there is a universal or not, such as the methods of type 4, is another issue altogether and does not affect our conclusion.

Earlier I said that a central part of the characterization of the notion of universal is that it is one thing that can occur many times, which already involves the notion of possibility. And we also concluded that a statement to the effect that there is a certain universal is an essentially modal statement: To say that there is a certain universal does not imply that the universal is instanced, though it does have implications for what is possible. We have now concluded that what is possible is determined by all the universals that there are. The notions of universal and possibility are fundamental metaphys-

---

44 If a modal truth is to be explained in terms of the sortal essence of a natural kind, then it is presumably explicable by the natural laws that govern the natural kind. If so, it is a form of natural necessity and not broadly logical necessity. That it is not possible for horses to have wings appears to be based on the genetic laws governing horses. Admittedly if something otherwise horselike had wings we would not call it a horse, but this sort of impossibility has something to do with reference and is therefore metaphysically not very important. Similarly, that it is impossible for something to have the mass of an electron and a charge of ten coulombs appears to be a matter of natural law, and we would not call it an electron. Cf., W. H. Newton-Smith, *The Rationality of Science*, p. 170.

ical notions and closely related. They have to be characterized in terms of one another, in the same way that the notions of point and line in geometry have to be explained and characterized in terms of one another.

6. POSSIBLE WORLDS

It follows from our conclusion that the modal cannot be explained in terms of the non-modal. The possible-worlds explanation of modality, on the other hand, can be regarded as an attempt to do just that, if the existence of possible worlds is taken to be a non-modal fact. I shall argue that this attempted explanation fails.

In other areas of philosophy people such as Frege and Wittgenstein have held that logic is a guide to ontology. If the purposes of logic require that sentences be recast in a different form, then that new logical form is a good guide to "what there is".[45] Those who argue for the existence of possible worlds are thinking in a way that is analogous: For them, what is good for semantics is good for ontology. Semantics is the strong point of the possible-worlds approach to modality, so much so that writers who explain modality in different ways try to vindicate their theories by reproducing possible worlds.[46]

Possible worlds provide truth-makers for modal statements in a fairly obvious way. It is possible that there be further examples of mice in my study, but we cannot name those possible individuals. They are what Armstrong calls 'alien individuals'. But on the possible-worlds approach they have more or less the same status as actual individuals and in a sense can be referred to – though, limited to the actual world as we are, we cannot in fact refer to them.

Although the theory of possible worlds provides a convenient semantics, it is not so clear that it provides an explanation of the nature of modality:

A model structure, for example, is a purely set theoretical construction that as such has no obvious connection with modal notions at all; it is just any ordered triple (G, K, R) where K is a set of which G is a member and on

45 Cf. Crispin Wright on the syntactic priority thesis, in *Frege's Conception of Numbers as Objects*, pp. 13, 14, and 51–3.
46 E.g., William Lycan and Stewart Shapiro, "Actuality and Essence"; Peter Forrest, "Ways Worlds Could Be"; and Armstrong, *A Combinatorial Theory of Possibility*, pp. 47ff.

which R is a reflexive relation. . . . To accept the pure semantics, therefore, is not, as such to acquiesce in any philosophical doctrine at all. The pure semantics commits itself to little more than a fragment of set theory.[47]

This is fine for pure semantics, but not for applied semantics; as Plantinga points out, pure semantics does not give us any "insight into our modal notions", nor does it tell us what the necessity operator means.[48] To do that we have to make the following identifications: K is the set of all "possible worlds", G is the "real world", and R the relation of "relative possibility" or "accessibility".

But what are *possible* worlds? Language does not tell us, nor does semantics. Intuition and mathematics tell us that some descriptions correspond to possible worlds while others do not. The worlds that are needed to explain modality do not include worlds that contain Escher staircases; those worlds are already excluded. It appears that for Lewis, the worlds he needs to explain modality are modal primitives.[49] But what is it that makes them possible worlds rather than simply other worlds? For example, someone might, for some totally different purpose, consider a world spatio-temporally and causally separate from this one. Would it be a "possible world" simply because it was disjoint from this one?[50] Isn't it at least possible that such a topologically disjoint world should at some stage become joined to this world? If this is impossible, in the appropriate sense of the word 'possible', does it thereby become a member of the set of possible worlds?[51] Perhaps a world is a possible world only if it is "impossible" for it to become joined to this one.

Sometimes, however, possible-worlds theorists write as if the worlds were simply given; and if given, how could they be impossible?[52] Their givenness is a non-modal fact that explains modality. But if they were simply given, we would need to know how they are relevant to what is possible in this world, for it is in this world that we can and cannot do certain things. It is in this world that we cannot make an object have two different velocities at the same time, and it is in this world that we cannot draw a square circle. It is in this world that there is a lump of clay that could possibly

47 Alvin Plantinga, *The Nature of Necessity,* pp. 126–7.
48 Ibid., p. 127.
49 Lycan and Shapiro, "Actuality and Essence", p. 358.
50 Cf. Armstrong, *A Combinatorial Theory of Possibility,* p. 16, where he mentions Broad's "island universes"; see also the note on p. 33.
51 Cf. David Lewis, *On the Plurality of Worlds,* pp. 71–2.
52 Cf. Richard Miller, "Dog Bites Man: A Defence of Modal Realism".

be given a certain shape; how we can mould it does not depend on what is going on in other worlds.

Like possible worlds, Plato's world of Forms was postulated to explain facts about this world while being totally separate from it. Like possible worlds the world of Forms provides an easy semantics; a general term simply refers to a Form, in much the same way that a proper name refers to a particular. Two of the traditional difficulties with the theory of Forms are the problems of "participation" and "separation". These are really two sides of the same problem. If the world of Forms is utterly separate from this world, how could its existence or non-existence be relevant to this world? And "participation" is just a metaphor, which if pursued leads to no elucidation of the relation between Forms and the objects of this world.[53]

"Imitation" is not much better than participation. A reproduction of a painting imitates or strives after the original painting, and the chalk circle imitates or strives after the true, perfect circle. Imitation is an asymmetrical relation, as it has to be for the theory of Forms to succeed, but the asymmetry derives entirely from the perfection of the original or the ideal. Perhaps Pythagoreans could make something of this notion of perfection, though in the end Pythagoreanism appears to appeal to a designer-creator; in other words, it appeals to productive, causal activity. From the point of view of metaphysics, however, it really does not matter that the true circle is more perfect than the chalk circle – they are both equally shapes; and it really does not matter that the original painting has more to it than the reproductions – they are both equally pictures. If the relation between a Form and an object in this world of appearances that exemplifies it is merely one of resemblance, a symmetrical relation, then the Forms make no contribution to the theory of universals. The Form is simply another object with the same status as the objects of this world that exemplify it; its existence is irrelevant to whether an object has a certain property or not.[54]

Intuitively, we imagine that the relation between Forms and the objects of this world is a productive one, that a Form is somehow responsible for the property an object has. But it is difficult to

53 Cf. Armstrong, Volume I, p. 66.
54 Cf. Armstrong, Volume I, pp. 71, 72. He points out that the modern Platonist would deny that the Form of a sphere was a sphere or spherical, so the intuitive motivation for Platonism from perfect or ideal patterns would disappear.

understand it as a productive relation on account of the separation of the transcendent world of Forms from this world.[55] And as Armstrong points out, once the difference between a productive relation and a constitutive relations is grasped, and the relation between Form and object is understood to be constitutive, then we have moved from transcendent realism to immanent realism.

There is a similar problem with possible worlds: How could things that are fundamentally of the same type as the things of this world explain modal facts concerning the things of this world? Moreover, for the explanation to work they have to exist in the same way as this world. Given their spatio-temporal and causal separateness, how could possible worlds be relevant to modality?[56]

The question of what are the truth-makers for modal statements is a different question from what is the basis of modality or the metaphysical explanation of modality. If there were possible worlds in any significant sense, then they would be the truth-makers for modal statements. It would still not be clear, however, that the set of possible worlds would be an explanation for the nature of modality. It is all very well calling them modal primitives as Lycan does.[57] There are, however, as I have shown, explanations of what makes some situations possible and therefore some worlds possible, and there are explanations of why other descriptions do not correspond to possible situations.[58]

55 Armstrong, Volume I, pp. 68, 69.
56 Cf. Armstrong, *A Combinatorial Theory of Possibility:* "These semantic postulations, however, in no way explain anything that happens in the natural world. Hence there seems no reason to make them" (p. 8). He then presents an argument about mathematics similar to mine about Forms.
57 Lycan and Shapiro, "Actuality and Essence", p. 358.
58 Some people who do not believe in literal possible worlds have tried to construct possible worlds out of other things, so that they too can have a semantics for modal logic. I have not tried to do this because I do not see the need. No doubt semantics is very interesting, but it all depends where the drive to provide semantics for modal logic comes from. If the thought is that from semantics insight can be gained into the nature of modality then the project is unlikely to be very successful.

4

The causal significance of basic attributes

1. BASIC UNIVERSALS

I have distinguished statements that say "there is" a universal from statements that say a universal occurs. If "there is" a universal, then it is possible that it occur any number of times, or not at all. The central characterization of the notion of universal is in terms of this possibility of multiple occurrence. This notion of occurrence is a primitive, intuitive notion based on a commonsense view of the world, but it is by no means alien to a scientific view of the world. The shape or mass to be found here, instanced by one object, is also to be found there, instanced by a second object. The shape or mass occurs in the sense that it can be "found".

In order to elucidate the notion of occurrence, or being found, it is natural to turn to causality. If a certain shape occurs, or is found, then we can interact with it in some sense, and it should be regarded as causally significant. If the shape of a body is changed from spherical to ellipsoidal, for example, then the particular concerned will interact causally in a different way. It is likely therefore that causality will be some sort of guide to the ontological status of universals.[1]

There are some predicates that appear to signify universals that are significant for causality, but that are dependent on other universals. For example, if a particular is spherical or polyhedral in shape, then it falls under a corresponding universal, which is certainly significant for causality, but there is also a more specific universal that it could fall under, for example, "spherical with radius five inches". The more general universal is different from the more specific universal, yet the two universals do not apply to the particular independently.

Shapes are an example of a hierarchy of related universals, which are such that if one of the more specific shape universals applies to

1 Cf. Armstrong, Volume II, Chapter 13, and "Towards a Theory of Properties".

a particular, then a number of other more general universals differing in generality also apply to the particular. That universals are arranged in hierarchies on account of differences in generality is a characteristic of universals, and a way in which they differ from particulars. This forms part of our characterization of the notion of universal. The notion of a hierarchy of universals will also play an important role in the discussion of the ways in which universals are real constituents of the world.

2. ONTOLOGICAL DETERMINACY

To say which attributes a particular possesses is to say what that particular is like as opposed to saying what sort of thing it is, which is why Strawson called attributes 'characterizing universals'. Among attributes there are what we shall call 'basic attributes'. Intuitively we can say that a basic attribute is a universal that is fully specified, such that if a particular possesses a certain basic attribute, then that basic attribute determines completely what that particular is like in that respect. More formally, a basic attribute is a perfectly determinate universal in the sense that it is classified by higher-level attributes but does not itself classify any lower-level attributes. We shall also require that a basic attribute not be a conjunction of other basic attributes.

There are, therefore, two ways that there could fail to be basic attributes. Firstly, if for any attribute, however specific, there is always a more specific attribute, one lower down the hierarchy, then there are no basic attributes. Secondly, there could fail to be basic attributes if any attribute can always be construed as a conjunction of attributes of the same level or lower in some ontologically significant way. The conjuncts would then be more basic or more fundamental. We shall show that there are basic attributes simply by producing some examples that satisfy both conditions.

A more general attribute classifies less general attributes. For example, the colour "red" classifies all the shades of red, such as scarlet, crimson, and claret; similarly, the shape "triangular" classifies all the different types of triangle. The relation between the lower-level attributes and the higher-level attribute that classifies them is called subordination (scarlet, for example, is subordinate to red). This relation is an example of an internal relation, and to describe it we would use our second interpretation of predicate calculus.

74

For any given attribute, if there is an attribute that is subordinate to it, then there is more than one attribute subordinate to it, where "there is" is used in the sense appropriate to universals. If there are basic attributes then they are attributes that do not classify other attributes; there are no attributes that are subordinate to them, so that they are at the bottom of their hierarchies (although in a different sense basic attributes can be said to classify the particulars they apply to).

In his book on McTaggart, Geach discusses what he calls the principle of ontological determinacy:

Nothing can have a determinable characteristic without having it in a perfectly determinate form. For example, nothing can have shape without having a perfectly determinate shape, or size without having a perfectly determinate size, or colour without having a perfectly determinate colour. Vagueness and fuzziness can infect only our descriptions, not the actual things we describe.[2]

A determinable characteristic is a higher-level attribute such as "spherical". A perfectly determinate shape is something like "spherical with radius five inches", which specifies exactly how a particular is as far as shape goes. No further details can be added. Intuitively, it does seem as though there are perfectly determinate attributes such as the aforementioned shape attribute. But all this amounts to is that there is a basic attribute in the sense that there is such a universal; it does not tell us about the characteristics of real particulars.

One important argument in favour of the principle of ontological determinacy is that physics always makes use of the principle; physics is the most appropriate discipline for describing the natural world, and physics is very successful. Classical physics, which deals with continuously divisible classical matter, assumes that a body possesses a perfectly determinate shape, and that bodies have perfectly determinate masses and charges and so on.

2 P. T. Geach, *Truth, Love and Immortality*, p. 55. McTaggart's name for the principle of ontological determinacy was 'Total Ultimate Presupposition'. Wittgenstein assumed the principle of ontological determinacy in the *Tractatus* (2.0131), but later came to deny it. The discussion of vagueness in language is not unrelated to how reality is, as the paradox of the heap shows. If we insist on discussing quantities of salt in terms of heaps, then there is indeed indeterminacy. But there are other ways of description that bring out that the distribution of the salt is perfectly determinate. It is conceivable that a perfectly determinate attribute of one sort could be the basis of predication of a vague predicate of another sort. Cf. Crispin Wright, "On the Coherence of Vague Predicates".

Quantum mechanics has so far not been given a widely accepted metaphysical interpretation, but nevertheless the principle of ontological determinacy plays an important role in quantum mechanics. Particles have determinate charges and rest masses, and in simple quantum mechanics atoms and molecules have determinate energy levels. The wave functions of quantum mechanics are also determinate functions. Those who interpret quantum mechanics as giving a fuzzy or indeterminate picture of the world are led to that view by the fact that the "state" of a system is often described by a superposition of wave functions. But they are in effect reifying the wave function, which is a perfectly determinate mathematical function. Reality is thought to hover because the wave function hovers, being a combination of incompatible eigenstates. If you do not reify the wave function, but merely regard it as something used to calculate the probabilities of the results of measurements, then you have no theory of the state of the system between measurements. If you have no theory of the state of the system, then you have no views about ontological determinacy.[3]

There is no doubt that there are perfectly determinate attributes. They include the perfectly determinate shape attributes and most of the simple properties dealt with by physics known as 'quantities', such as masses, charges, and quantities of energy. We shall show that these attributes are basic attributes in the sense explained at the beginning of this section, and we shall adopt them as our fundamental attributes.

There are such attributes, of course, in the sense of "there are" appropriate to universals. It is also true, however, that we use such attributes to describe reality, and use them very successfully too, though it is still conceivable, if unlikely, that physical reality is not

3 David Bohm has shown that hidden variables are possible. You do not have to agree that his theory of hidden variables is true to acknowledge that he has provided a logical demonstration that such theories are consistent with quantum mechanics. To object that Bohm's hidden variables are unacceptable is irrelevant unless it can also be shown that his hidden variables are the only way in which quantum mechanics is consistent with hidden variables. Bohm shows that you have to take into account the hidden variables of the apparatus as well as of the system. His hidden variables are non-local, and it appears from the work of J. S. Bell that hidden variables have to be non-local. D. Bohm, "A Suggested Interpretation of the Quantum Theory in Terms of 'Hidden Variables', Part I". It is also worth noting that many interpretations assume that at some stage in the measurement process reality is classically describable. For the various interpretations of Heisenberg's indeterminacy relations, see Max Jammer, *The Philosophy of Quantum Mechanics*, pp. 79ff.

in itself like this. On the other hand, the argument for ontological determinacy from the success of physics is a good one. So far there is no alternative to assuming the truth of the principle of ontological determinacy, certainly no alternative that explains the success of physics.[4]

What we have to choose between are metaphysical theories of physical reality. It would be nice if we had a number to choose from, some that fell under the principle of ontological determinacy and some that did not. Unfortunately, we have very few. The theory of classical, infinitely divisible matter, which does fall under the principle of ontological determinacy, is perhaps the best example of a metaphysical theory of physical reality. Perhaps a metaphysical theory could be developed for classical fields; it too would fall under the principle of ontological determinacy.[5] And that is about it. There are no generally accepted metaphysical theories that apply to quantum reality. Nevertheless the universals common to physics – mass, charge, and quantity of energy – also apply to quantum reality. Indeed, they are guaranteed to apply by the correspondence principle, whatever we finally make of that mysterious principle.[6] We may conclude, therefore, that on most occasions and to all intents and purposes, the universals appropriate to classical matter do apply to reality.

The simple properties or quantities of physics are the same in classical mechanics or quantum mechanics or relativity, in the sense that the property itself existing in the world is the same property, the same universal. If there are differences they are conceptual or intensional differences. Adopting Putnam's language, we can say that though the syntactic and semantic markers are the same, the stereotype, understood in terms of the exact form of the laws governing the attribute, will differ. The universal itself plays for us the role played by the extension in Putnam's original version.[7]

That physical quantities are measured in the same way is corroborating evidence for their being the same. Take force, for example.

4 Cf. Alexandre Koyré, *Galileo Studies*, pp. 201–4.
5 Cf. H. Reichenbach, *The Philosophy of Space and Time*, p. 270.
6 Cf. Paul Feyerabend, "Problems of Empiricism, Part II", pp. 296–300. The problem of the interpretation of the correspondence principle seems to be neglected today.
7 See Putnam, "The Meaning of Meaning", pp. 268–71. For the application of Putnam's theory to science see W. H. Newton-Smith, *The Rationality of Science*, Chapter 7.

The vacuum state of quantum field theory exerts a measurable force in the Casimir effect that is measured in the way forces are usually measured.[8] To see that forces are measured in the same way in relativistic mechanics as in classical mechanics, imagine a particle accelerated to relativistic speeds by a single linear accelerator. The force exerted on the particle is the same as that exerted on the accelerator, and the force on the accelerator could be balanced by a weight on a string, at least in theory. I can see no reasons for denying that mass and charge are the same universals in quantum mechanics as in classical mechanics, and it seems obvious that distance relations are the same universals.[9]

Someone might object to the principle of ontological determinacy by suggesting that matter is a rough and imperfect thing, and that no material object is ever likely to be perfectly spherical, for example. And it is true that on closer examination material objects are found to be pitted and jagged over short distances, and always slightly out of true over longer distances. But this does not count against ontological determinacy. It should be noted that "spherical with radius five inches", for example, approximates to the actual irregular shape, as opposed to classifying such irregular shapes. It may approximate to many actual irregular shapes, but that does not imply that it stands to them as a higher-level universal. The actual irregular shape is not subordinate to the universal "spherical". The actual irregular shapes and "spherical with radius five inches" are equally perfectly determinate shape attributes. If the object were made of classical matter, then its shape, however irregular and even if not mathematically describable, is nevertheless perfectly determinate.

Classical matter can be determinate in two ways: if the matter stops abruptly, bounded by a geometrical line or surface, or if the density function goes to zero in a determinate fashion. Real matter is understood in terms of classical fields, which are determinate, and in terms of quantum states whose determinacy we have already discussed, though these two concepts probably do not exhaust it.

Sometimes objections are made to the principle of ontological determinacy on what look like linguistic grounds:

8 I. J. R. Aitchison, "Nothing's Plenty: The Vacuum in Modern Quantum Field Theory", and M. J. Sparnaay, "Measurement of Attractive Forces Between Flat Plates".
9 For further discussion of "mass" see Chapter 5, Section 5.

I want to argue that it is part of the grammar of a word like "jumps" that it shall be inadmissible to speak of "jumps" that are indefinitely small or indefinitely brief. . . . But I want to argue that there is a logical absurdity in saying that a man jumps a thousandth of an inch, if the word "jump" is understood in any of its ordinary, everyday, uses. When we normally speak or think of a jump made by a man, we have in mind primarily the kind of change of position that can be observed with the unaided senses. . . . But try now to imagine a jump of atomic dimensions! We no longer have any plausible way of connecting a means of verification with the sentence, which does not have and cannot plausibly be given a use. [10]

In this passage Max Black associates the logical grammar of the word 'jump' with how we normally think about jumping. He seems to think that how we think about jumping is inevitably tied not merely to what we can perceive but to what we can discriminate. In this roundabout way he appears to tie the principle of ontological determinacy to a form of the principle of perceptual determinacy. In other words, he appears to be arguing that reality is not determinate because perception is not determinate – which simply does not follow. He also appears to be a verificationist.

Perceptual determinacy is, however, relevant in the discussion of colour attributes. If shades of colour are understood in terms of what is perceived, then the principle of perceptual determinacy says that what is perceived is a "definite, absolutely determinate, colour – regardless of whether the percipient's colour-vision was perfect or not, and of whether he had any name for this definite colour". [11] To illustrate perceptual indeterminacy Geach cites the problem of seeing a speckled hen: Must I see it as having a definite number of speckles? Here perception is indeterminate and reality determinate.

If we did perceive determinate colours, then we would expect colour discrimination to be straightforward, but unfortunately it is not. Consider two shades of colour, one definitely a red, the other definitely an orange. It is possible to find a series of shades of colour that starts with the red one and ends with the orange one, such that any two neighbours are only just discriminable. As we proceed along the series we find no point where the shades of colour cease to

10 Max Black, "Is Achilles Still Running?" pp. 116, 117. There is something intuitively appealing about what Black is saying, based perhaps on our understanding that a human being is a spatially rough and imperfect thing. A physicist will say, however, that he has a perfectly determinate centre of mass.
11 Geach, *Truth, Love and Immortality*, p. 125.

be red and become orange. Red and orange are higher-level colour attributes, both at the same level. Any two neighbours in our series of colour shades appear to be examples of the same determinable colour such as red, but the end points of the series are not.[12] In the (indefinite) class of shades of colour that are all reds there is a transitive resemblance relation, which as an equivalence relation characterizes the class of shades of colour that are all reds. Unfortunately, there is also, as Hume noted, a form of colour resemblance that is non–transitive and that cuts across the usual resemblance–equivalence classes.

It is also possible for there to be a series of shades of colour where any two neighbours cannot be discriminated from each other, but where the end points can definitely be distinguished from each other. Indiscriminability for colour shades is non–transitive. This example has persuaded some people to suggest that non–observational changes are taking place, though we normally understand colours as purely observational.[13]

Colour perception is a difficult subject, and so is the semantics of colour predicates. To try to construct a coherent metaphysics for colours would be a mistake. The problems associated with colour perception do not affect the principle of ontological determinacy, since colours only have a phenomenal existence, though they have an objective basis; they are secondary qualities, to use the old terminology.[14] It is true that we see colours as properties of particulars, in effect projected on to them; we also think of them and speak of them *as though* they were genuine properties of particulars, but it is only *as though*.

The second way in which there could fail to be basic attributes was if any attribute could be construed as a conjunction of attributes, and so *ad infinitum*. However, they would only fail to be basic attributes if the analysis were ontologically significant: The conjuncts would have to be either basic attributes at the same level or at a lower level. If the conjuncts are higher-level attributes the analysis is not ontologically significant. My position is that higher-level at-

12 Cf. Crispin Wright, "On the Coherence of Vague Predicates": "Colour predicates as a class are semantically incoherent" (p. 333).
13 Ibid., pp. 338–40. Cf. Armstrong, Volume II, pp. 125–6, who thinks that colours have hidden depths that we do not perceive!
14 Cf. Hardin, *Color for Philosophers*, pp. 59–67.

tributes have a secondary ontological significance relative to basic attributes, which have a primary ontological significance.

The possibility of an analysis of a perfectly determinate attribute in terms of a conjunction of other attributes is difficult to rule out in general terms. It appears, however, that the universals we have chosen as basic cannot be regarded as conjunctions of other attributes. Consider the basic attribute "spherical radius five inches", which we shall represent by C^5. It is true that spheres themselves are not atomic, because spheres are divisible; but it is not the universal that is divided, it is a particular that is cut into two particulars. Consider a spherical object a, with shape C^5, being cut along a plane into two segments b and c. Let S^h and S^k be the shape attributes of the two segments where h and k are perpendicular heights of the segments perpendicular to the plane base, and $h + k = 2 \times 5$. If C^5 were to be a conjunction of the new shape attributes we would have $C^5 = S^h \& S^k$, which is not a possibility since it is not the case that $C^5a \leftrightarrow S^ha \& S^ka$. It follows that C^5 cannot be regarded as a conjunction of shape attributes, and it is hardly likely that it can be regarded as a conjunction of attributes of another type.

Similarly, a body with mass m can be divided into two bodies with mass $\frac{1}{4} m$ and $\frac{3}{4} m$, but it is not the case that the mass attribute (i.e. "having mass m") can be regarded as a conjunction of having mass $\frac{1}{4} m$ and having mass $\frac{3}{4} m$, since the three mass attributes are incompatible.

Our argument against the possibility of all hierarchies of attributes being extended downwards indefinitely likewise works by producing examples. The universals we have chosen as basic attributes do not classify any other attributes. This is apparent because they are, in an intuitive sense, perfectly determinate attributes, and it may become more apparent in our discussion of hierarchies of attributes in the next chapter. These fully determinate attributes are by no means insignificant, since they are the universals that are basic to our understanding of the physical world. It is, of course, conceivable that there could be other types of basic attributes.

It follows that the determinate shapes and determinate quantities are examples of basic attributes, since they satisfy the abstract characterization of the notion of basic attribute, which can be summarized as follows: Basic universals are fully determinate, first-order universals; they do not classify other attributes. They are not conjunctions of other fully determinate, first-order universals, and they

81

are causally significant. Basic attributes are monadic, attributive basic universals. Our basic attributes are therefore "basic" only in this limited, specific sense. This is why we have used the term 'basic attribute' rather than 'atomic attribute'.

The choice of basic attributes is *a posteriori*, as Armstrong would put it. It has to be, since it appears that it is not possible to give a purely abstract account of what is real; there has to be some lead-in. The simple properties of physics are real constituents of the world if any universals are; but the recognition of this fact is *a posteriori* and does not arise from our characterization of the notion of universal or basic attribute. It arises from the findings of science.

Although the basic attributes of physics are my starting point, it is conceivable that some other philosopher might have chosen a different starting point. Leibniz might have chosen the properties of monads as his fundamental type of universal, and Aquinas might have chosen the personal attributes of God, angels, and human souls. These universals, however, might not be basic attributes in my specific sense. Nevertheless, it is possible that a theory with some other starting point might connect with mine. It would have to be shown that the other attributes gave rise to causal relations that could change a particular's basic attributes.

3. CAUSALITY AND BASIC ATTRIBUTES

Consider a long strip of polished metal, like a sword blade, which is slowly bent to form various shapes that are all arcs of circles. Each different shape will have different causal effects. For example, if a beam of light strikes the strip it will be focussed in a different way by each different shape of the strip.

Let C be a shape attribute that applies to a particular if its shape is an arc of some circle, where the arc length is fixed. Let S^r represent determinate shape attributes subordinate to C that are indexed by the radius of curvature r. It is the determinate attributes, S^r, that are basic attributes, which are the most important for causality. The slightest change in shape from one S^r to another very close to it produces a different causal interaction, whereas the general attribute C applies to the particular throughout a range of different causal interactions. However, the general attribute C is not irrelevant to causality, since if the blade is bent sharply so that it is no longer circular at all, it will take part in a different class of causal interactions.

It could perhaps be argued that it is only the general shape that is significant for the focussing of light by reflection, whereas the actual determinate shape is in fact irregular and not circular. But it is in fact a determinate circular shape that approximates to the actual shape; it is not more general and it does not classify it. One perfectly determinate attribute is being used as an approximation to another.

In general we would expect basic attributes as perfectly determinate attributes to give rise to perfectly determinate causal relations, another type of basic universal. And we would expect different types of basic attributes to give rise to correspondingly different types of causal relations.

Causality can be used as a criterion of identity only for basic attributes:[15] If X and Y are basic attributes, then X is identical with Y if and only if they have exactly the same causal interactions – that is, give rise to exactly the same (determinate) causal relations and are changed in exactly the same way by causal relations.[16] This criterion of identity does not apply to higher-level attributes such as C, since particulars that fall under C can have a range of different causal interactions. To C there corresponds a set of causal relations of a certain type, each of which produces different states and changes.

Causality can only be a way of characterizing basic attributes, since our intuitive understanding of perfectly determinate attributes is probably based originally on causal ideas. Since basic attributes are significant for causality they have a very good claim to be real constituents of the world. In general, a criterion of identity for something cannot fix the nature of that thing, as can be seen from the fact that Frege was unsuccessful in using his criterion of identity for numbers to fix the nature of number.[17] Similarly, I do not think that the criterion of identity for basic attributes in terms of causality fixes what a basic attribute is, but it does contribute to the characterization of the notion of basic attribute by expressing the fact that a basic attribute is perfectly determinate in a way that has to do with causality.

The examples given of basic attributes are all quantitative; they can all be represented to some extent by the real numbers. But there

---

15 I have already defended criteria of identity for universals in Chapter 2, Section 3.
16 Cf. Sydney Shoemaker, "Causality and Properties", and Armstrong, Volume II, Chapter 16. Our analysis of causality will ultimately be in terms of causal relations between particulars.
17 See Frege, *Foundations of Arithmetic*, Section 63, and cf. P. Benacerraf, "What Numbers Could Not Be".

is in fact no reason why basic attributes have to be quantitative.[18] It should also be noted that basic attributes such as masses are quantitative in a different way from basic shape attributes.

As the blade bends it takes on a series of new ontologically significant features. It is difficult to see how a nominalist could explain this, and there are difficulties for the particularist as well. Ockham, for example, thought that certain qualities of a substance were things distinct from substance, though not themselves substance.[19] Presumably he thought of them as tropes, as understood by modern particularism. What worried him about the bending of a blade was that if the shape attributes were regarded as entities distinct from substance, then those entities would come into existence and go out of existence at a great rate. He concluded that qualities that could be changed by the local motion of parts, such as the shape of the blade, could not be things distinct from substance. Ockham is right that the example counts against particularism, but he does not say how his, presumably nominalist, account of shapes explains causality.[20]

Our account of basic attributes implies that a conjunction of basic attributes cannot itself be a basic attribute, so we need to show that a conjunction of basic attributes is of no ontological significance, in other words, that a conjunction of basic attributes is not a universal in its own right. Even according to our stipulation a basic attribute can be a conjunction of higher-level attributes, so there is at least one way in which a basic attribute can be a conjunction of other universals.

If a certain particular has two basic attributes, F and G, then this can be expressed by the true sentence 'Fa & Ga'. The connective "&" joins two propositions, not two basic attributes. It is true that we can syntactically form something like '$F(\ )$ & $G(\ )$', which will combine with the proper name 'a' to give the original conjunctive sentence, but there is no reason to suppose that this symbol refers to something ontologically significant in the way that 'F' itself does. For one thing, the symbol '$F(\ )$ & $G(\ )$' can, as far as syntax goes,

18 Suppose perchance that the basic attributes we have chosen were shown not to apply to the physical world we live in. Nevertheless there are such universals, and since they conform to the abstract characterization of the notion of basic attribute, they show the coherence of that notion.
19 Ockham, *Summa Logicae, Part I*, 55. We could call the example Ockham's blade.
20 For a discussion of the notion of change see Roderick M. Chisholm, "Coming into Being and Passing Away".

equally well combine with two proper names to form the sentence '*Fa & Gb*', which does not involve any reference to anything that can be understood as a "conjunctive universal".

In order for a conjunction of universals to be itself a universal there must be something that binds the two conjuncts together into a single ontological unit, as opposed to merely being properties of the same particular.[21] Let us write a conjunctive property with brackets to indicate that it is an ontological unit: $P = (F \& G)$. If a particular possesses the conjunctive property $(F \& G)$, then it also possesses F and G, but there is something in addition, something ontologically significant, that makes possessing F and G a matter of possessing the conjunctive property. If this is not the case, then a particular that possessed a number of simple properties would also possess a larger number of conjunctive properties; there would be conjunctions of properties taken two at a time, three at a time, and so on. Although perhaps not an insuperable objection, there is a multiplication of entities when there is no real need, and it makes conjunctive properties look arbitrary, whereas a true property should not be something arbitrary. It is true that some overlap, but that does not help their credibility as ontologically significant things.

The doctrine that there are conjunctive universals can take two forms: Either all pairs, triples, and so on of properties instanced by the same particular form a conjunctive property merely in virtue of being instanced by the same particular, or only some pairs, triples, and so on of properties instanced by one particular form conjunctive properties in virtue of some further ontologically significant factor. Both versions face the difficulty of explaining what makes a conjunction an ontological unit. The second version has to explain how the additional factor works.

One of Armstrong's reasons for believing in conjunctive properties is his recognition of the (doxastic) possibility that every property might be a conjunctive property, not only every property we recognize as a true property at the moment, but all the conjunct properties of those properties, and so on all the way down, however far the analysis in terms of conjuncts is taken. In other words, there would be no such things as simple or atomic properties. Because we cannot settle whether this is the case or not, Armstrong thinks

---

21 Cf. Albert Casullo, "Conjunctive Properties Revisited", p. 290.

that "we need to keep open the possibility that there are properties which do not reduce to complexes of simple properties, we need to admit conjunctive properties".[22]

Indeed, if there were no atomic properties, then it would be very convenient if there were conjunctive properties, because then conjunctive properties would be ontological units and we could deal with them as such without worrying about their components. It would be convenient, but it does not follow that if there are no atomic properties, then there are conjunctive properties. To be of any use in this eventuality, conjunctive properties have to be ontological units, and Armstrong has not said anything to explain which properties occurring together form conjunctive properties and what it is that makes them an ontological unit.

In general, what makes any property an ontological unit for Armstrong is its causal powers: "Armstrong who holds that difference in causal powers is a necessary condition for difference of properties is hard pressed to explain the need for a single conjunctive property (F & G) as opposed to two distinct properties F and G which are coinstantiated."[23] In order for a conjunction of properties to be itself a property there must be something that binds the two conjuncts together into a single ontological unit as opposed to merely being properties of the same particular; there must be something in addition, something ontologically significant, that makes possessing F and G a matter of possessing the conjunctive property. For Armstrong, as well as for us, that something would have to be an additional causal power. But if (F & G) possessed an additional causal power it would cease to be a simple conjunction. In the absence of a general account of additional causal powers there is no case for conjunctive properties.

Armstrong's case for conjunctive properties seems to be based on trying to avoid one form of metaphysical atomism for properties: If what we take to be a genuine property, that is, an ontological unit, is subsequently discovered to be a conjunction of properties, then those conjuncts now have to be taken as the new ontological units.[24] From this it seems to follow that if anything is to be real there must be simple, non-conjunctive properties. He wants to avoid this conclusion by claiming that a conjunction of properties is

22 Armstrong, "Towards a Theory of Properties", p. 153; cf. Armstrong, Volume II, Chapter 15.
23 Casullo, "Conjunctive Properties Revisited", p. 290.
24 Cf. Armstrong, Volume II, pp. 32 and 33.

itself an ontological unit with a similar sort of significance as its conjuncts. But, there is no reason to believe in this form of metaphysical atomism, though a basic attribute, which is an ontological unit, can sometimes be represented as a conjunction of universals that because they are higher-level attributes are not ontological units.

4. STRUCTURAL UNIVERSALS

A structural universal is one that corresponds to the repeatable structure of complex particulars. The problem of structural universals is posed in terms of parts and wholes. A particular with a complex structure has parts, and it is assumed that the corresponding universal must also have parts – an assumption that plays into the hands of the particularist. A complex particular such as a molecule of methane has as spatial parts an atom of carbon and four atoms of hydrogen, and so it is thought that the universal "methane" has as parts the universal "carbon" and the universal "hydrogen". The assumption is that the structural universal is isomorphic to the structured particular, and so presumably the part–whole relation appropriate to the universal is isomorphic to the spatial part–whole relation appropriate to the particular.[25] It cannot be exactly the same relation, since a relation that takes particulars as its terms cannot be the same as a relation that takes universals as its terms; they are, however, said to be isomorphic.

The problem is that a molecule of methane as a structured particular has four hydrogen atoms as spatial proper parts, and therefore the universal "methane" should have the universal "hydrogen" four times over as proper parts. But there is only one universal "hydrogen". There is, of course, no problem with there being four hydrogen atoms, since the universal "hydrogen" can be instanced any number of times; the problem lies in explaining the structure of a universal as composed of other universals. The universal "methane" does involve the universals "carbon" and "hydrogen" in some sense; the problem lies in explaining the mode of composition.

Unfortunately there are not many relations available that might explain the mode of composition of structural universals. Campbell

25 See David Lewis, "Against Structural Universals", p. 33. See also Campbell, *Abstract Particulars*, pp. 45–51; Bigelow and Pargetter, *Science and Necessity*, pp. 82–92, and D. M. Armstrong, "In Defence of Structural Universals". Armstrong now denies that the part–whole relation appropriate to a universal is the spatial part–whole relation (private communication).

claims that the relations we do have a good understanding of are the part–whole relation and the set membership relation,[26] though as we noted earlier the part–whole relation for universals is not the same as that for particulars. There is also a widespread opinion that universals can be joined together by conjunction. But the notion of conjunction of universals is really parasitical on the notion of conjunction of sentences.

Suppose that *a* is the name of a methane molecule. If we write:

a is methane ↔ (a has a carbon atom) & (a has a hydrogen atom) & (a has a hydrogen atom) & (a has a hydrogen atom) & (a has a hydrogen atom),

then it is clear that this is equivalent to:

a is methane ↔ (a has a carbon atom) & (a has a hydrogen atom),

which gives us the problem of structural universals. In fact, any formulation of the problem works in a similar way. If we use brackets to signify some mode of composition of universals, we can write:

methane = (carbon, hydrogen, hydrogen, hydrogen, hydrogen),

which is equivalent to

methane = (carbon, hydrogen)

– given that there is no mode of differentiation between the different instances of hydrogen, which, of course, is the point.

In effect, the formulation of the problem of structural universals does not use any account of the mode of composition of universals more sophisticated than that of set membership. It may be that in the conjunction formulation of the problem, '(a has a hydrogen atom)' is understood mereologically as "a has a hydrogen atom as a part", but it plays no role in the formulation of the problem. The formula fails to capture the way in which the molecule has parts. In any event, "being a part of" is a fairly non-specific sort of relation; it does not by itself explain how the particular is put together.

Consider a simple shape universal such as "circular radius *r*". A particular that is this shape can be resolved into spatial proper parts in an infinite number of ways, each of which is in a sense arbitrary.

26 Campbell, *Abstract Particulars*, p. 49.

It could, for example, be regarded as divided into two semicircles, or four quadrants, or two equal caplike segments formed by parallel chords with another sort of shape in between them. The proper parts of a circular particular are real, independently existing things only in the sense that the particular *could* be cut along those lines.

If a shape universal were isomorphic to the particular that instances it, then the shape universal should also have parts. But in this case one division into parts is as good as another, and none of the suggested divisions represents the true structure of the universal "circular radius r", simply because there are so many possible divisions.[27] The problem of structural universals arises here too. If the universal "circular" is thought of as having the universal "quadrant" as a proper part, then it should have it as a proper part four times over, despite the fact that there is only one universal "quadrant".

Consider a cross made from five squares so that one is in the middle and the other four are the arms. A particular with this shape can be regarded as having five proper parts, and unlike the proper parts of the circular particular they can perhaps be regarded as natural parts because there is a fairly obvious way in which to cut it up. For this reason the cross example is nearer to the standard example of methane, because a methane molecule is also divided into parts in a natural way. Nevertheless the way in which the cross-shaped particular is composed of proper parts is exactly the same way in which the circular-shaped particular is composed of proper parts. Therefore the universal "cross-shaped" is constituted out of its parts in the same way that the universal "circular" is constituted out of its parts – if, indeed, universals have parts.

It is not clear that the standard spatial part–whole relation is of much use in explaining how a particular is constructed out of its proper parts; if so, then *a fortiori* it is not clear that the isomorphic part–whole relation for universals explains how a universal is constructed out of its parts. Consider a circular particular constructed out of two semicircular proper parts. When the two parts are stuck together in the right way they are indeed proper parts of the circular particular, but they could equally well be proper parts of an infinite number of other particulars with unusual shapes. The construction

27 Campbell is aware that there is a similar problem for particularism; see *Abstract Particulars*, Section 6.2. His solution is to regard shape tropes as not being among the basic tropes; see p. 146.

89

of the whole is not explained by the simple part–whole relation, since the relation "being a proper part of" does not explain how the parts are put together.

It is only if the whole and its structure are taken as a given that we are in a position to understand the part–whole relation. The structure of a spatial whole depends on its proper parts and the spatial relations between them. If the problem of structural universals is one of individuating natural proper parts that are exactly alike, then the individuation of the proper parts is explained by the situation of the parts within the whole – in other words, by the spatial relations between the parts.

The structure of a spatial whole consisting of five proper parts could be analysed in terms of the shape of its parts and the arrangement of the parts, where the arrangement is a five-place relation. If C is a basic cross-shape universal, S a basic square universal, and R a five-place relational basic universal, then the formula

$$(\exists x)Cx \leftrightarrow (\exists x_1)(\exists x_2)(\exists x_3)(\exists x_4)(\exists x_5)$$
$$(Sx_1 \& Sx_2 \& Sx_3 \& Sx_4 \& Sx_5 \& R(x_1, x_2, x_3, x_4, x_5))$$

gives necessary and sufficient conditions for C being instanced in terms of other universals being instanced. The formula shows what it is for C to be instanced in terms of the instantiation of other universals, namely, R and S. No other universals are relevant to C being instanced, so in a sense the universals R and S are the components of the universal C.

The preceding formula does not (and need not) make mention of the part–whole relation, but the part–whole relation is implied. If a is a cross-shaped particular and p_1, p_2, p_3, p_4, and p_5 are its square-shaped proper parts, then

$$Sp_1 \& Sp_2 \& Sp_3 \& Sp_4 \& Sp_5 \& R(p_1, p_2, p_3, p_4, p_5) \rightarrow Ca.$$

a would still be cross-shaped however the parts were permuted within the arrangement universal. The permutation of this formula is not the only one that makes a cross shape; hence the direction of the arrow.

Lewis sets up the problem of structural universals by claiming that a structural universal is isomorphic to the structured particular that instances it. The particular has particular parts that are put together by the part–whole relation; therefore the corresponding universal has parts that are universals and that are put together by the part–whole relation appropriate to universals. Our formulas, on the other hand, show that though the particular and its parts are subject to the spatial part–whole relation, that is not exactly how the parts are put together; they are put together by an arrangement universal. The corresponding universal, C, is composed of the universals S and R, where R is a first-order arrangement universal, but I see no reason for saying that there is a part–whole relation between R and C or between S and C.[28]

By analogy we would expect the universal C to be put together by a second-order arrangement universal. Can a second-order arrangement universal prevent multiple instances of a first-order universal from collapsing into each other? One account of the second-order arrangement universal would take it to be the universal corresponding to the right-hand side of the first of the preceding formulas with the predicates R and S understood as argument places. That formula does appear to prevent multiple instances of a universal from collapsing into each other, so it does at least seem possible to avoid the problem of structural universals by considering second-order arrangement universals.

It is difficult to understand our analysis as a fundamental one because the cross shape can be analysed in any number of ways involving different sorts of parts, and the same is true of all shape universals. It could also be argued that it is not really the second-order arrangement universal that encapsulates the structure but rather the first-order arrangement universal. The five-place arrangement relation R is a relation that takes squares, instances of S, as its terms, and it also governs the orientation of the squares and the way in which edges coincide. Understood in this way it gives us the structure, which in this case is just a shape, without any help from other universals.

Methane differs from our cross-shaped particular because the parts of a methane molecule are natural parts (because of this our formulas may be more appropriate for describing the structure of methane than for describing the shapes of particulars), and with methane there is form of necessity of essence. A molecule would not be a methane molecule unless it had four hydrogen atoms and one carbon atom and the usual structure. This sort of necessity partly

28 Naive isomorphism pictures R as having S as its terms, but R is a first-order universal and has particulars as its terms.

has to do with the laws of nature that permit only certain stable structures, and partly arises from what we are prepared to call methane.[29] The cross example shows, however, that the problem of structural universals is not related to forms of necessity associated with essence.

I also doubt that the foregoing formulas do tell us how the universals are put together, because I doubt whether logical formulas in general tell us about how universals are instanced together. Consider a conjuction of universals $F(\ )$ & $G(\ )$ where it is understood that both component universals apply to the same particular. If two universals, for example, a certain shape and a certain mass, are instanced by the same particular, this fact is expressed by the sentence Fa & Ga. Metaphysically this sort of conjunction corresponds to two universals *inhering* in the same particular or, on some understandings, two universals *mutually inhering;* for example, the shape and the mass fit together in the way appropriate to them.[30] But we understand nothing about inherence from our understanding of logical conjunction, even though we may draw some true conclusions from it. The problem of structural universals also concerns universals being instanced together. Our formulas tell us nothing about how the universals are instanced together, though it may enable us to draw some true conclusions.

I do not claim to have said very much to explain the structure of universals; my aim rather has been to attack the way the problem of structural universals has been set up in terms of isomorphism and the part–whole relation. There is an interesting problem here, but not a knock-down argument against structural universals, or against universals in general. The admission that basic shape universals can be regarded as having components does not affect the characterization of basic attributes, because the mode of composition, whatever it may be, is not conjunction.

The way the problem of structural universals is set up appears to play into the hands of the particularist. A cross-shaped concrete particular has five square concrete particulars as proper parts, and its shape trope also has five square shape tropes as proper parts, so there is indeed an isomorphism between a particular and its shape

29 See Chapter 3, note 44.
30 Cf. Chapter 9, Section 5.

trope. The shape trope is also a part of the concrete particular, so the part–whole relation crops up everywhere, commending particularism to the mereologists.

The parts of a concrete particular are put together by an arrangement relation that takes concrete particulars as its terms. The shape trope for the whole is also put together by an arrangement relation, one that takes tropes as its terms. These two arrangement relations are tropes and different tropes. I do not think they can be the same type of trope, but even if they are of the same type they must be numerically different tropes. Therefore, how a concrete particular is put together spatially is explained by two arrangement tropes, since it is explained by the relation between the concrete parts and by the shape trope, and therefore by the relation between the shape trope's parts. I think that this is one relation too many and that it counts against particularism. Although I am aware that Campbell for one can be very strong-minded in the face of the multiplication of entities,[31] the issue is one of explanation, not of how many entities one can put up with.

5. NATURAL KIND UNIVERSALS

There is no single determinate attribute or combination of determinate attributes that makes something to be a lemon. Lemons vary in shape, in colour, and in acidity. They all have the same general structure; but not only is that structure not a determinate attribute, it is something they share with all citrus fruits. Similarly, there is no determinate pattern of stripes that all tigers share. All tigers may have the same general pattern of stripes or general skeletal structure, but neither can be regarded as a determinate attribute. Something is a lemon or a tiger, not because it possesses a certain conjunction of determinate attributes, but because its determinate attributes fall within the ranges appropriate to lemons or tigers.

Although a hydrogen atom has as its parts a proton and an electron, the existence of a proton and an electron is not enough to give a hydrogen atom. There must also be an appropriate energy-level relation between the proton and electron. The range of allowable energy-level relations is determined by Schrödinger's equation, and any energy-level relation chosen from the infinite number within

31 Cf. Campbell, *Abstract Particulars*, p. 38.

93

the range would give us a hydrogen atom. Even with a precisely determined natural kind such as "hydrogen atom", where the laws governing it are well known, there is no conjunction of determinate properties that all members of the natural kind must possess. Hydrogen is a paradigm case for the other atoms and for the simple molecules dealt with in textbooks on spectroscopy.

It is conceivable that a natural kind correspond to a conjunction of determinable universals. The determinate colours in the range of possible colours could all be yellows so that they are all subordinate to the determinable "yellow"; the determinate shapes in the range of possible shapes could all be circular so that they are all subordinate to the determinable "circular". Normally a conjunction of universals is not itself a universal; but if there is something to bind them together, as there is for a natural kind, there is a case for regarding the conjunction of determinables as a universal – in Chapter 5 I argue that determinables are themselves universals. And since all the members of the natural kind and only its members fall under this universal, it can be regarded as the natural kind universal.

In general, however, the range of shape determinates that members of a natural kind can possess is narrower than the set of all determinates that are subordinate to the appropriate determinable. And the same will be true for the other types of determinates. All the members of the natural kind may still fall under a certain conjunction of determinables, but there will be, or could possibly be, individuals that fall under the conjunction of determinables that are not members of the natural kind because their determinates fall outside the applicable ranges. It follows that in general the conjunction of the appropriate determinables cannot be regarded as the natural kind universal.

Instead of the determinable itself we must consider the property of having a determinate taken from a limited range of the determinates that are subordinate to the determinable. We shall call it a 'range property'. All members of a natural kind will therefore have the same shape range property, the same colour range property, and so on. Normally a range property would not be regarded as ontologically significant, but since the nature of the range property is determined by natural law, there is a case for regarding range properties as ontologically significant. And since natural law determines that certain range properties occur together, there is also a case for regarding the conjunction of a natural kind's range properties as being the natural kind universal, and as being ontologically significant.

In Chapter 5 I argue that determinables are universals that have a secondary ontological significance, as opposed to the primary ontological significance of basic attributes. It follows that ontologically significant conjunctions of determinables and ontologically significant conjunctions of range properties also have secondary ontological significance.

Natural kinds are clearly ontologically significant in some way, and they are based on determinables, as opposed to determinate attributes; my theory at least has the virtue that it takes these two facts into account. Where I have doubts is about the nature of the combination of the range properties. For the sake of argument I have described it as conjunction, but it is probably some other mode of combination. And since structure is also important for natural kinds, an adequate account of natural kinds must await a satisfactory account of structural universals.

Consider the sentence 'Fa', which says that a certain material object has a certain mass, or perhaps a certain charge. The proper name 'a' refers to the material object. The predicate 'F' refers to the characteristic or property the object possesses and which is asserted of a by the sentence 'Fa'. A sentence such as 'Fa' is not saying that the object belongs to a certain set, such as the extension; it is not a sentence about set membership at all. It says that a certain particular has a certain property.[32]

The question of what a predicate such as 'F' refers to is partly a metaphysical question, in the same way that the question of what a proper name refers to is partly a metaphysical question. A proper name in the first interpretation of predicate calculus refers to something that is at least a particular, and the notion of particular as something that can occur only once is a metaphysical notion, if a fairly thin one. Similarly, what you take predicates, such as 'F', to refer to also depends on your ontology. If you follow Russell, as I do, in thinking that objects have ontologically significant features that are the basis of predication and that those features are to be understood as universals, then you will conclude that some predicates

32 For the notion of what is said by a sentence see Bell, *Frege's Theory of Judgement*, pp. 112–18.

95

at any rate refer to universals. There are no other things in our ontology that predicates could refer to.[33]

If there is no reason to think that '*F*' refers to its extension when '*F*' is an attribute predicate, then there is likewise no reason to think that a natural kind predicate refers to its extension. If '*F*' is a natural kind predicate, then '*Fa*' is saying that the object *a* is an example of that natural kind, not that *a* belongs to a certain set. You do not have to know which set is currently the extension of '*F*' to know what is meant by the sentence. It is not a sentence about set membership. Putnam cannot be right when he says that a natural kind predicate sometimes "means" its extension.[34]

Whatever '*Fa*' is saying when '*F*' is a natural kind predicate, it is not saying that *a* has certain *definite* – that is, determinate – properties, because the properties of members of the same natural kind can vary considerably. To know what '*Fa*' is *saying* you merely have to know which object *a* is, and what it is to be an example of the natural kind. It follows that if '*F*' is a natural kind predicate, then it refers neither to a set of determine properties nor to its extension.

According to E. J. Lowe, there are no bare particulars, only examplars of certain kinds. The notion of individual and kind can be understood only in terms of one another. Lowe believes that realism with respect to individuals implies realism with respect to kinds, though he suggests that thoroughgoing realism about kinds should be restricted to natural kinds.[35] We may add that for non-natural kinds realism about their attributes may be sufficient. For Lowe, the "crucial distinguishing feature of natural kinds is that they are subject to *natural law*".[36] It is the relationship of the kind to natural law that distinguishes natural kinds from classes of non-natural kinds such as artefacts.

Now if there is a natural kind, then at any given time there will usually be a class of distinguishable individuals belonging to that kind. The members of the natural kind are distinguishable from members of other kinds because they possess combinations of properties that always go together in such a way that certain similar combinations are forbidden, with the result that one kind does not

---

33 Cf. the discussion in Chapter 2.
34 "Although the verb 'means' sometimes means has as extension, the nominalization 'meaning' never means extension." Putnam, "The Meaning of Meaning", p. 224.
35 E. J. Lowe, *Kinds of Being*, p. 5.   36 Ibid.

merge continuously into another.[37] That this should be the case is the result of natural law. And how the members of that class behave and interact is also governed by natural law.

The existence of a distinguishable class, and how the members of that class behave and interact, is thought of as arising from a common nature. But the hypothesis that there is an ontologically significant common nature that explains the existence of a distinguishable class *and* how its members behave and interact is equivalent to the hypothesis that there is a certain universal. Further, when it comes to an individual that belongs to a natural kind there is a most fundamental kind of answer to the question "What is it?"[38] If the answer is to be ontologically significant, then some sort of realism about natural kind sortals is implied – in other words, some sort of belief in natural kind universals. The common nature also gives rise to a law-based principle of unity that governs how the individual persists through time.

It seems that it should be possible to give conditions for an object falling under a natural kind universal, though this cannot be done for all cases at present. But it is at least determined in most cases whether or not an object falls under a given natural kind universal. If conditions for being a member of a natural kind can be given, then a contextual account can be given of the natural kind universal in terms of what it is for an object to fall under the universal. In general, the principle of unity of a natural kind has to do with the properties associated with the natural kind *and* their lawlike variation.

We can form a picture of the principle of unity of a natural kind by considering the work of Mayr on fruit flies.[39] A single quantitative character, such as the number of abdominal bristles of a fruit fly, varies within a range and about a norm and can be represented by a distribution curve. The average number of abdominal bristles is about 36. Under artificial selection the number was pushed up as far as 63 and down as far as 25. When artificial selection was stopped and mass lines continued, the number dropped to 44 or rose to 32 depending on where the mass line was started from. Biologists call this phenomenon 'genetic homoeostasis' or 'genetic inertia'. It is an example of a property varying within a range. There are also indications that it is an example of variation about a norm, since the

37 This is not always the case in practice.
38 Cf. David Wiggins, *Sameness and Substance*, p. 24; cf. pp. 78–80.
39 See Ernst Mayr, *Animal Species and Evolution*, pp. 285–93.

region 32–44 seems to be preferred in some way. In other words, there are signs of stability; it would be strange if all values within the range were equally probable or equally accessible. Despite the fact that we do not know the laws concerned, it seems to be an example of lawlike variation, though it is likely that we are observing the effects of many factors acting together, governed by many laws.

Animal species possess a number of quantitative characters. If the distribution of two or more of these characters is plotted on a graph, then different species can be distinguished by the way the points cluster together. This is sometimes used as a method of discrimination between species, or as a test for whether there are indeed two species.[40]

Two or more quantitative characters plotted on a multi-dimensional graph should define a closed multi-dimensional hypersurface corresponding to the range in the one-dimensional case. The vast majority of the members of the species should fall within that hypersurface, and members of other species should not fall within it.[41] This is of course something of an ideal, but it is one that is approximated to in practice. And I think it could be claimed that when we think of an animal species as a natural kind we presuppose something like this.

Speaking very generally we can say that the basic attributes of individual members of a natural kind can vary in a number of ways. For example, they can vary about a norm or within a range or within a discrete spectrum. The electron is unusual in that its properties of mass and charge are precisely fixed, presumably by natural law, and its spin varies within a discrete spectrum of two values, whereas with atomic hydrogen the energy level varies within a infinite discrete spectrum.

When F is a natural kind term, F does not refer to anything isolable in the way that a basic attribute is isolable. We can say that F refers to a universal understood as *defined contextually* in terms of *what it is to be* an example of the natural kind as suggested in the previous paragraphs. There is a basis in the basic attributes of an individual for saying that it belongs to a certain natural kind, but that basis can only be understood in terms of *what it is to be* a member of the natural kind, which itself can only be understood

40 See E. O. Wiley, *Phylogenetics,* Chapter 10.
41 For animal species, how they reproduce is also part of the principle of unity of the species.

in terms of the characteristic attributes *and* their characteristic law-like variation.[42]

Our account of natural kind universals is in some ways analogous to the account we shall give of higher-level universals. It is not possible with either to point to an isolable feature of an individual as you can with basic attributes, yet in both cases there are natural classes corresponding to the term – roughly speaking. With both we resort to some kind of characterization or contextual account, yet both have an objective basis in basic attributes. Higher-level universals and natural kind sortals are examples of universals that are dependent in different ways on other universals. Although these two are probably the most important examples, it is at least conceivable that there are other universals like this.

Like Aristotle I do not think that a natural kind, considered as a universal, inheres in a particular in the way that a basic attribute does.[43] On the other hand, unlike Aristotle I do regard a natural kind as a universal that has a basis in the particular in a way parallel to the way that higher-level universals have a basis in particulars.[44] The combination of range properties (initially thought of as a conjunction) mentioned at the beginning of this section could well be the universal we are looking for.

42 David Wiggins, *Sameness and Substance,* pp. 78–80, gives a contextual account.
43 Aristotle, *Categories,* 2, 1ᵃ 20–23.
44 Cf. Joseph Owens, *The Doctrine of Being in the Aristotelian Metaphysics,* p. 390.

5

Hierarchies of universals

1. DETERMINATES AND DETERMINABLES

Determinate attributes of particulars can be gathered into types; there are mass determinates, temperature determinates, length determinates, and so on. Not only do all mass determinates have something in common, but all particulars that have a mass determinate have something in common – they are all massive particulars. It follows that at least one type of universal other than determinate attributes is required.

There have been a number of accounts of what the extra common factor is, the two most obvious being what I call the second–order theory and the second–level theory. According to the second–order theory, all determinates of a certain type have a second–order attribute in common, a property of a property; what the particulars that have determinates of that type have in common has to be explained in terms of the second–order attribute. According to the second–level theory, all particulars that have determinates of a certain type have another attribute in common, a second–level attribute; what the determinates of a given type have in common is explained, in my version of this theory, by a relation of "subordination" between the determinate and a second–level attribute. The term 'determinable' is often reserved for what I have called the second–level attribute, which is a determinable in the classical sense, though the problem, irrespective of proposed solution, is usually called the problem of determinables.[1] Although both determinate

Some of the sections of this chapter are based on Andrew Newman, "The Material Basis of Predication and Other Concepts".

[1] See W. E. Johnson, *Logic, Part I*, Chapter 11; and J. Searle, "Determinables and the Notion of Resemblance" and "Determinables and Determinates" in *The Encyclopedia of Philosophy*. For the second-order theory see A. N. Prior, "Determinables, Determinates and Determinants". For other accounts see Armstrong, Volume II, Chapter 21, Part IV, and Chapter 22, and Bigelow and Pargetter, *Science and Necessity*, Chapter 2.

and determinable are first-order attributes, the relation between them of "subordination" is a second-order relation. Indeed, it seems likely that any solution of the problem will involve second-order universals of some sort.

The relationship between a determinate and a determinable is frequently called the 'determinable relation', particularly when one is trying to explain what the problem is. It is initially characterized as not being like the species–genus relation. A species is defined in terms of its genus by means of a *differentia;* it is defined *per genus et differentiam.* The particulars that are members of the species are also members of the genus, except that unlike the other members of the genus they possess a certain attribute called the *differentia.* The species universal can therefore be understood as the conjunction of two other universals, the genus universal and the *differentia.*

The relation between determinate and determinable is like that between species and genus in the way that their extensions are related; they form hierarchies in the same sort of way. The difference is that in most cases a determinate cannot be understood as a conjunction of the determinable and some *differentia.* A determinate mass attribute cannot be understood as a conjunction of "being a massive particular" and some other universal. A determinate shade of red cannot be understood as a conjunction of the determinable universal "red" and some other universal. Recent work on structural universals has made this failure to understand a determinate as a conjunction of components easier to live with because it appears that conjunction is not the mode of composition for universals.[2]

Shape universals are an exception, since a more specific shape can often be understood in terms of general shape attribute and some other attribute. For example, triangles that are similar have the same general shape but differ in size. The general shape is the genus, and the size can be understood as a *differentia.* The determinate shape attributes are important examples of determinate attributes, and so more general shape attributes are often called determinables. Although the "determinable relation" is an important feature of most hierarchies of determinates and determinables, we need not regard it as the defining characteristic.

Armstrong would like a theory of determinates and determinables to be able to explain certain difficulties about similarity and

2 See Chapter 4, Section 4. Cf. D. M. Armstrong, "Are Quantities Relations? A Reply to Bigelow and Pargetter", p. 312.

difference in what looks like the same respect, as well as certain characteristic entailment patterns. Two particulars with different masses are both similar with respect to mass and different with respect to mass; and the two mass determinates are both similar with respect to mass and different with respect to mass. The characteristic entailment patterns are as follows: If a particular possesses a certain determinate, then it also possesses the corresponding determinable; and if a particular possesses a certain determinable, then it possesses one and only one determinate that is subordinate to that determinable. My view is that the demand for an explanation of all these things is excessive.

The similarities and differences and the entailment patterns for determinates and determinables are exactly paralleled by similarities and differences and entailment patterns for species and genera. In fact, the classical second-level theory of determinates and determinables works by analogy. In effect, it understands the hierarchy of determinate and determinable attributes as analogous to the hierarchy of species and genus universals, except of course that determinates and determinables are attributes, not sortals, and determinates cannot, in general, be defined *per genus et differentiam*. If there is an analogy, as I think there is, then the second-level theory should work, in the sense of being consistent with the similarities and differences and entailment patterns for determinates and determinables. Whether the second-level theory can actually explain these things is another matter. In fact, the similarities and differences and entailment patterns for species and genera are to a large extent explained by the relevant *differentiae*, which are attributes. For determinates and determinables the explanations are bound to be limited, and most theories appear to "explain" at least some things by simply saying that there is a fundamental rule to that effect.

2. GEACH'S FUNCTION THEORY OF HIERARCHIES

The next few sections will be devoted to a discussion of hierarchies of universals with the aim of giving an account of the classical second-level theory of determinates and determinables. The focus will be on giving a characterization of the second-order relation between a determinate and a determinable called 'subordination'.

I propose to use colours as the main example. Let us use the word 'claret' to refer to a fully determinate shade of colour, even though in ordinary language 'claret' could be used to classify a number of shades of red. The word is no longer an ordinary language word; we have converted it to our own use. Then the relation between claret and red is a determinable relation, since claret cannot be understood as the genus red plus some *differentia*. Red is in turn an example of a colour, but cannot be understood as the genus "colour" plus some *differentia*. We have, therefore, three levels of attributes represented by "claret", "red", and "colour".

The reason for using colours is that with colours there are these three definite levels, whereas with quantities like mass and temperature there are only two levels, and the upper level is in both cases controversial and involves certain technical difficulties. The upper level is also difficult to grasp intuitively, whereas with colours the idea of something being red is relatively easy to grasp, because we can see it. Colours should therefore be regarded as an abstract example of the determinable relation, which unlike most abstract examples is intuitively accessible. On the other hand, I do not propose to entirely ignore other determinables. Section 5 is devoted to the notion of mass, and I shall mention shapes here and there throughout the discussion, though the problem with shapes is getting clear levels.

For the purpose of providing an example of determinates and determinables we shall maintain the usual way of thinking and speaking and treat colours *as though* they were genuine properties of particulars, though they are not. We shall also make some simplifying assumptions about the nature of shades of colour. We shall assume that the principle of perceptual determinacy applies to shades of colour, and that if two shades of colour are distinct they can be perceived to be distinct. We shall also assume that each shade of colour is subordinate to a definite higher-level colour attribute.[3]

In *Mental Acts* Geach uses a function theory to explain how the attributes of a hierarchy of colour attributes all apply to one particular. For example, a particular can be a certain determinate shade of colour such as claret, and also be red. Such a particular is also chromatically coloured, where the chromatic colours are all the colours except black, white, and grey. The particular in one sense possesses three different colour attributes, and in another sense it is only one colour.

3 Hardin, *Color for Philosophers*, gives details about "real" colours.

Geach argues first that the notion of chromatic colour cannot be obtained by abstraction, where abstraction "is a process of singling out in attention some one feature given in direct experience – abstracting it – and ignoring the other features simultaneously given – abstracting from them".[4] Without getting involved in the discussion of how we come to understand colour attributes, we can observe that Geach is right about colours. Red, blue, and green do not have anything in common that we can single out in attention and call 'chromatically coloured'. "Red" is not composed of a genus "chromatic colour" and some *differentia*. Similarly it can be argued that the different determinate shades of red do not have anything in common that can be singled out in attention, and thus give rise to the more general notion of "red".

According to Geach, a particular is said to be both red and chromatically coloured because of the same feature:

Now it is quite impossible that I should form this concept, *chromatic colour,* by discriminative attention to a feature given in my visual experience. In looking at a red window-pane I have not two sensations, one of redness and one barely of chromatic colour; there are not, for that matter, two distinct sense-given features, one of them making my sensation to be barely a sensation of chromatic colour, the other making it a sensation of redness. If I abstract from what differentiates red from other chromatic colours I am abstracting from red itself; red is not chromatic colour *plus* a *differentia,* so that we can concentrate our attention upon chromatic colour and abstract from the *differentia.*[5]

We have two attributes, red and chromatic colour, which apply to the same particular; the reason that both attributes apply is a single feature that the particular possesses. If there is only one feature, which cannot be divided, why do we think of the particular as possessing two attributes? If universals are real constituents of the world, how is it that the particular possesses only one relevant feature, which it is natural to interpret as a single universal inhering in the particular. In the next section, 11, Geach asks the same question:

4 P. T. Geach, *Mental Acts,* p. 18. In Section 10 Geach criticizes the idea of obtaining colour concepts by abstraction. On page 13 he defines a concept as "mental capacity belonging to a particular person", where a sufficient condition for a person to possess a concept is to have mastered the intelligent use of the word for the concept. In Section 11 he starts talking about attributes without explaining the change. However, predicates refer either to Fregean concepts or to universals; they do not refer to mental capacities, though there are such things.

5 Geach, *Mental Acts,* p. 37. I talk about "chromatic colour" rather than "colour" because Geach does.

If the glass has not two distinct attributes, redness and chromatic colour, how can these attributes be distinct anywhere? and then how can anything be chromatically coloured without being red?" This objection, natural as it is, rests upon a false Platonistic logic; an attribute is being thought of as an identifiable object. It would be better to follow Frege's example and compare attributes to mathematical functions.[6]

Geach's point in this paragraph is that there is something in the particular in virtue of which we say that it possesses a certain attribute, but attributes do not correspond to features of the world in a one-to-one fashion, in the same way that not every element of a sentence names a piece of reality.[7] Instead, Geach suggests that Frege's function theory of concepts can be adapted to show how the two predicates describe reality. This is how he thinks Frege's approach applies to this problem:

Since what is chromatically coloured is often not red, "the chromatic colour of x" or "x's being chromatically coloured" does not in general stand for the same thing as "the redness of x"; but if x is red, then it is by one and the same feature of x that x is made red and chromatically coloured; the two functions, so to speak, assume the same value for the argument x.[8]

In arithmetic there are two functions – "the square of . . ." and "the double of . . ." – and they both map 2 into 4:

$$S(\ ): 2 \rightarrow 4, \ D(\ ): 2 \rightarrow 4.$$

Similarly Geach suggests that there are two functions – $C(\ )$ = "the chromatic colour of . . ." and $R(\ )$ = "the redness of . . .". We can therefore write:

$$C(\ ): a \rightarrow e, \ R(\ ): a \rightarrow e$$

where a is a red particular, and e is some feature of that particular, which is the basis of both predications. We can also write $C(a) = R(a) = e$.

Although he does not say so explicitly in *Mental Acts,* it is clear that Geach intends that e be a particular. In "Form and Existence" Geach argues that the attributes of a particular, as they exist in the particular, are themselves particulars, so we would expect him to

6 Ibid., pp. 38–9.   7 Cf. ibid., p. 41.
8 Ibid., p. 39. Geach says that attributes are only analogous to functions. It should be noted, however, that the function theory is meant to do some serious explanatory work.

think that e was a particular.[9] The attributes of particulars, as they exist in particulars, are what Geach calls 'individualized forms'; in other words, they are the tropes of particularism.

If an analysis of this sort could be made to work, then it seems to count in favour of Frege's theory of concepts, which must be combined with particularism to explain the actual features of particulars. As always with particularism, we shall want to know what it is about the tropes that makes them to be like other tropes. In this case, there is a class of tropes that are alike in that they are responsible for particulars being not only claret, but red and chromatically coloured!

However, the functions Geach introduces, $C(\ )$ and $R(\ )$, are not concepts as functions in the way Frege understands them, which is why I have written them with brackets. For Frege a one-place concept maps a particular into a truth-value, and the result of combining a concept term with a proper name is a sentence. If we wish to understand Geach's functions in terms of Frege's concepts as functions, we shall have to consider definite descriptions.

'The capital of Germany is Berlin' is a sentence that is sometimes used to illustrate unsaturatedness. The expression 'The capital of . . .' is incomplete. When we fill the empty space with 'Germany' we obtain a referring expression that refers to the same thing as 'Berlin'. Let us use the notation '$(\imath x)Fx$' for a definite description used referentially, so that it is a proper name and not defined contextually as in Russell's theory of descriptions.[10] In effect, we are using Frege's theory of proper names.

This is how we should understand the sentence 'The capital of Germany is Berlin':

> 'bCg' = 'Berlin is capital of Germany.'
> 'Cg' = '. . . is capital of Germany.'
> '$(\imath x)(xCg)$' = 'the capital of Germany.'
> '$(\imath x)(xCg) = b$' = 'The capital of Germany is Berlin.'

The last sentence allows us to understand how "the capital of . . ." works as a map or function:

$$(\imath x)(xC \ . \ . \ .): g \rightarrow b,$$

9 P. T. Geach, "Form and Existence".
10 According to the argument of Chapter 2 there is no problem in using proper names in the right context to refer to universals.

which indicates simply that "the capital of . . ." maps Germany into Berlin.

The definite description and definite description-type function we have just discussed are based on a relation that relates two different sorts of particulars. "Being a capital of" relates cities and countries, in the same way that the definite description 'the king of France' is based on the relation "being a king of", which relates persons and countries. The definite descriptions refer to particulars, and the relations they are based on are relations between particulars. But how you understand a definite description such as 'the direction of line a' depends on your ontology. There is a general notion of direction, and there is a specific direction that line a possesses, and there is also some sort of connection between the specific direction and the general notion of direction. The definite description 'the direction of line a' is based on this connection. The moral, then, is that definite descriptions and definite description-type functions are based on a connection or relation between two different sorts of things.

Let us now apply this analysis to Geach's account of colours. If 'the redness of a' refers to the trope e, then the relation on which the definite description is based is a relation that relates particulars – as it must be in particularism. Using our symbolism, 'The redness of a is e' should be written '$(\imath x)(xRa) = e$'. And the function $R(\ )$ is the function:

$$(\imath x)(xR \ . \ .): a \rightarrow e.$$

We can also write 'eRa', which says "e makes a red", or "e reddens a", or "e is a redness of a". Using Geach's language it would read "e is a feature in virtue of which a is red". If we just want to say that a is red, then the correct logical form is presumably:

$$(\exists x)(xRa).$$

In other words, there is some feature of a in virtue of which a is red. Since e is a particular there are presumably any number of exactly similar particulars, e', e'', . . . , in virtue of which a would be red. e is the basis; it inheres in the particular. Curiously, R must be that relation of inhering.

Now the point of Geach's theory is that not only is the redness of a the trope e, but the chromatic colour of a is also e. So e is a feature of the particular a in virtue of which it is both red and chromatically coloured. The original problem was to explain ontologically how a particular could possess three attributes – claret, red, and chromatic colour – which all seemed to correspond to one feature of the particular. Geach has transformed the problem into one of explaining why the three functions map the particular into one trope. In virtue of what is the trope *e* a suitable target for these three different maps?

The problem is not peculiar to colours. If a particular has a certain determinate triangular shape, then in virtue of that one trope it is that determinate shape, and it is also right-angled triangular and also just triangular.

For Keith Campbell, a more recent defender of particularism, that two things are alike means there is a primitive equivalence relation between them that is not based on anything in its terms. For colour tropes that relation is, presumably, that they look alike. Campbell explains determinables by "resemblance requirements of increasing stringency".[11] This is in effect an appeal to different types of resemblance relations. The best the particularist can do to explain what the distinctions are based on is to say that there are three different classes of resemblance relations, one for each of the terms 'claret', 'red', and 'chromatically coloured', where these resemblance relations differ from each other on account of possessing three different second-order tropes.

Similarly, for a triangular particular there would be one shape trope and three resemblance relations, one for each of the terms 'triangular sides (*abc*)', 'right-angled triangular', and 'triangular'. The explanation for the significance of the term 'triangular' lies in the resemblance relation, not in the fact that all particulars to which the term applies have three sides. This approach puts considerable strain on our intuitions, since the explanation is always provided by a trope of higher order.

Criticism of Geach's particularism

Let us return to the sentence '*eRa*', which says that *e makes a* red. Does the redness arise from the trope *e,* or from the relation of inhering *R?* The above analysis, based on Geach, does not give a clear answer. The consideration of these alternatives occupies the remainder of this section.

11 Campbell, *Abstract Particulars,* p. 84.

Consider several tropes, e, e', e'', and so on. They are exactly alike; they could only make a particular claret or red or chromatically coloured. There also has to be a relation of "reddens" that is different from the relation of "whitens" and different from the relation of "claretens". The trope e is responsible for three attributes; it does three things for the particular, and so there are presumably three relations, of which "reddens" is the easiest to say. Perhaps the consistent way to develop Geach's view is to say that redness arises both from a trope and from a relation of red-inhering.

Is the trope e itself coloured red? If the particular lacked the trope e, then it would cease to be red. It would certainly sound strange to say that e itself was not red, but instead had some sort of "red-making attribute" that enabled it to redden a particular. For particularism a "red-making attribute" would be some sort of trope and it would be a new and different sort of trope. On the other hand, if the trope is itself red, then to explain this predication we must suppose that the first-order trope possesses an exactly similar trope that functions this time as a second-order trope, and so *ad infinitum* – which is quite unsatisfactory as an explanation.

Perhaps the trope e is red in virtue of itself, so we would say "e reddens e" or "eRe". But then either the redness arises from the trope (in other words, the trope is red), which runs into the difficulties outlined earlier, or it arises from the relation R. At any rate, it seems strange to say that a trope inheres in itself.

If redness arises, perhaps only partially, from the relation of inhering, R, then it too should be a trope. There are two particulars, a and e, related by a relation, R, which would also be a particular. Not only are a and e related by the relation R, they are also related by the relation corresponding to "claret" and the relation corresponding to "chromatically coloured", which is strange to say the least. There would also be a relationship between the particulars a and R, to which there would correspond a secondary relation, another trope, and so *ad infinitum*.[12]

We conclude then that Geach's particularist account of determinates and determinables is unsatisfactory; we now try to convert his function theory into one consistent with immanent realism and the second-level theory of determinables.

12 Cf. Ockham, *Summa Logicae, Part I*, 51, and F. H. Bradley, *Appearance and Reality*, Chapter 2.

3. THE HIERARCHY OF COLOUR CONCEPTS

As before, let "claret" be a fully determinate shade of red, a determinate attribute, so that any two particulars that are claret are exactly the same shade of colour. "Red" is a determinable attribute of particulars that also classifies determinate colour attributes, so, relative to claret, it is a general attribute. We are used to saying that "red is a chromatic colour" or that "red is numbered among the chromatic colours"; we also want to say that "claret is a red" or that "claret is numbered among the reds". We call this relation between a determinate attribute and a determinable attribute 'essential subordination' and write it as follows:

$$\text{'}R\text{sub}C\text{'} \text{ and } \text{'}C'\text{sub}R\text{'}.$$

It is essential, since "red" would not be what it is unless it were a chromatic colour, and "claret" would not be what it is unless it were a red.

R sub C entails $(x)(Rx \rightarrow Cx)$; that is, (x)(if x is red, then x is chromatically coloured).

It is not entailed by it, however. This view of essential subordination differs, therefore, from any view that understands subordination as extensional.[13] Essential subordination will be discussed further in Section 4.

Instead of calling red a chromatic colour, let us be more precise and call it a spectral chromatic colour. The standard chromatic spectral colours are the colours of the rainbow, R O Y G B I V, which must be extended to include other attributes at the same level, so that shades of colour such as browns, pinks, magentas, and so on, are subordinate to determinable attributes in the same way that shades of red are subordinate to the determinable attribute "red". We shall assume for the sake of argument that such groupings exist, and that they divide the shades of colour exhaustively and exclusively – even though this is questionable and something of an idealization.

In ordinary language there is an ambiguity: We say that claret, a determinate shade of colour, is a chromatic colour, and we also say that red, a spectral colour, is a chromatic colour. We have then two higher-level attributes, spectral chromatic colour, C', and shade of

13 Cf. Frege, *Posthumous Writings*, p. 181.

chromatic colour, C''. The ordinary language term 'chromatic colour' is ambiguous between these two: C' and C''. The ordinary language notion of chromatic colour cannot be understood as a composite attribute: for example,

$$C'\text{sub}C = (C'\text{sub}C'' \lor (\exists F)(C'\text{sub}F \ \& \ F\text{sub}C'))$$

does not define a composite attribute; it merely expresses the ambiguity. It is possible, however, that shade of chromatic colour, C'', might itself be understood as some sort of constructed attribute.

Returning to Geach we can see that his arguments are assisted by an ambiguity in his use of the term 'chromatic colour', which could classify either all the spectral colours minus black, white, and grey, or all the shades of colour minus the shades of black, white, and grey.

Geach wishes to say that "the redness of a is e" and that "the chromatic colour of a is e", which he understands in terms of the maps:

$$R(\ ): a \to e \text{ and } C^h(\ ): a \to e.$$

Following this way of speaking it would also be possible to say "The claretness of a is e". Unfortunately all these locutions are unnatural because e is not really an attribute in the usual sense; it has too many tasks to perform since it makes the concrete particular claret, red, and chromatically coloured. Indeed, the unnaturalness of Geach's expressions counts against his theory. Instead, we want to say that "the redness of a is claret", "the chromatic spectral colour of a is red", and "the shade of chromatic colour of a is claret".

Geach's analysis, which we have considered and criticized, has the advantage that it requires only the logical forms of some version of the first interpretation of predicate calculus. For Geach, "The redness of a is e", which is understood in terms of an attribute mapping one particular into another, is talking directly about particulars. On the other hand, the form "The redness of a is claret" is talking about attributes and particulars and so does not fit in with either the first or the second interpretation of predicate calculus; but it appears that such forms are needed.

Let us write:

'Red is a spectral chromatic colour of a' as '$R\text{sub}C' \ \& \ Ra$'

and

'Claret is a red colour of a' as '$C'\text{sub}R \ \& \ C'a$'.

111

Using our symbolism we can also write the following expressions:

'The spectral chromatic colour of a' as '$(\imath X)(X\text{sub}C' \ \& \ Xa)$'

and

'The redness of a' as '$(\imath X)(X\text{sub}R \ \& \ Xa)$'.

So the sentence 'The redness of a is claret' can be written:

$$(\imath X)(X\text{sub}R \ \& \ Xa) = C''.$$

Instead of the functions the Geach-based theory leads to, we have the following functions:

1. The redness of . . . = $R(\ )$
   $R(\ ) = (\imath X)(X\text{sub}R \ \& \ X \ . . .)$: $a \rightarrow C'$
2. The spectral chromatic colour of . . . = $C'(\ )$
   $C'(\ ) = (\imath X)(X\text{sub}C' \ \& \ X \ . . .)$: $a \rightarrow R$
3. The shade of chromatic colour of . . . = $C''(\ )$
   $C''(\ ) = (\imath X)(X\text{sub}C'' \ \& \ X \ . . .)$: $a \rightarrow C'$.

Definite descriptions and definite description-type functions are based on a connection or relation between two different sorts of things. Here the relation is the second-order relation of essential subordination between determinates and determinables.

These functions indicate that it is the determinate attribute, claret, that is the basis for predicating the higher-level attributes of the particular. It is also indirectly the basis for predicating the attribute "has a spectral chromatic colour" of the particular. R and C'' are second-level attributes, whereas C' (has a spectral chromatic colour) is a third-level attribute. It is not clear that Geach's view allows for a true hierarchy.

The preceding functions recover something of Geach's original function theory of attributes, and they correspond to locutions that are more natural than Geach's. In accordance with Geach's original intention they show that not every element of a sentence names a piece of reality. Not every predicate corresponds to something isolable. It is really only particulars that are strictly speaking isolable, since even a determinate attribute is not isolable in the way a particular is.

Higher-level predicates do not correspond to anything in reality in the way that a proper name corresponds to a particular, nor do they correspond to anything in reality in the way that a determinate predicate corresponds to a determinate attribute, but that is not to say that they do not have a basis in reality. When we say that to a certain higher-level predicate there corresponds an attribute, we mean that the use of the predicate within a sentence has a basis in reality. All attributes at whatever level equally apply to particulars, but only the determinate attributes as such inhere in a particular. The higher-level attributes apply to a particular in virtue of a determinate attribute, and in virtue of the nature of that determinate attribute – in other words, in terms of the non-isolable structural features of the determinate attributes.

4. ESSENTIAL SUBORDINATION

We have introduced the notion of essential subordination as a relation between two attributes without having said much about it. It is unlikely that a definition could be found for the notion of essential subordination as it is *sui generis*. It can be characterized by saying things about it, however, and by saying what it is not.

Essential subordination is to be distinguished from accidental subordination. "All swans in the Northern Hemisphere are white" is an example of accidental subordination; it could have been otherwise and might be false in the future. It is usually interpreted as being about present extensions. "The whale is a mammal" is an example of essential subordination. What is being said is that "the whale is a kind of mammal", which is about two universals, two natural kind sortals.[14]

Accidental subordination is extensional and is adequately represented by $(x)(Ax \rightarrow Bx)$, whereas essential subordination, $A\mathrm{sub}B$, entails $(x)(Ax \rightarrow Bx)$ but is not entailed by it. Similarly, "Red is a chromatic colour" entails $(x)(Rx \rightarrow Cx)$ but is not entailed by it. To see that the reverse entailment does not hold, consider:

$$(x)(\text{if } x \text{ is red, then } x \text{ is extended}),$$

which is an example of accidental subordination. This sentence is not only true, but like the essential subordination "Red is a chromatic colour" it appears to be necessarily true. Now if $(x)(Rx \rightarrow Cx)$ entails "Red is a chromatic colour", then we would

14 Cf. Frege, *Foundations of Arithmetic*, Section 47.

expect (x)(if x is red, then x is extended) to entail "Red is an extension", which is false. Therefore, $(x)(Rx \to Cx)$ does not entail "Red is a chromatic colour".[15]

Essential subordination is an internal relation between two universals, and as such is true even when there happen at present to be no particulars that instance the two universals concerned. It is true that a sentence expressing accidental subordination, such as $(x)(Fx \to Gx)$, can be regarded as true when there are no instances of F or G because $\to$ is the material conditional. But this actually counts against accidental subordination entailing essential subordination. If there are no instances of F and G, then the accidental subordination, $(x)(Fx \to Gx)$, is true whatever F and G might be. F might be "perfectly triangular", and G might be "perfectly circular", and even if F and G were not instanced at present it would still be absurd to say that F is essentially subordinate to G.

It can be shown that essential subordination for colour attributes is not a transitive relation. Consider the following arguments:

$$(x)(C'x \to Rx)$$
$$(x)(Rx \to C'x)$$
$$\therefore (x)(C'x \to C'x)$$

C' sub R	claret is a red
R sub C'	red is a spectral colour
$\therefore C'$ sub C'	$\therefore$ claret is a spectral colour

The first argument is about particulars and is valid. If $(x)(C'x \to Rx)$ is considered as expressing a relation between attributes, which we have called accidental subordination (Russell called it formal implication), then that relation is transitive. The second argument is invalid, as claret is not a spectral colour. Therefore we can conclude that essential subordination for colour attributes is not transitive. It also follows that essential subordination for colour attributes is not extensional: For if it were extensional, it could be represented by an expression about particulars, such as $(x)(Rx \to C'x)$, which would make the relation between R and C' transitive. Essential subordination is not transitive, and therefore it is not extensional. Essential subordination is thus not a form of accidental subordination. It is quite distinct from it.

15 Cf. Armstrong, Volume I, p. 60, where he cites Frank Jackson, "Statements about Universals".

Consider these arguments:

$C'a$	a is claret
$C'\mathrm{sub}R$	claret is a shade of red
$\therefore (x)(C'x \rightarrow Rx)$	$\therefore (x)(\text{if } x \text{ is claret, } x \text{ is red})$
$\therefore Ra$	$\therefore a$ is red
Ra	a is red
$R \text{ sub } C'$	red is a spectral chromatic colour
$\therefore (x)(Rx \rightarrow C'x)$	$\therefore (x)(\text{if } x \text{ is red, then } x \text{ is spectrally coloured})$
$\therefore C'a$	$\therefore a$ is spectrally coloured

These arguments make use of the fact that essential subordination entails accidental subordination, and they illustrate the fact that the higher-level attributes apply to particulars. It is not possible to say that claret is spectrally coloured, since only particulars can be spectrally coloured according to the way ". . . is spectrally coloured", etc., is used in these arguments.

There is nevertheless some relationship between the attributes "claret" and "spectral chromatic colour", which we can write

$$(\exists F)(C'\mathrm{sub}F \ \& \ F\mathrm{sub}C').$$

This is a true statement, but there is no ordinary language way of expressing it. It appears that attributes such as C', R, C', and C'' *apply* to particulars, and are related to other attributes, via essential subordination or more complicated forms.

Essential subordination is also a necessary relation. The whale is necessarily a mammal, and red is necessarily a spectral chromatic colour. Essential subordination cannot be represented by something like $(x)(Rx \rightarrow C'x)$, where " $\rightarrow$ " is material implication, since considered as a relation between attributes material implication is not a necessary relation, as well as being transitive. Neither can R sub C' be understood as $(x)(Rx \Rightarrow C'x)$, where " $\Rightarrow$" is entailment, even though entailment is a necessary relation. For one thing, the relation between attributes generated by entailment is transitive, and essential subordination, as we have seen, is not transitive.

There is another reason similar to the one used for material implication. If $(x)(Rx \Rightarrow C'x)$ entails "red is a colour", as well as being entailed by it, then $(x)(x \text{ is red} \Rightarrow x \text{ is extended})$ should entail "red is an extension", which is false. Therefore R sub C' cannot be understood as $(x)(Rx \Rightarrow C'x)$. In fact, no formula that quantifies

115

over particulars can adequately represent essential subordination, which is what one would expect with a second-order relational universal.

The second-level theory as we have developed it can answer some difficulties about similarity and difference. If particular a is claret and particular b is scarlet, then they are alike with respect to colour and also different with respect to colour. And the determinates "claret" and "scarlet" are alike in being shades of red and also different in being different shades of red. Similarly, red and blue are alike in being spectral chromatic colours, but the way in which they differ is also with respect to colour.[16]

The particulars a and b are alike in that they possess the same spectral chromatic colour and different in that they possess different shades of chromatic colour. They are alike in one respect and different in another:

1. $R(a) \neq R(b)$, i.e. the redness of $a \neq$ the redness of b, since $C^r \neq S^c$;
2. $C''(a) \neq C''(b)$, i.e. the shade of chromatic colour of $a \neq$ the shade of chromatic colour b;
3. $C'(a) = C'(b)$, i.e. the spectral chromatic colour of $a =$ the spectral chromatic colour of b.

Explaining similarity and difference for universals is not so easy. "Claret" and "scarlet" are alike in that they are both subordinate to "red", though they are different shades of red. Neither "claret" nor "scarlet" can be represented as a conjunction of the determinable "red" and a *differentia,* so the differences between determinate shades of colour subordinate to one determinable colour cannot be explained by *differentiae* in the traditional sense; it does not follow however, that "claret" and "scarlet" do not have components in some sense.[17] If "claret" and "scarlet" were to differ only in hue, then there appears to be no further explanation of how their hues differ; the hues appear to differ *simpliciter.*

Not only is this an acceptable state of affairs, it could be argued that if differences are to be explained at all there must be attributes that differ *simpliciter.* The difference between two particulars can be explained in terms of their possession of different attributes; and the

16 Armstrong criticizes second-order theory for not being able to explain similarities and differences; Volume II, p. 106.
17 For how shades of colour differ from each other see Hardin, *Color for Philosophers,* pp. 42–3 and 113–20.

difference between the attributes can be explained in terms of their possession of different component attributes, whatever the mode of composition of attributes might be. Such explanations can be acceptable within certain contexts, but if there is to be an ultimate explanation of difference this process cannot go on *ad infinitum;* it must terminate, and the only way it can terminate is with attributes that differ *simpliciter.* It follows that reference to attributes that differ *simpliciter* can be an acceptable explanation. I am not claiming that all determinate shades of colour differ from each other *simpliciter;* I am merely claiming that at some stage it can be an acceptable type of explanation.

This is not the explanation of the differences between determinate quantities, however. The determinate mass attributes "mass five kilograms" and "mass three kilograms" are alike in that they are both subordinate to the mass determinable, and though it is clear that they differ, that difference cannot be explained in terms of *differentiae* – that is, in terms of different monadic attributes.

Determinate quantities of a certain kind are ordered in the same way that real numbers are ordered, the difference being that determinate quantities are usually only mapped into the positive reals. Determinate quantities of a certain kind are similar to the real numbers in that there are order internal relations between them. Being internal relations, the order relations constitute the differences between the determinate quantities of a certain kind, rather than explaining them; and order relations also constitute the differences between real numbers, rather than explaining them.[18] I will argue in the next chapter that the order relations between determinates of a certain kind and between real numbers are ungrounded relations, so that they are not to be explained in terms of the monadic attributes of the things they hold between.[19]

For the real numbers it can be plausibly maintained that the order and proportion relations alone do constitute the differences between them. And for determinate quantities of a certain kind, it could also be plausibly maintained that the order and proportion relations alone constitute the differences between them. On the other hand, it must

18 The internal relations between determinate quantities are proportion relations that can be mapped into the real numbers, or are the real numbers on some views; there are also internal relations between the proportion relations themselves that can be mapped into the real numbers and so on.

19 See Chapter 6, Section 1.

not be thought that the real numbers are a special sort of quantity; they are not attributes of particulars.

In contrast, the determinate shades of colour do not have proportion relations between them in the way that determinate quantities of a certain kind do. The ordering relations between shades of colour are resemblance relations, both transitive and intransitive. Although very different from proportion relations, they are internal relations, as Moore pointed out. As internal relations we might expect them to be constitutive of the differences between the determinate shades to some extent, but resemblance relations alone cannot be said to constitute those differences.

Even greater difficulties surround explaining the differences between determinables, such as the difference between "red" and "blue" or the difference between "mass" and "charge". They do appear to differ *simpliciter*. It is true that masses and charges give rise to causal relations in characteristically different ways, but causal relations cannot be used to explain the difference between the determinables "mass" and "charge". Causal relations are grounded relations, and the differences between the two types of determinate quantity explain differences between causal relations, not the other way round. Any type of theory that admits a second type of universal in addition to determinates will have the same problem.

Criticism of the second-order theory of determinables

In the second-order theory, essential subordination, which is a relation between two first-order attributes, is replaced by the predication of a second-order attribute of a first-order attribute. So "chromatic colour" would be an attribute of "red", and "red" would be an attribute of "claret". On this view, the resemblance of "claret" and "scarlet" is explained in terms of the possession of a common attribute, namely, "red".

The second-order theory can also give an account of definite descriptions involving colour terms. Corresponding to

$$(\imath X)(X \text{sub} R \ \& \ Xa) = C'$$

of the second-level theory, the second-order theory has

$$(\imath X)(R(X) \ \& \ Xa) = C'.$$

And corresponding to

$$(\imath X)(X \mathrm{sub} C' \ \& \ Xa) = R$$

of the second-level theory, the second-order theory has

$$(\imath X)(C'(X) \ \& \ X(C')) = R.$$

A definite description involves a relation or connection between two different sorts of things. Instead of a relation in the strict sense, the second-order theory has the instantiation of one sort of thing by a different sort of thing.

Armstrong notes that the second-order theory does not correspond to the way we talk;[20] we do not say that "red" is coloured or redness is coloured. This is more than an appeal to ordinary language; it is an appeal to intuition and one that is, I think, well founded. In order to focus that intuition let us confine ourselves to simple material objects, which I shall just call 'objects'.

The attribute "triangular" is not a determinate attribute, since there are many ways in which objects can be triangular. It is the attribute that applies to things when they have three straight sides. Now it is objects that are triangular in the sense of having three straight sides; determinate shape attributes are not triangular in this sense. If the determinate shape attributes of triangular objects have anything in common, it is on account of their connection with the general, but first-order, attribute "being triangular".

Similarly it is objects that are spherical in shape. Determinate shape attributes such as "spherical with radius five inches" are not spherical in shape. All spherical objects, whatever their size, have something fundamental in common: They are all basically the same shape in the same way that similar triangles are the same shape. It is also objects that are massive, since it is only objects that have mass. Determinate mass attributes such as "mass five kilograms" cannot be described as massive or as having mass; it would not make any sense. There is something wrong with a theory that denies this and tries to say that what these objects have in common is not a fundamental feature but something derived from a common attribute of their determinate shape attributes.

Particularism does the same sort of thing. It says that what all spherical objects have in common is not a fundamental feature but is

20 Armstrong, Volume II, p. 106.

derived from a less stringent form of resemblance between tropes that are not exactly alike.

It is true that we cannot perceive or imagine determinable attributes such as "spherical" or "triangular" as isolated things. But our thought does not deal only in things that can be perceived or imagined as isolated. And the things that can be isolated can be isolated in varying degrees. As far as perception or imagination goes, a determinate shape attribute cannot be perceived or imagined in isolation; it must always be perceived or imagined as instanced with some other determinate attribute such as a colour. But what can be perceived or imagined does not always have a lot to do with how things are or how they are understood. A determinate shape attribute is always perceived or imagined as having some size, but size as perceived or imagined is size in perceptual space and as such is incommensurable with real size.

According to the second-order theory, two particulars with different masses are similar because their determinate masses possess the same second-order attribute. Strictly speaking the particulars themselves do not have any ontologically significant attribute in common. It is true that they share the attribute of "having a determinate which possesses the property of being a determinable mass", but this is an indefinite first-order property that is not itself of ontological significance.[21] Possession of a determinate mass would not entail that the object itself was a massive particular, for in a sense, on this view, it is not a massive particular.

It has also been suggested that essential subordination is merely set membership, that C' sub R is to be understood as $C' \in R$.[22] There certainly is such a set, the set of all determinate shades of colour that are subordinate to red. This view does admit that there are common features, because C' is a common feature of particulars. But there also appears to be another type of common feature: All the particulars that are red have something in common, and all the different shades of red also appear to have something in common. To explain red as a set is in effect to deny that there is another common feature, since the members of a set need not have anything in common. There are indeed sets whose members all have something in common, and there are also sets whose members are arbitrarily chosen

21 Cf. Bigelow and Pargetter, "Quantities", pp. 292–4.
22 Cf. Armstrong, Volume II, Chapter 22.

and do not have anything in common. If red is a set, it is either of the first type or the second type. If it is of the first type, then some other explanation of what the members have in common is available; if it is of the second type, then there need be no naturally given reason why they are members of the same set.

On this view only determinates would be true universals; the higher-level predicates would refer to nothing but sets of determinate attributes. Such a theory would be a form of immanent realism about determinates, but class nominalism for higher-level attributes, with all the problems associated with explaining the principle of unity of the set.

If the higher-level attributes such as red are sets, then they do not apply to particulars, contrary to what we have concluded so far. To say that a particular is red would be to say that $(\exists F)(F \in R \ \& \ Fa)$ and no more. Circularity and three-sidedness are higher-level shape attributes, but they clearly apply to particulars and so cannot be sets. Our view, then, is that besides determinate universals there are also determinable universals, both of which apply to particulars.

5. MASS UNIVERSALS

Colours are an interesting and instructive example of universals that are attributes, but they are secondary qualities. Mass is a primary quality if anything is, and it is also a quantity, an important type of attribute. Although there are various ways of mapping the set of determinate shades of colour into a bounded subset of ordered sets of real numbers, there are no natural proportion relations between determinate shades of colour. Determinate masses are quantities because of the natural relations of proportion between them. Unlike the colour attributes, it appears that with mass attributes we have at most only two levels. There is a set of determinates and one determinable.

Each material object has mass. And each material object has only one mass, though any number of objects can have exactly that mass. That mass is specified by an arbitrarily chosen unit of mass and a positive real number. We can never know exactly what the mass of an object is, but physics with its commitment to the principle of ontological determinacy always supposes that each object has an exact mass. We have then a set of determinate mass universals that can be put into one-to-one correspondence with the positive real numbers.

In physical equations 'm' is in effect a variable that ranges over the set of determinate masses.

There is also a "concept" of mass. In fact, speaking somewhat informally, we can say that there are several concepts of mass: In Newtonian mechanics there is inertia, quantity of matter, and active and passive gravitational mass. It is possible that it is only convention that assigns them the same magnitude, with nature merely telling us that they have a constant ratio. It seems unlikely, however, that a body would have four properties so closely related. There is no reason why a single attribute should not be responsible for a number of different effects; for example, it is a body's charge that governs how it interacts with both an electric and a magnetic field.

If we remember that a ratio scale is a function that maps a set of determinates into the real numbers

$$f: \{M^k\} \rightarrow R,$$

and that scales are unique up to the choice of unit, then it would be odd to posit the existence of several different kinds of determinates without any other distinctions.[23]

In Newtonian physics there would be no point in saying there is more than one determinate attribute that the object actually possessed. In relativistic physics, quantity of matter (or rest mass or proper mass) should be regarded as the fundamental attribute and the same attribute that is recognized by Newtonian physics, and inertia should be regarded as an important, but derived, quantity, in the same way that momentum is a derived quantity.

Since mass is a fundamental quantity, it is not possible to define it, and though we know very well how to measure it, it is difficult to know how to explain or characterize the notion of mass. It is interesting to compare mass with temperature. There are practical ambiguities that arise in trying to establish a scale of temperature using the properties of materials such as the resistance of a piece of platinum or the length of a column of mercury enclosed in glass. The proportion relations between temperatures are different for each

23 For ratio scales the admissible transformations are linear similarity transformations. The difficulty with non-linear transformations is that they would not be additive; if f and $f*$ were related by a non-linear transformation and $f(M_1) + f(M_2) = f(M_1 + M_2)$, we would not have $f*(M_1) + f*(M_2) = f*(M_1 + M_2)$. There would also be a change in the form of the physical equations in which those quantities appear.

property so that it seems that there are no naturally given proportion relations for temperature based on such scales.[24] It is quite different for mass: There are no practical ambiguities because there are naturally given proportion relations.

That there are naturally given proportion relations for masses is probably connected with the fact that mass, unlike temperature, is an extensive magnitude. There is a physical correlate of adding masses – namely, the putting together of two massive particulars to make one massive particular – in the same way that the adding of lengths corresponds to the concatenation of rods. If two equal volumes of a uniform fluid are combined, we would expect the quantity of matter to be doubled, and it turns out that all the effects of its mass are doubled.

Is it possible for different theories to introduce different universals that are different kinds of mass, and do we then have a higher mass determinable to which all these different mass determinables are subordinate? Consider a set of possible worlds all governed by the same set of natural laws, say those of Newtonian mechanics; in those worlds only one mass determinable, M, will be instanced by all material objects. In another set of possible worlds, governed by different laws, another universal will be instanced by all material objects. It is probably best to regard these two universals as simply different universals, as different as charge is from mass, unless some reason can be given for saying that they have something in common. It appears that we have no reason to believe that there is a further determinable to which the usual determinable "mass" is subordinate; in other words, the determinable, M, is an absolute determinable.

For example, Newtonian mass, which is also called 'inertia', seems to have something in common with relativistic inertia, since it approximates to it at low speeds. But in fact they are always distinct. Newtonian inertia is a fundamental quantity that is the same as mass, whereas relativistic inertia is a derived quantity. In New-

24 Temperature scales based on properties of materials are interval scales, so that a fixed point as well as a unit has to be chosen by convention. Thermodynamic temperature establishes naturally given proportion relations as well as a naturally given zero point, effectively making it a ratio scale. For the distinction between interval and ratio scales see David H. Krantz, R. Duncan Luce, Patrick Suppes, and Amos Tversky, *Foundations of Measurement*, pp. 9–12.

tonian mechanics "mass" is responsible for the effects we ascribe to "inertia", whereas in relativistic mechanics "mass" is only a contributing factor, along with the body's speed, to the same effects.[25]

There are three theories about the nature of mass universals: (1) the classical theory of determinables or the second-level theory, according to which there is a set of determinate monadic attributes of particulars, $\{M^k\}$, and there is also a second-level monadic attribute, M, which is also an attribute of particulars; (2) the second-order theory, according to which there is a set of determinate monadic attributes of particulars, $\{M^k\}$, and there is also a second-order monadic attribute, M, which is an attribute of the determinate attributes, a property of properties; and (3) the relationist theory, according to which there is only a set of determinate dyadic relations between particulars, $\{M^k\}$, which stand in topic-neutral relations of proportion to each other – the Bigelow–Pargetter view.[26]

Our previous study of the nature of colour attributes and shape attributes led us to some general conclusions about determinates and determinables that suggest that the first view is correct, that M is a true determinable, an attribute of a particular. On this view 'Ma' says that a is a massive body, or a has mass.

On the second-level view the relation between M^k and M is not an example of the genus–species relation where the species is explained *per genus et differentiam:* There is no X that is an attribute of a particular such that M^k is the conjunction of X and M. M^k is related to M by the second-order relation of essential subordination.

When we say that a body has mass we are saying that it is a massive body, which is expressed by the sentence 'Ma'. When we say that the mass of a body is M^k we are saying something like

$$M(a) = (\imath X)(X \text{ sub } M \ \& \ Xa) = M^k.$$

When we wish to say that two objects differ in mass, we are saying something about their determinate mass attributes:

$$M(a) \neq M(b).$$

a and b are alike in being massive bodies; they both have M; and they differ in that one has M^k and the other M^l.

25 Cf. John Earman, "Against Indeterminacy", and Arthur Fine's appendix. Earman is answering Hartry Field, "Theory Change and Indeterminacy of Reference".
26 John Bigelow and Robert Pargetter, "Quantities" and *Science and Necessity*, pp. 51–71.

Bigelow and Pargetter explain mass attributes in terms of determinate relations between particulars, such as "being twice as massive as". Instead of possessing a monadic determinate attribute a particular enters into a number of mass relations, such as "being twice as heavy as".[27] Each mass relation stands in what Armstrong calls a "topic neutral" relation of proportion to every other mass relation, but a mass relation cannot stand in a proportion relation to a universal of a different type such as a volume relation. The mass relations "being twice as massive as" and "being four times as massive as" have the proportion relation of 1:2 to each other.

If a particular a is k times more massive than particular b, then this can be represented by 'aM^kb', where M^k is a determinate "mass" relation. The set of determinate mass relations, $\{M^k\}$, can be put into one–to–one correspondence with the positive real numbers. The terms of the relations $\{M^k\}$ are what are normally thought of as massive bodies, but on the Bigelow–Pargetter view the notion of massive particular is explained in terms of the relations $\{M^k\}$: Massive bodies are particulars that are the terms of the relations $\{M^k\}$. One way out would be to say that all the M^k have the second–order attribute of being a mass relation, but Bigelow and Pargetter do not take this route, since for them virtually everything is a relation.

If one mass relation M^k is h times greater than another mass relation M^l, then this can be represented by '$M^kR_hM^l$', where R_h is a relation of proportion between two universals. It is essential to Bigelow and Pargetter's theory that the relations $\{R_h\}$ are topic neutral; in other words, the same relations $\{R_h\}$ hold between determinate mass relations and between determinate volume relations. On the other hand, we are told that a relation such as R_h only has terms of the same type: Determinate mass relations only enter into proportion relations with other determinate mass relations. But we were looking to second–order properties or relations to explain the differences between the different classes of determinate relations, whereas the order we are presented with is this: Massive bodies are particulars that are the terms of the determinate mass relations, and determinate mass relations are a class of relations that can stand in proportion relations only to each other. There is nothing that explains the division of determinate quantities into different types, the

27 Their need to explain all quantities as relations seems to come from their theory of real numbers; see *Science and Necessity*, p. 79.

determinate masses, the determinate volumes and so on; there is nothing that explains what the determinate masses have in common. The relations of proportion are topic neutral, and in the end Bigelow and Pargetter want to identify them with the real numbers,[28] but because they are topic neutral they do not explain what certain determinates quantities have in common.[29]

We expect monadic properties to explain relations of proportion, not the other way round, in the same way that we expect the resemblance of two objects to be explained by their monadic properties. As Armstrong points out, Bigelow and Pargetter have inverted the usual order of explanation: They have a superstructure hanging on nothing.[30]

In the Bigelow–Pargetter theory there is only one type of mass universal – the determinate mass relations $\{M^k\}$. What takes the place of a determinable mass universal is an indefinite first-order attribute, the property of "entering into determinate mass relations with other particulars". Being a massive particular is merely a matter of "entering into determinate mass relations with other particulars". After a fashion it can explain similarity and difference in mass. Two particulars differ in mass because they enter into different determinate mass relations with other particulars; the same two particulars are similar in that they are both massive particulars – as understood earlier in this section. But the ontological significance of the indefinite first-order attribute arises from whatever it is that mass relations have in common, and for that no explanation has been offered; it is not in itself an ontologically significant attribute of a particular.

The relationist theory of quantities understands determinate masses and, it seems, all other determinate quantities, as relations between particulars without any monadic foundations in those particulars. In other words, there is nothing intrinsic to or peculiar to the particular that is the basis for those relations holding. If all the determinate quantities possessed by a particular constitute it in some way, then it follows that on the relationist view a physical particular is constituted out of ungrounded relations, the particular in itself being simply a bare term.

There are indeed ungrounded relations between particulars; spatial relations are the best example, and in fact Bigelow and Pargetter em-

28 Ibid., p. 353.
29 Cf. Armstrong, "Are Quantities Relations? A Reply to Bigelow and Pargetter".
30 Ibid.

phasize this analogy. Perhaps uniqueness of mass for a physical particular is supposed to be analogous to uniqueness of position for a physical particular.[31] The spatial relations a physical particular enters into do not constitute it in any way; they are accidental to what it is. But it is impossible to understand the attributes of physical particulars as relations that are accidental to what it is and that do not constitute it in any way; there must be some monadic attributes. On the other hand, a spatial position or spatial point, considered as a particular,[32] only has relational properties. And in this case the relations do constitute it, but at the expense of being internal relations – relations necessary to their terms. The physical attributes of particulars are not necessary to their terms, however, so they cannot be understood as relations in this way.

Normally we think of an object entering into causal relations on account of the properties it has, such as its mass. We expect causal relations to be grounded relations. On the relationist account of mass, causal relations would be grounded in other relations, which is not how physics understands causal relations.

Suppose that all the masses of all the bodies in the universe were suddenly doubled; all their mass relations (that is, their masses according to Bigelow and Pargetter) would remain the same, but their accelerations due to electrical forces would be halved, and so would their rates of fall of temperature due to radiation losses. The Bigelow–Pargetter theory does not, therefore, reproduce standard physics.

6. THE BASIS OF HIGHER-LEVEL ATTRIBUTES

Our account of the second-level theory of determinates and determinables has been in terms of the relation of essential subordination, certain definite descriptions, and functions based on those definite descriptions. The definite descriptions are themselves ultimately based on the relation of essential subordination, which is a second-order internal relation between first-order attributes of different levels. And we were able to say some things about the nature of the relation of essential subordination. The notion of level for attributes comes from the analogy between the way in which determinates and determinables classify particulars and the way in which species and genera classify particulars, mentioned at the beginning of this chapter.

31 Cf. ibid., p. 308.   32 In fact, it is not my view that they are particulars.

127

This theory was not able to explain all the similarity and difference difficulties that were also mentioned at the beginning of this chapter. I argued that an explanation of differences in terms of attributes that differed from each other *simpliciter* could in certain circumstances be regarded as an acceptable form of explanation. And it does appear that determinables differ *simpliciter* from other determinables. Determinate quantities belonging to the same determinable do not differ from each other *simpliciter,* or an account of *differentiae;* they differ from each other on account of internal relations.

Similarly, the entailment patterns cannot be completely explained. It seems that there are merely rules to the effect that if a particular possesses a certain determinate, then it also possesses the corresponding determinable, and if a particular possesses a certain determinable, then it possesses one and only one determinate, which is subordinate to that determinable. The first rule can be seen as a consequence of the fact that essential subordination is an internal relation between first-order attributes, but it is difficult to see the second as a consequence of anything else. Intuitively we are certain that a material object can have only one mass and one velocity, though we cannot explain it by referring to a different fact about universals.

As we noted at the beginning of this chapter, the similarity and difference problems and the entailment patterns for determinates and determinables have parallels for species and genera. Even for species and genera there are some things that cannot be explained. We are certain that one individual belonging to a genus cannot belong to more than one species subordinate to that genus. Although we cannot explain it in terms of the species and genus universals, it will depend on a similar property of the attributes which the species universals are based on; in other words, it will depend on the second entailment pattern for determinates and determinables.

Despite the fact that the second-level theory of determinates and determinables cannot completely explain the characteristic similarity and difference difficulties and the entailment patterns, there seems to be no problem with the consistency of the theory arising from these issues, and there is some doubt as to what further facts could explain them.

A higher-level predicate such as 'red' does not correspond to a feature of a particular in the way that a determinate predicate does. But there is a basis in the determinate attributes for the use of such predicates, a basis we have characterized in various ways. To say that a predicate does not signify anything isolable, but that its use in a sentence has a basis, sounds a little like Frege's context principle. Semantically, number terms have to be treated as proper names, but numbers themselves cannot be regarded as self-subsistent objects in the usual Platonist sense. Nevertheless, there is an objective basis for true statements containing number terms.

We cannot point to an isolable feature that corresponds to a higher-level colour predicate or to a quantity determinable. But we have to treat all determinables as attribute terms that apply to particulars, and there is an objective basis in the determinate attribute for true statements containing determinable terms. We have a sort of contextual account of what it is for a particular to possess a higher-level colour attribute. Moreover, there does not seem to be any other way to deal with such attributes.

The difficulties concern isolability. There is no reason to think that each element of a sentence refers to a separate – that is to say, isolable – piece of reality. And it is also important to note that there are different degrees of isolability.

There are similar difficulties for shape attributes, even though determinate shape attributes have components that function as *differentiae*. Distance, considered as a monadic attribute, can be regarded as a sort of one-dimensional shape, but when we come to true, three-dimensional shapes we lose the simple structure typical of the quantities. Consider a triangular particular and its determinate shape attribute, "triangular (*abc*)", where '(*abc*)' signifies the lengths of the sides of the triangle. This determinate attribute has certain component attributes such as, "three-sided", "rectilinear closed figure", and "sides (*abc*)". All of these component attributes are attributes of the particular; they are not properties of the determinate attribute.[33] Some of them are higher-level attributes, but not all.

The attribute "closed rectilinear figure" cannot be isolated, in the sense that no particular can simply have "closed rectilinear figure" as its shape attribute without further determination. If we have a particular with determinate shape attribute "triangular (*abc*)", then neither in perception nor in imagination can we isolate the attribute "closed rectilinear figure". What we can do perceptually is isolate

33 Cf. Frege, *Foundations of Arithmetic,* Section 53.

parts of the particular, such as its sides, which is not the same thing. In this way a higher-level shape attribute is similar to a higher-level colour attribute. The difference is that a determinate shape attribute can in a sense be regarded as a conjunction of various sorts of attributes. For example, '*a* is triangular (*abc*)' can be understood as the conjunction '*a* is a closed rectilinear figure & *a* has three sides & *a* has sides (*abc*)'. This does not imply that "triangular (*abc*)" is not a basic attribute as the conjuncts are higher-level attributes, except for "has sides (*abc*)" and it is not clear what that is.[34] It seems to presuppose that the shape is triangular, which raises similar problems to those raised in the discussion of the cross-shaped particular in Chapter 4, Section 4.

In a sense the higher-level shape attributes cannot be isolated, any more than the higher-level colour attributes or determinable quantities can be isolated. If higher-level shape attributes can be isolated at all, it is only a conceptual sort of isolation. In all cases we can say that there is an objective basis for the higher-level attribute in the nature of the determinate attributes. The difference is that for the determinate shape attributes there are also *differentiae*.

If we consider a globe of white marble, in the way David Hume did,[35] we find that we can perceive two determinate attributes. From the point of view of perception, which is Hume's point of view, the two determinate attributes cannot be isolated from each other. We do, however, have two totally different types of causal interaction, and this is one reason for regarding the two determinate attributes as different, real constituents of the world. Further, the shape can occur with any number of different shades of colour. The shape may have to occur with some colour, but it is independent of the actual colour of the marble. On the other hand, the shape cannot occur without all the higher-level shape attributes to which it is subordinate also applying to the particular.

Hume uses a Scholastic term, 'distinction of reason', to describe the distinction between the colour and the shape of the globe of marble. Usually there is said to be a distinction of reason when one thing is looked at from two different points of view; the evening star and the morning star are often given as an example. In fact, this seems to be Hume's idea:

34 Cf. George Bealer, *Quality and Concept*, p. 182, who does not appear to make the distinction between determinate attribute and higher-level attribute.
35 Hume, *A Treatise of Human Nature*, I, I, vii.

After a little more practice of this kind, we begin to distinguish the figure from the colour by a *distinction of reason;* that is, we consider the figure and colour together, since they are in effect the same and undistinguishable; but still view them in different aspects, according to the resemblances, of which they are susceptible.[36]

We have here someone who seems to understand very well the implications of extreme nominalism, in this case a form of resemblance nominalism.

Our reasoning, however, leads to the view that there is a *real distinction* between the determinate shape attribute and the determinate colour attribute. This is because, using causal interaction as a criterion of identity, we have concluded that the two determinate attributes are different and causally independent real constituents of the world. Basic attributes therefore are ontological units, and with respect to basic attributes our view amounts to a form of metaphysical atomism. It does not follow that basic attributes do not have components; it is that their components are not causally significant in the same sort of way.

Armstrong says that there is a *formal distinction* between the determinable shape of a triangle and its size.[37] The determinable shape is shared by all similar triangles with the size functioning as a *differentia*. A determinate triangular shape could then be regarded as having the determinable shape as a component. This does not explain the mode of composition of determinate shapes, but it does point to the fact that there are degrees of isolability.

The full title is *distinctio formalis a parte rei;* in other words, there is some objective basis in the thing for the distinction, which fits in with what we have said so far.[38] Consider a set $s = \{a, b, c\}$. There is something like a formal distinction between s and a. We cannot present s and a together as separate, because s would not be s unless a were one of its elements. This is not a very pertinent example as a set has an arbitrary principle of unity. We would get a better example if s were a material object having a, b, and c as essential

---

36 Ibid. Hume is no stranger to Scholastic distinctions; see Ronald J. Butler, "*Distinctiones Rationis,* or the Cheshire Cat Which Left Its Smile Behind".
37 Armstrong, Volume I, p. 110.
38 On the formal distinction see F. Coplestone, *A History of Philosophy,* Volume II, Part II, pp. 232–3; P. Skagestad, *The Road of Inquiry,* pp. 68–9; and particularly Francisco Suarez, *Disputationes Metaphysicae,* Book VI. According to the Scholastics, things that are formally distinct cannot be separated even by God; we can say that it is logically impossible to separate them.

proper parts. Again we cannot present *s* and *a* together as separate things, because *s* would not be *s* unless *a* were part of it.

These examples should probably be regarded only as analogies as they deal with simple particulars, whereas the formal distinction is usually applied to things having to do with universals and essences. The typical Scholastic example is to say that there is a formal distinction between the individual essence of Socrates (his haecceity) and his humanity. Although humanity is a universal that occurs many times, it is not possible to have the individual essence of Socrates without humanity, since it is essential to Socrates that he is human.

A triangular determinate shape has a number of components such as, "three-sided", "rectilinear closed figure", and "sides *(abc)*". There is a formal distinction between each of the components, and between the determinate itself and each of the components. It could also be claimed that there is a somewhat tighter formal distinction between a determinate colour and the corresponding determinable and between a determinate quantity and its determinable. Although the notion of formal distinction does not explain the mode of composition of shape determinates it is a useful way of pointing to the fact that there is a distinction that has an objective basis, which is different from the real distinction between two different elements of reality.

Armstrong has suggested that determinate quantities have components and a structure analogous to that of structural universals. In contrast to the usual structural universals, which he calls 'relational structural properties', he calls determinate quantities 'non-relational structural properties'. A relational structural property is one like "being methane" where the parts stand in certain relations to each other.

Non-relational structural properties involve the proper parts having certain properties, but do not involve any relations between these parts. *Being two kilograms in mass* appears to be such a structural property. For an individual, *X*, (which may be a scattered individual), to be two kilograms in weight there must exist innumerable pairs, triples, etc. of non-overlapping individuals, where the N-tuples are such that each member is less than two kilograms in mass, and such that the sum of the members is the individual *X*.[39]

39 Armstrong, "Are Quantities Relations? A Reply to Bigelow and Pargetter", p. 312.

This analysis of what it is to be two kilograms in weight is very similar to the analysis of relational structural universals that was given in Chapter 4, Section 5, except that the multi-place arrangement relation is replaced by a "sum of members".

For a pair of non-overlapping parts Armstrong's analysis appears to correspond to the following formula:

$$(\exists x_1)(\exists x_2)(M^l x_1 \ \& \ M^m x_2 \ \& \ S(a = x_1 + x_2) \ \& \ k = l + m) \rightarrow M^k a$$

where $k = l + m$ says that certain real numbers are added together, and $S(a = x_1 + x_2)$ says that two component parts, x_1 and x_2, are added together to give the whole, X.

Now it is true that mass is an extensive attribute and is therefore additive. No sense can be made, however, of adding determinate mass attributes such as M^l and M^m, since strictly speaking it is the real numbers that represent them that are added. Two massive particulars are "added" in the sense of being put together to form one massive particular, so that the whole has one determinate mass attribute; the mass of the whole is the sum of the masses of the parts so that $k = l + m$. It is difficult to know what it is to add scattered particulars in this way, though we know what the mass would be if the particulars were to be actually "added" together, although they would have a common centre of mass.

The adding of massive particulars is similar to the putting together of rods in such a way that the length of the whole is equal to the sum of the lengths of the parts. This problem is more acute with lengths, and if the theory is to work it would also have to apply to lengths and the combination or rods. If a combined rod is to instance the length that is the sum of the lengths of its components, the component rods have to be actually combined together. And the rods have to be put together in a certain way – namely, laid end to end.

When two material objects are put together to form one material object they are always put together in a certain way (i.e. with a certain arrangement), even though that arrangement does not affect the mass. Many different arrangements of the same parts would result in the same mass, but only a few would result in the same particular – it depends on the identity conditions for that type of particular. Armstrong's notion of summation, which I have represented by $S(a = x_1 + x_2)$, is a sort of indeterminate putting together of parts to form an "object". It is the part–whole relation of mereology.

In a scattered object there are naturally given parts that are connected lumps. If the analysis is to apply to one of those connected lumps, then according to usual mereological practice the lump can be resolved into parts in any number of ways, each of which is in a sense an arbitrary division of the lump. The analysis, therefore, explains a determinate mass in terms of arbitrarily given components, each of which can be given any number of similar analyses.

In the formula that I have used to represent Armstrong's analysis the predication of a mass attribute appears on both sides of the formula. The analysis does not explain what it is for the component parts to have mass. In effect, the analysis shows something about how masses are additive, and though that is an essential aspect of mass the nature of the addition is still left obscure. It follows that Armstrong's analysis does explain how determinate mass attributes are composed of component universals.

7. WHAT IS A CONCEPT?

For Geach a concept is "a mental capacity belonging to a particular person". A sufficient condition for a person to possess a concept is to have mastered the intelligent use of the word for the concept.[40] In this way concepts are objective, since many people can possess the same mental capacity or skill. It is presumably the concept considered as a type that is objective, though we should remember that Geach is a particularist. Geach's use of the term 'concept' corresponds to those ordinary language locutions where we speak of persons possessing and acquiring concepts, and of persons applying concepts.

There is no doubt that there are such mental capacities and that they are important. What is questionable is whether there is a reasonable interpretation of logic, or fragment of ordinary language, which understands predicates, such as F, as referring to mental capacities. Perhaps this is why in Section 11 Geach talks about red and chromatic colour as attributes.

We often speak as though there were a distinction between claret as something existing in the world, and a "concept of claret", and we speak of mass as an attribute of objects and also speak of a "concept of mass". I suggest the following analysis: The statement

40 Geach, *Mental Acts,* pp. 12, 13.

'Claret is the basis of the concept claret' should be parsed as 'Claret is the basis for a person applying the concept claret', which, finally, should be parsed as 'Claret is the basis for a person judging that "*a* is claret".' In making such a judgement the person will, of course, make use of that mental capacity Geach insists on calling a concept. The ordinary language locution "possessing a concept" is simply to be understood as having that mental capacity that enables you to make such a judgement.

6

Causal relations

1. REAL RELATIONS

We are happy to say that certain particulars exist and are real, and this lends credibility to the idea that basic attributes are real constituents of the world. The reason is that basic attributes inhere in particulars and are thought of as in some way constituents of particulars, contributing to their reality. Relations, on the other hand, seem to have a shadowy sort of existence; they seem to hang between particulars. Intuitively, it is difficult to regard relations as real constituents of the world.

According to Gottfried Martin this intuition found expression in mediaeval metaphysics. For Aquinas the being of an accident (i.e. an attribute) was a matter of its existing in an individual being "Esse accidentis est inesse"[1] – for an accident, to be is to inhere: "A relation, considered as a real accident, would be an accident which stood so to speak with one foot in one substance and the other in another, and this contradicts the idea of an accident as inherent in a particular individual being."[2] This point of view leads to the doctrine that all relations are "relations of reason", in other words that they are things produced by thought and that there are no such things as "real relations".[3] The argument is that since relations cannot be independently existing things – if they were, they would cease to be relations – and since they do not exist *in* their terms, then the only place left for them to exist is in the knowing subject.[4]

Some sections of this chapter and the next are based on Andrew Newman, "The Causal Relation and Its Terms".
1 Gottfried Martin, *Leibniz: Logic and Metaphysics,* pp. 144–58.
2 Ibid., p. 149; cf. Spinoza, *Ethics,* Axiom I.
3 Ockham notes that the distinction between relation of reason and real relation is not to be found in Aristotle, *Summa Logicae,* Part I, 52.
4 Cf. Russell, "On the Relations of Universals and Particulars": "Relations, obviously, do not exist anywhere in space. . . . General qualities such as whiteness, on the contrary, may be said to be in many places at once" (p. 107).

The other point of view, the doctrine of real relations, is the view that "every relation is a thing distinct from its foundation, so that the similarity by which white Socrates is like white Plato is a thing really and totally distinct from both Socrates and the white which grounds the similarity."[5] The doctrine of real relations was understood as positing an independent sort of existence for a relation, not the independent sort of existence appropriate to a substance but that appropriate to the particularized properties or tropes of particularism; hence the expression *res absoluta realiter distincta*. The argument just given against real relations seems to be based on the essentially intuitive idea that a trope can only exist, or hold up, if it is compresent with other tropes to form a concrete particular, but not if it is suspended between two or more concrete particulars. This argument, which questions the location or support of real relations, need not influence an immanent realist, since it depends on intuitions about tropes as particulars having a semi-substantial sort of existence.

The argument is particularly compelling, however, to a modern particularist who sees a substance as composed of tropes, which are its constitutive parts. It is one of the reasons why Keith Campbell, a modern particularist, has misgivings about relations despite the importance of the relation of resemblance for particularism.[6] He is also worried that a relation depends for its existence on its terms, so that all its terms have to be present.

Campbell is also a foundationist; he believes that all relations have foundations in monadic properties of particulars – which Russell calls the "monadistic view". He thinks Ockham's razor dictates that relations and their foundations should not be regarded as equally real constituents of the world. For him a relation is not a thing of reason, but has a secondary ontological significance, being "supervenient" on its foundational monadic properties. We need to look, then, at the foundationist doctrine that all relations have monadic foundations.

According to Gottfried Martin, it is unlikely that Leibniz was influenced directly by Ockham, but it does seem that ideas about

5 Ockham, *Summa Logicae*, Part I, 54. In this section he gives an account of the doctrine of real relations, which he calls the view opposed to Aristotle's. But compare Aristotle, *Metaphysics*, 1088[a] 22. For a discussion of Ockham's arguments against real relations see Julius Weinberg, *Abstraction, Relation, and Induction*, pp. 103–8.
6 Campbell, *Abstract Particulars*, p. 98.

relations similar to Ockham's came down to Leibniz through his teachers.[7] The following passage gives Leibniz's account of the relation between two line segments, L and M. L has one length and M another, and the relation between them is given by the ratio of the two corresponding numbers:

> The ratio or proportion between two lines L and M, may be conceived three several ways; as a ratio of the greater L to the less M; as a ratio of the lesser M to the greater L; and lastly, as something abstracted from both, that is, as the ratio between L and M, without considering which is the antecedent, or which is the consequent; which the subject, and which the object. . . . But, which will be the subject, in the third way of considering them? It cannot be said that both of them, L and M together, are the subject of such an accident; for if so, we should have an accident in two subjects, with one leg in one, and the other in the other; which is contrary to the notion of accidents. Therefore we must say, that this relation, in this third way of considering it, is indeed out of the subjects; but being neither a substance, nor an accident, it must be a mere ideal thing, the consideration of which is nevertheless useful. . . . And 'tis this analogy, which makes men fancy places, traces and spaces; though those things consist only in the truth of relations, and not at all in any absolute reality.[8]

In effect, Leibniz is denying the doctrine of real relations; for him spatial relations are merely well-founded phenomena. Leibniz was a foundationist; he believed that all there is in reality is the foundation in the substances that are the terms of the relation.

Consider two particulars a and b, which have basic length attributes L''' and L''. a is greater than b, although to be precise we should say that a is greater than b with respect to length; in other words, a is longer than b. a is not greater than b with respect to mass or temperature, nor indeed are we talking about a relation between pure numbers. The relation between a and b has foundations, since the relation depends on a and b having certain lengths, which are monadic properties and which determine that the relation should hold.[9]

Not only do the two particulars a and b bear a certain relation to each other; the two basic attributes L''' and L'' also have a relation with respect to each other, and so do the two real numbers that are used to represent the basic attributes. We therefore have three "greater than" relations. There is the relation $>_2$, which holds be-

7 Martin, *Leibniz: Logic and Metaphysics*, p. 148.
8 Leibniz's Fifth Paper, 47, *The Leibniz-Clarke Correspondence*, pp. 71–2.
9 The basic length attributes can also be looked at as relations, with their terms being end points, point objects with finite mass, or centres of mass.

tween two particulars when one is greater than the other with respect to length. '$a >_2 b$' should be understood as saying that "a is longer than b"; it is a spatial relation. There is the relation $>_1$, which is an ordering relation on the set of all basic length attributes, and there is the relation $>_0$, which is the well-known ordering relation on the set of real numbers. Although it is clear that $>_2$ is a spatial relation and that $>_0$ is not a spatial relation, it is not clear what $>_1$ is. L''' cannot be said to be longer than L'' in the way that a is longer than b. $>_2$ is a first-order relation that has particulars as its terms, whereas $>_1$ is a second-order relation that has universals as its terms. [10]

Corresponding to the three "greater than" relations there are three types of proportion relations. There are relations such as R_k^2, which holds between two particulars when one is k times greater than the other with respect to length. '$a R_k^2 b$' should be understood as saying that "a is k times longer than b". There are also relations such as R_k^1, which are proportion relations between basic length attributes: '$L''' R_k^1 L''''$ says that "L''' is k times greater than L''''" and it follows that $m/n = k$. R_k^0 is a proportion relation between real numbers. The proportion relations are similar to the "greater than" relations in that R_k^2 is a first-order relation that has particulars as its terms, whereas R_k^1 is a second-order relation that has universals as its terms. R_k^0 has the real numbers themselves as its terms.

The view of Armstrong and Bigelow and Pargetter is that the proportion relations are topic neutral; in other words, it is the same relations that hold between determinate quantities of all kinds. This makes it clearer that R_k^2 is a different relation from R_k^1, since R_k^2 is not topic neutral. If this view is right, then the $\{R_k^1\}$ are the same relations as the $\{R_k^0\}$, and $>_1$ is the same relation as $>_0$.

Now the relation two particulars bear of one being greater than the other with respect to length can in a sense be explained by monadic properties the particulars possess, namely, their basic length attributes. As a consequence of the nature of determinate quantities there is a relation between any two particulars that possess determinate quantities of the same type: One of them is greater

10 If there were negative length attributes, then the set of all the basic length attributes should satisfy the real number axioms; see Raymond L. Wilder, *The Foundations of Mathematics*, p. 150. Wilder's informal description of these axioms is: (1) simple order axiom, (2) Dedekind cut axiom, (3) separability axiom, (4) unboundedness axiom.

than the other in that respect. So in a sense $a >_2 b$ is explained by $L''' >_1 L''$. But there is a difference: $a >_2 b$ is a contingent truth, whereas $L''' >_1 L''$ is a necessary truth. The relation ">$_1$" is an internal relation that holds between the universals whether they are instanced or not: A basic length attribute would not be the universal it is without all the order and proportion relations it has with the other basic length attributes.[11] The full explanation is that $a >_2 b$, a contingent truth, is explained by the combination of $L''' >_1 L''$, which is a necessary truth, and $L'''a$ and $L''b$, which are contingent truths.

I am not sure whether this explanation of $a >_2 b$ is the monadic reduction looked for by foundationists. The relation between two particulars has been explained in terms of monadic properties of those particulars, but the explanation involves acknowledging the existence of relations between universals that are essential to the nature of those universals. As far as I can see, the explanation can be taken no further, although I am aware that foundationists will want to explain the relation between the basic attributes in terms of properties of basic attributes, as Russell suggests on their behalf.[12]

It might be possible to explain the relation $>_1$ between two basic attributes L''' and L'' by the fact that the basic length attributes can be put into one-to-one correspondence with the positive real numbers, but that would not be the sort of explanation required by foundationism, since the real numbers used to represent L''' and L'' are not monadic properties of L''' and L''. Since a set of determinate quantities can be represented by real numbers in an infinite number of ways, the real number used to represent L''' on a given occasion is not any sort of intrinsic property of L'''.

The basic length attributes obey the real number axioms, and like the real numbers themselves they do not have any properties that are relevant other than those given by the real number axioms, despite what Keith Campbell suggests.[13] And those properties are not monadic; they are essentially relational. The basic length attributes do have one further property that is the same for all of them: They are all subordinate to the length determinable. As for the real num-

---

11 Cf. G. E. Moore, "External and Internal Relations", particularly p. 286, and Wittgenstein, *Tractatus*, 4.122–4.1252. We do not usually think of particulars as entering into internal relations, since it implies that they have individual essences.
12 Russell, *The Principles of Mathematics*, Section 214.
13 Campbell, *Abstract Particulars*, p. 103.

bers themselves there is no reason to suppose that they have any further properties. It follows that the foundationist programme does not work for quantity determinates.

Campbell suggests that an order or proportion relation between two particulars supervenes on the determinate quantity attributes, since it is they that determine the relation between the particulars – Ockham and Leibniz regarded it as a "thing of reason". Unfortunately the notion of supervenience is a formal one that is conceptually obscure, and its formal conditions are difficult to satisfy.[14] It seems to me that the metaphysically important notion here is that of internal relation between basic attributes, though I agree with Campbell that the relations between basic attributes have secondary ontological significance. It is the basic attributes themselves that are causally significant; the relations between basic attributes can only be causally significant via the basic attributes.

When Russell and Moore argued that there were such things as universals, they gave certain relations as examples of things that they thought were undoubtedly universals. Russell suggested resemblance and then spatial relations, and Moore also suggested spatial relations.[15] Russell was in effect arguing against resemblance nominalists. Resemblance nominalists take various types of resemblances to be primitive, and they have to admit that given a certain type of resemblance, many pairs of particulars resemble each other in the same way. Any type of resemblance can occur many times; in other words, it is a universal. It is not possible, however, to explain the multiple occurrence of the resemblance relations themselves in terms of higher-order resemblance, since that move gives rise to an infinite regress, which is not only cumbersome but also fails to explain anything.[16]

The particularist relies heavily on the notion of resemblance, and Campbell's response to Russell's objection is to be strong-minded.[17] If a set of concrete particulars resemble each other, then the dyadic relations of resemblance between the particulars are all different tropes; the set of these tropes also have dyadic relations

14 See Chapter 9, Section 4.
15 Russell, *The Problems of Philosophy*, pp. 95–105; Moore, *Some Main Problems of Philosophy*, pp. 303–4, but cf. pp. 312–19.
16 Cf. Russell, *The Problems of Philosophy*, p. 96, and Armstrong, Volume I, pp. 54–6.
17 Campbell, *Abstract Particulars*, p. 38.

141

between them, and so on all the way up. Being strong-minded is a matter of tolerating the hierarchy: "It proceeds in the direction of greater and greater formality and less and less substance."[18] But what we are looking for is explanation.

Two things resemble each other if they look alike, and they always look alike in some respect. Looking alike, though intuitively appealing, is not good enough because there are too many properties that are not observed by the senses, so "looking alike" has to be replaced by "being alike". The particularist or the resemblance nominalist has to regard "being alike" as an ungrounded, primitive equivalence relation. It is ungrounded in that it is not based on the nature of its terms or the properties of its terms, for if it were we would turn to the nature or properties of its terms for an explanation of the relation of "being alike" and it would cease to be primitive. On the other hand, Campbell has no time for other ungrounded relations, and he sometimes speaks as though tropes have natures or are natures.

If the relations of "being alike" do not have foundations in the tropes that are their terms, then if two tropes differ, their differences are grounded in different primitive relations of "being alike"; in fact, they are grounded in two different networks of such relations. Instead of a relation being grounded in a property, the property is grounded in the relation. This makes the relation of "being alike" ontologically more important than the monadic tropes, so as we go up the hierarchy we are supposed to find more and more substance, not less. But however far we go, we find no explanations, because similarities and differences are always explained by the next level up. It is also difficult to understand why the primitive relation tropes of "being alike" should be regarded as real constituents of the world, since as relations they have no causal effects.

Although Russell has given a good argument against nominalism, it does not follow that the relation of resemblance has to be admitted as a real constituent of the world. The immanent realist, as opposed to the nominalist, says that two particulars resemble each other – that is, look alike to some perceiver – because they have similar attributes. The relation of resemblance is one that has a foundation in its terms as the mediaevals would put it; or, as we would say, there is a basis in the terms for predicating resemblance of them.

18 Ibid., p. 34.

Admitting to the existence of hierarchies of universals helps to explain resemblance. For example, two particulars can resemble each other exactly in shade of colour because they are both exactly the same shade of colour. Or they could resemble each other more distantly because they are both shades of scarlet, or because they are both red. It explains the different ways in which two things can resemble each other. It is the possession of a common universal that explains why the two look alike to a perceiver. The perceiver is aware of the common universal; he is not, at the same time and in the same way, also aware of a distinct relation of resemblance. Non-transitive resemblance is difficult to explain on any account, particularly for resemblance nominalism, for which it presents a fundamental problem.

2. SPATIAL RELATIONS

There are, of course, those who deny the reality of space and time, and assert that they are mere illusions. But for most people, space and time are in some sense real constituents of the world; even for Leibniz, space and time, though phenomena, still had good foundations. What is difficult is understanding in what way space and time are real.

Suppose we have three pairs of particulars that are spatially related as follows:

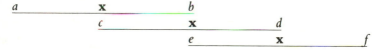

It seems that the three pairs have something in common – namely the distance between them and the orientation of that distance, which is why '**x**' is used to represent the relation, which is a vector displacement.

We perceive three pairs of particulars and three expanses or spaces separating each member of a pair from the other. We perceive that the spaces resemble each other. And as Moore points out, "The respect in which they are all alike is obviously not identical with any one of them, but is something common to them all."[19] Even Hume has to admit that we can attend to the respect in which different

19 Moore, *Some Main Problems of Philosophy*, p. 313.

143

particulars resemble each other, so that the best he can do is to maintain that "whenever we think of a general idea, we must also have a particular one before our minds".[20]

We can write the relationship between the particulars a and b as

$$(a)\mathbf{x}(b),$$

where the brackets are added merely for emphasis, to show where the proper names go. In three-dimensional space the vector displacement, which is written $\mathbf{x}$, is represented by an ordered triple of real numbers (x, y, z).

There are two ways of understanding the relation $(\ )\mathbf{x}(\ )$. Either it is a fundamental universal, or it is based on something else, something more fundamental. Moore's conclusion was that $\mathbf{x}$ was an indirect relation, since he regarded the space separating the particulars as itself a particular, "something substantive", as he puts it.[21] For Moore the relation between a and b consists in the fact that "each is at one end of *this* space".

For the absolutist, space itself is a something – that is, a something that is a self-subsistent particular, intervening between bodies.[22] A region of space is a self-subsistent particular, and so is an expanse of space between two bodies; and presumably the points of space are also self-subsistent particulars. A region of space is constituted out of points of space, an example of a non–atomic particular being constituted out of atomic particulars. I shall not decide here between the absolutist and the relationist; I shall merely argue that even an absolutist has to regard distance universals as real constituents of the world in their own right.

Moore wanted to say that the spatial relation between a and b was a matter of a and b being at either end of a particular expanse of space. However, since there is also a spatial relation between the two spatial points that a and b occupy, that relation must also be a matter of the spatial points being at either end of the same particular expanse of space. There is also a relation of "occupation", since body

---

20 Ibid., p. 314.   21 Ibid., p. 317.

22 Strictly speaking we should discuss space-time since absolutism about space itself is no longer an option, but it is easier and more convenient to talk about space. Most of our remarks will carry over to space-time. There is also something fundamental about purely spatial relations considered as universals. My own are views given in Andrew Newman, "A Metaphysical Introduction to a Relational Theory of Space". That paper is related in part to Peter Alexander, "Incongruent Counterparts and Absolute Space".

a "occupies" a certain point. So the absolutist *could* analyse the spatial relation between bodies *a* and *b* in terms of the relation of occupation, and the distance relation between two spatial points.

The only way in which distance relations could be eliminated altogether is if the distance between two spatial points can be analysed in terms of the number of points between them. But we know that this cannot be done, since the number of points between any two non–identical points is the same. Instead, Moore wanted to see distance relations as in some way secondary or subordinate to regions of space as particulars, but it is not clear how this could be done.

The absolutist, since he sees a point of space as a particular distinct from all other points, must think that points have some sort of identity as points. Each point of space must differ from every other point of space in a fundamental way. This is how Newton explains how regions of space differ from each other:

So the parts of space are individuated by their positions, so that if any two could exchange their positions, they would simultaneously exchange individuation, and each would be converted numerically into the other. By their mutual order and positions alone are the parts of duration and space understood to be just what they are in fact; nor have they any other principle of individuation besides that order and those positions, which therefore they cannot change.[23]

By 'order' Newton means the order of points, and by 'position' he means position within that order; in other words, the position of a certain point would be its relations with all the other points. This is more than an account of individuation; it is an account of the essence and individuation of spatial points. Even if space were made up of grainlike points that are particulars and fundamental entities, nevertheless spatial relations, such as order relations and distance relations, would be also, and equally, fundamental things. On this account of how spatial points are individuated from each other, spatial relations such as ( )**x**( ) are real constituents of the world.

23 Newton, "On the Gravity and Equilibrium of Fluids", p. 103 (Latin), p. 136 (English translation). The translation I have given is that of Howard Stein, "Newtonian Space-time", p. 194, which I have modified. Note that Newton is using the term 'individuation' in the mediaeval sense. If points of space are particulars as the absolutist believes, then their relations with other points are internal relations. Here, apparently, we have an example of particulars entering into internal relations; see note 11, this chapter. Newton's position does give a foothold to the relationist.

A foundationist, however, could not accept this account of the nature of spatial points.[24] For the sake of simplicity consider a real one-dimensional continuum of space or perhaps of time, and let us take the absolutist view that the points of that continuum are self-subsistent particulars. Those points have a number of properties or characteristics. The most important characteristic is that they obey the real number axioms, but they also have at least one further characteristic: The points in a real continuum are all spatial points or all temporal points. It is conceivable, of course, that a point could have further unknown properties, but we have no knowledge of what they might be. For the absolutist each point is different from every other point, and it is conceivable that the points differ in virtue of the hypothesized further unknown properties. This hypothesis has the consequence that space has essential characteristics we are unaware of and probably cannot become aware of, which is an unwelcome hypothesis. However, for the absolutist who is not a foundationist this is an unnecessary hypothesis, since the points are fixed in their positions by their relations with all the other points in the continuum and are therefore adequately individuated by them – as Newton suggested.

The foundationist has to show that the distance relation between two points is in some way founded on monadic properties of points. The characteristic that all spatial points have in common (namely, that they are all points of space) is not a suitable monadic foundation for spatial relations, simply because it is the same in all of them. We can say that the points possess certain characteristics in virtue of satisfying the real number axioms, but those characteristics are essentially relational and so are not the required monadic characteristics. Moreover, those relations are ordering relations; in the case of spatial points they will be spatial ordering relations, but they are not distance relations. Distance relations between a set of points in one dimension give rise to ordering relations, but not vice versa. Ordering relations determine which point is after another and which points are between two distinct points, but not how far apart points are. For this reason the real number axioms, even when the ordering relation is a spatial ordering relation, do not determine distances between points.

24 For a foundationist account of spatial relations see Campbell, *Abstract Particulars*, pp. 126–30.

It is not possible, therefore, to find monadic foundations for distance relations in any of the properties of points that we know about. The foundationist is left with the hypothetical unknown further properties of points. This is Leibniz's way out. These unknown properties are not spatial properties as we usually use the term 'spatial'. To say that they provide monadic foundations for the spatial relations we do understand is to offer no explanation at all.

We can conclude that spatial relations such as **x** are fundamental constituents of the world, in the sense that they cannot be explained by or reduced to anything more fundamental. Among spatial entities distance relations are the most important real constituents of the world. They are also basic universals since they are fully determinate; they do not classify any lower-level relations, and they are non-conjunctive. It is true that there are any number of ways of breaking **x** up into components by the usual method of vector addition:

$$\mathbf{x} = \mathbf{y} + \mathbf{z}.$$

But it is not true that

$$(a)\mathbf{x}(b) \leftrightarrow (a)\mathbf{y}(b) \ \& \ (a)\mathbf{z}(b),$$

which is what it is for a relation to be conjunctive.[25] In Chapter 8, Section 2, I shall argue for the significance of distance relations in causality.

3. CAUSAL RELATIONS

Causality has to do with things happening in the world – that is, the real world. We do not look for causal explanations, or causal relations, in the realm of ideas or in the realm of propositions or in mathematics. Causality is also used as a criterion for what is real, so that there is a certain amount of inevitable circularity here. In starting to talk about causality we have to start with intuition and common knowledge, if not common sense. And in this we can look to the more general conclusions of modern science for assistance.

Causality has to do with things happening in the world, and with explanations for those happenings in terms of other things in the

---

25 Campbell, who is a particularist, thinks that tropes have proper parts, so that a certain height has other heights as proper parts. It seems to me that he is modelling tropes too closely on ordinary particulars; *Abstract Particulars*, p. 109.

world. Causality also has to do with states of things in the world, and with explanations for why those states continue. Causal explanations are therefore explanations in terms of relations – causal relations. Even Hume's notion of constant conjunction can be understood as giving rise to a sort of causal relation: Impression A belongs to a class of impressions whose members are constantly conjoined to the members of another class of impressions, of which impression B is a member. It is not a relation that has any explanatory value; we would not expect there to be true causal relations between impressions.

Not everyone agrees that all examples of causation are lawlike, but everyone does agree that lawlike examples of causation are among the most important examples of causation. In lawlike causation, similar properties produce similar effects, where effects are understood in terms of properties or changes in properties. Lawlike causation must therefore be understood in terms of repeatable features of the world; in other words, lawlike causation must be understood in terms of universals. This argument seems a little slick, and it seems to ignore all the possible manoeuvres open to the nominalist. But it is in effect how Armstrong argues at the end of each of his chapters that deal with the various forms of nominalism.[26] The only viable alternative to the immanent realist account is particularism, which understands the repeatability of properties in terms of the similarity of tropes.

If similar causes produce similar effects on account of causal relations, then causal relations are also repeatable features of the world and should be understood as universals. If there were no causal relations, then there would be no ontological explanation for why things happen in the world, and there would be no explanation for why some situations in the world remain static. If there were no causal relations things would just happen, and it would be a total mystery as to why they happen. There may be regularity, but regularity by itself is no explanation.[27] This is not the only argument that can be brought against Hume, though it is an important one.

In fact, we must think of similar properties as giving rise to similar causal relations. This is what is expressed by the equation:

$$F = GM_1M_2/r^2,$$

26 Armstrong, Volume I, Chapters 2–5.
27 Cf. John Bigelow, Brian Ellis, and Robert Pargetter, "Forces", p. 619.

which can be interpreted as saying that particulars with properties, mass M_1 and mass M_2, and a distance relation between them of r, give rise to a force relation F.

It is the basic attributes of particulars, and other basic universals such as the spatial relations between particulars, that give rise to causal relations, such as the force relation of Newton's law of gravitation. The relation between the basic universals that are properties of particulars and the causal relation itself is a lawlike relation, something expressed by an equation. On this view causal relations relate particulars, and laws of nature relate universals.[28] This is similar to Armstrong's view that laws of nature are second-order relations between universals. Laws of nature are therefore about universals, and they are expressed in the immanent realists' second interpretation of predicate calculus as described in Chapter 2.

Causal relations, therefore, have as good a claim as anything to be real constituents of the world. If we can give an account of the different types of causal relation, then we are giving an account of some of the most important constituents of the world. From such an inventory, even if it is not complete, we can hope to draw some conclusions about which particulars are significant for causality, since the types of particulars that are the terms of causal relations are going to be very significant ontologically. We shall eventually conclude that it is particulars such as physical objects that are the terms of causal relations, and not particulars such as events or facts.

4. TYPES OF CAUSAL RELATION

Unfortunately, examples of causality do not fall under a single type, nor can they be easily resolved into a limited number of types. On the other hand, if causality is to be taken seriously, then causal analysis must be a possibility. It must be possible to break down a causal situation into a series of basic physical and mental interactions, and among these we may be more fortunate in finding a limited number of types of causality.[29]

28 Cf. Armstrong, Volume II, Chapter 24, and *What Is a Law of Nature?*, Chapter 6.
29 Today our analysis of physical phenomena terminates with quantum descriptions. It is the lack of a conceptual understanding of the correspondence principle that provides a difficulty for causal analysis. Bigelow et al., "Forces", p. 627, suggest that macroscopic interactions are supervenient upon microscopic quantum interactions, but see Chapter 9, Section 4, for comments on supervenience.

I suggest, therefore, that there are at least five basic types or ideals of causality. They are "force relation", "energy exchange", "mechanical trigger", "information trigger", and "free-will initiative". What makes them examples of causal relations is that if any of these relations holds between two particulars, then one of the particulars can change its basic attributes on account of that relation. This, however, does not rule out static causal situations, since a relation that is responsible for something changing can also be responsible for something remaining static.

My claim is that these five types are good and typical representatives of causal relations. Even though it might not be the case that all examples of causality fall exactly under one or other of these headings, these types are basic to our present understanding of the world. I am not claiming that there are no other types of causal relation, and I am certainly not claiming that other types are impossible. But since these types are typical they can be used to guide general conclusions about causality.

These types will show that our intuitions about causality in terms of "produce" or "bring about" or "be responsible for" are to some extent well founded. If these types are indeed all examples of causal relations, then there is no one simple mechanical ideal of causality, such as Quine's notion of energy flow, which is what causality is. From an examination of these representative types of causality it will be seen that there are indeed relations that are productive relations and that we cannot really refuse to call causal relations, and it will also be seen that it is physical objects and not things like events that are the terms of those relations.

Force relation

It is easy to understand forces as being causes: A force is something that causes an acceleration. Physicists would agree with such a statement. Most other people regard the body responsible for the force as the cause: The horse caused the cart to move, the sun causes the motion of the earth, and so on. It seems permissible to say that a force caused the cart to move, and it also seems permissible to say that the horse caused the cart to move. We do seem to have a choice here.

If there is to be an explanation of why bodies accelerate or why some bodies stretch or contract under certain conditions, then there must be forces in reality. If anyone should doubt the physical significance and reality of forces, they should note that so austerely a quantum mechanical entity as the vacuum is capable of exerting a measurable force, as in the Casimir effect.[30]

A force cannot be regarded as something in its own right, however, since it is neither an object nor a property of an object. Suppose two qualitatively identical bodies, A and B, approach each other along a straight line, exert a repulsive force on each other for a short time, and then return whence they came. If we ask the cause of the acceleration of body A, then it is the force exerted on it by body B; and if we ask the cause of the acceleration of body B, then it is the force exerted on it by body A. And Newton's third law tells us that those forces are equal and opposite.

Newtonian mechanics looks at each body in isolation, and draws an imaginary boundary around the body so that it can be determined which forces "cross" that boundary and act on the body. Newton's third law also tells us that forces only occur in pairs: A force on one body is not possible without an equal and opposite force on another body. The explanation for this phenomenon is that there is a relation between the two bodies that we can call a 'force relation'. A "force" as it is discussed in Newtonian mechanics is a force relation looked at from a one-sided point of view. Such a force is neither an object nor a property of an object. It is merely a one-sided way of looking at a force relation, and it is the force relation that has the claim to being an element of reality. A force relation is an example of a causal relation, and it is something mutual, holding between bodies, not between events.[31]

The forces that are dealt with in mechanics are vectors, and vectors present certain difficulties because any vector can be resolved into components in an arbitrary number of ways. Which then is real, the resultant vector or some preferred set of components? Nancy Cartwright argues that it is only the resultant that is real, whereas

---

30 See I. J. R. Aitchison, "Nothing's Plenty: The Vacuum in Modern Quantum Field Theory". The vacuum should be regarded as a physical entity. See Bigelow et al., "Forces", pp. 623–4, for arguments that forces are real constituents of the world.

31 There are also force relations that are looked at one-sidedly as tensors that have more than three components. They were first discovered by physicists working on stresses in crystals; see L. Brillouin, *Tensors in Mechanics and Elasticity*, Chapter 1.

Lewis Creary argues that it is only the naturally given components that are real.[32]

Consider velocity as a vector. If a body has a velocity, then that velocity can be resolved into components in an infinite number of ways. It is only physical objects that have velocities, because it is only physical objects themselves that cover so much distance at a certain rate in a certain direction. Since it is physical objects that have velocities, what physical objects do is a guide to the ontological status of velocities. Any components into which the velocity of a physical object is resolved should therefore be regarded as fictional, since the physical object does not actually cover distance in those directions. And the same considerations apply to acceleration considered as a vector.

A line of reasoning based on the same principles can be applied to forces. Although a force can be resolved into components in an infinite number of different ways, and though the effect of forces acting together has to be assessed from combining them to give the resultant, forces arise only when physical objects act on each other in pairs. This is why centrifugal forces and Coriolis forces should not be regarded as real forces. There is reason to think, therefore, that it is the forces that are combined to obtain the resultant that are real, rather than the resultant itself.

To get an intuitive feel for how forces combine to give a resultant consider two rubber strings at right angles exerting forces of equal magnitude on a body. We know where the real force relations are: They are in the strings; there is no force relation as such between the body and anything else.[33] The body accelerates in a direction of forty-five degrees to both strings, but there is no physical object in the direction towards which it is accelerating.

The difficulty with this approach is that the real acceleration is in a direction in which there is no real force relation, whereas Newton's second law says that a force causes acceleration and they are both in the same direction. Newton's law in fact treats forces and accelerations as though they were the same sort of thing; it treats a force as though it were something monadic acting on a body, almost as a

32 Cf. Nancy Cartwright, "Do the Laws of Physics State the Facts?", and *How the Laws of Physics Lie*, Essay 3; see also Lewis Creary, "Causal Explanation and the Reality of Component Forces".

33 According to Cartwright: "The 'component' forces are not there, in any but a metaphorical sense, to be added"; *How the Laws of Physics Lie*, p. 59.

property of a body. It is only by treating forces in this way that we can regard them as vectors in the usual way – that is, as subject to the operations of being resolved into components or being combined to form resultants.

This is no doubt a correct way of proceeding. But a force relation is not like an acceleration; it may be something that is directional in the sense that it acts along a directed line, but it is either an attractive force relation or else a repulsive force relation. It does not have direction in the same way that a vector has direction. And a relation is the property of two things, not one thing, and so the only force relations that could plausibly be combined as relations are force relations between the same two physical objects, such as an electrostatic force and a gravitational force.

It follows that the force that is the subject of Newton's law is not a force relation but something constructed out of real force relations. It appears that for the purpose of calculating the combined effect of a number of force relations we have to consider vectors that are monadic reductions of force relations and then take their resultant. Creary claims that it is the resultant force as opposed to its components that is a mathematical fiction;[34] not only is this right, but the forces that appear in Newton's laws are mathematical fictions anyway because they are monadic reductions of relations that are real constituents of the world. Although the method of calculating the effect works, it does not follow that there is in nature anything that corresponds to the method itself.

In his criticism of Nancy Cartwright, Creary suggests that forces are real physical causes because they are important explanatory factors. An explanation in terms of forces uses two types of physical law: There are *laws of causal influence,* which govern the exertion of forces, and *laws of causal action,* which govern the effects of such forces on states of motion including how forces combine together.[35] In this way the laws can be understood to state the facts. I agree with this approach except that I would understand *laws of causal influence* as laws that say how certain factors give rise to causal relations. And I would understand *laws of causal action* for forces as consisting of two laws, one saying how to obtain the resultant monadic reduction force from a network of causal relations, and the

---

34 Creary, "Causal Explanation and the Reality of Component Forces", p. 151.
35 Ibid.

other giving the effect of the monadic reduction force on the state of motion. Generalizing to all causal relations, Creary says that "causal influences need not combine in accordance with a scalar or vector addition law in order for an explanation by 'composition of causes' to be possible".[36]

In opposition to Hume, Nancy Cartwright makes a distinction between a *power* and the *exercise* of that power. The distinction between two sorts of laws of nature implies that there are two different kinds of powers and the two different kinds of the exercise thereof. If a body has mass, then it always has a power to enter into a causal relation, which it cannot exercise unless there is another body. If there is a causal relation such as a force, then that force has a power to alter a state of motion or produce a strain, but a force is never inactive, as Brian Ellis observes; it always exercises its power in some way.[37]

Neil Sheldon makes the point that an electromagnetic wave can be resolved into components in a number of different ways, and that those different ways can each be regarded as physically significant because apparatus can be constructed to detect the wave considered as analyzed in those different ways.[38] It is similar to someone hearing a chord first as a whole and then making a *gestalt* switch to hearing it as separate notes. The answer to this objection, which was posed as a difficulty for both Cartwright and Creary, is that fields are not forces. Ellis argues that forces always have an effect: "There is no such thing as an inactive or ineffective force",[39] which I interpret to mean that there is a force only if there is a force relation between two physical objects, and that relation always has an effect in a general sense: It either produces an acceleration, or a strain, or is balanced by other forces. A field on the other hand need not be active or have an effect on anything else. An electrostatic field exerts a force only when a charged particle is introduced into it, and it produces a force only at the particle. This is an argument for regarding fields as physical objects in their own right – that is, as things that enter into force relations. This conclusion is strengthened by the fact that electromagnetic fields possess an energy density and a momentum density. It is not yet clear whether the gravitational field has an energy density or not.

36 Ibid., p. 153.   37 See note 39, this chapter.
38 Neil A. Sheldon, "One Wave or Three? A Problem for Realism".
39 Brian Ellis, "The Existence of Forces", p. 172.

If electromagnetic fields, oscillating or otherwise, act on a particle, then the number of force relations there are depends on the number of physical objects (i.e. on the number of fields that are present). The problem is, when do we have one field or many? When two distinct fields of the same type are superimposed on each other in the same place the intensity is the combination of them both. So do the two fields exist mixed together, or do they coalesce to form one field? It might be thought that there is one field rather than many because fields are understood in terms of their effects – that is, in terms of the forces they exert; we combine fields as though we were combining forces. The problem, then, has to do with the ontology of fields and does not affect the ontology of forces directly.

If two bodies exert a force on each other, where are those forces? There are no forces in the space between two bodies if the force is due to a field, since there is no force where there is no body for the field to act on. If a field acts on a body, there is a force between a field and the body, though it is not a relation that spans any distance, because field and body are contiguous.[40] As a first approximation we can often adopt the non-contiguous Newtonian point of view and speak of a force relation between two bodies separated by a distance, even if we believe that ultimately they must be connected in a contiguous fashion. Perhaps in the last analysis all force relations are contact relations.

We habitually make a distinction between the cause and the conditions for the effect to occur. A certain movement of the cart is caused by a certain force, the nature of the origin of the force being of no consequence to the effect. But that determinate movement would not have occurred unless certain other conditions had obtained, namely, the reaction of the road, the friction of the road, and the air resistance. These are all forces, but acting by themselves they will not cause movement because they are reactive forces. We could call these other forces "conditions" for the effect, as opposed to the cause of the effect. Other conditions for the effect include the mass of the body the force is acting on, and perhaps the laws of mechanics, and so on.

40 Bigelow et al., "Forces", p. 616.

A force relation is a relation that is quite symmetrical and mutual.[41] On the other hand, in the energy exchange type of causality what we call cause is very often prior in some sense to the effect, as the energy very often has to be sent at a finite speed across a finite distance.

Physical interactions can be understood in two ways, either in terms of forces or in terms of the exchange of energy.[42] The orthodox interpretation of quantum mechanics, however, usually understands interactions in terms of energy exchange.

If the sun's rays fall on a body, its temperature will rise. In classical physics you could analyze it in terms of forces produced by oscillating electromagnetic fields, but even in classical physics it is natural to understand the causal interaction in terms of energy exchange. Here also we have a choice as to what we call the cause. Either we can say that the incident radiation caused the rise in temperature, or we can say that the body was warmed by the sun; we can also say that the sun caused the flow of radiation, and the flow of radiation caused the rise in temperature. In this case the causal relation between the sun and the body amounts to an exchange of energy, in the same way that according to the force type of causality, the causal relation amounts to a force relation. Admittedly we can say that the sun causes a flow of radiation; in other words, it causes a region of space to contain a certain intensity of radiation energy flowing in a certain direction. But this radiation is a "something" in motion.

If the rise in temperature has a cause it also has conditions. For example, the body will have been exchanging energy with its local surroundings, though these exchanges would not by themselves have led to a temperature rise. Other conditions include the nature of the surface of the body, its mass, and specific heat.

If we do a causal analysis of a force relation we often find that at whatever level we examine we are still dealing with forces. If two

---

41 One of Kant's categories was that of community, or reciprocity between agent and patient; *Critique of Pure Reason,* B 106.

42 There are other ways of looking at Newtonian mechanics, but only these two provide ideals of causality; cf. H. Hertz, *The Principles of Mechanics,* the Introduction.

classical bodies exert a force on each other via a connecting string, then the action of one part of the string on another part can be understood in terms of forces. Similarly, if we do a causal analysis of an energy exchange interaction, we find there is energy flow at whatever level we examine.

In the energy exchange type of causal interaction the terms of the causal relation are emitters and receivers of energy, which are physical particulars, typically bodies and not events, since events are just not the sorts of things that possess energy. But perhaps an event theorist could urge that "events consist in the transfer of energy, and so do not themselves do any transferring out of their own interiors, but that sequences of transfer are the ontological basis for causal descriptions". Imagine then a circle of children passing a parcel from hand to hand. They can only pass it on because they possess it, if only momentarily. Notice that they are not passive bystanders; they actively cause the parcel to move on. Consider now the passage of a beam of light divided into events. Those events do not actively cause the light to move on; they are passive if they are not exactly bystanders – they are not the ontological ground of anything else. The light is caused to flow by the object that emitted it. If any further explanation is required it lies in the laws that govern such interactions.[43]

It is tempting to regard physical causality as the only type of causality and to say that the energy exchange type, as it is the one favored by modern physics, is all there is to causality. We know what the cause is and we know what the effect is, because there is a net energy flow from cause to effect; and since energy flow takes time, the cause is always prior to the effect. This is Quine's view of causality.[44]

David Fair has presented a more sophisticated version of Quine's theory by suggesting that to a first approximation the causal relation "is a physically-specifiable relation of energy-momentum flow from the objects comprising the cause to the objects comprising the effect".[45] In effect there are four cases: (1) Energy and momentum are both transferred from cause to effect; this is the typical case. (2)

43 For further discussion of events and energy flow see Chapter 8, Section 2.
44 See W. V. Quine, *The Roots of Reference,* Section 2, but in *The Ways of Paradox,* he says that "the notion of cause itself has no firm place in science" (p. 229). W. D. Hart defends Quine's original view in *The Engines of the Soul,* pp. 65–8.
45 David Fair, "Causation and the Flow of Energy".

Energy is transferred but no momentum. Macroscopically the transfer of heat energy is often understood in this way. (3) Momentum is transferred but no energy. When a charged particle moves in a circle at right angles to a uniform magnetic field momentum is transferred but no energy.[46] (4) Neither energy nor momentum is transferred, because the forces are static. When a billiard ball rests on a table the gravitational force on the ball is balanced by the reaction force of the table.

It is this last case that presents a difficulty for his theory, so Fair insists on understanding this case also in terms of momentum flow. The gravitational force transfers momentum to the ball at a certain rate, which is exactly balanced by the rate of transfer of momentum by the reaction force. It is a dynamic equilibrium in which the net momentum of the ball remains zero. It is one thing for David Fair to insist that this happens when one force balances another, even though it is something of a mathematical fiction; it is quite another to claim that the causal relation amounts to a balancing of momentum flows in the same way that equilibrium for cases involving thermal radiation is a balancing of equal radiation energy flows. The causal relation amounts to forces balancing as forces, not to the balancing of rates of flow of momentum.

Besides producing accelerations and balancing other forces, forces have another type of effect: They also deform elastic bodies; in other words, they produce strains. In fact, whenever static forces act on elastic bodies strains will be produced. The body that the force acts on deforms until the elastic reaction force equals the applied force, not until there is a balance of rates of transfer of momentum. Here the causal relation cannot be understood in terms of the transfer of momentum. If cases where there is elastic deformation cannot be so understood, then neither can any case of balancing of forces.[47]

Mechanical trigger

The difficulty with the energy flow or energy-momentum flow account of causality is that there are certain counter-examples that it is

---

46 Ibid., p. 230.
47 We have not mentioned probabilistic causality where there is an interaction and a range of possible outcomes, but where the actual outcome is a matter of chance and it is not supposed that there is any underlying determinism. Such cases will probably fall under "force relation" or "energy exchange".

difficult not to regard as examples of causality, such as the example of static forces mentioned previously.

Consider a large concrete ball lodged precariously near the top of a building. When we ask what causes it to remain there, the answer is in terms of certain forces, which, of course, do no work, and therefore no energy is exchanged. Despite the fact that the cause and effect are contemporary, there is a definite order of dependence that has nothing to do with the direction of flow of anything.[48] This example should be regarded as an example of the force relation type of causality. We know exactly what things the causal relation holds between – they are certainly not events – but it is difficult to categorize the effect.

When we turn on the light switch we cause the light to come on, but we do not thereby contribute any energy to that effect. The work done in moving the switch does not involve electrical energy; it is a form of a mechanical work that is then dissipated. Similarly, turning on the tap causes a flow of water, but it contributes no energy to the flow of water. These are examples of triggers. They are instances of causal relations where the cause contributes no energy to the effect – contra Quine.

When we were discussing the force relation and the energy exchange type of causality we made a distinction between the cause and certain other "conditions", even though those conditions included forces (where the cause was a force) and energy interactions (where the cause was an energy interaction). It is clear that in cases where we have mechanical triggers, there are other important conditions that are productive of the effect. If the tap is on and the water is flowing when we enter the bathroom, and someone asks, "What causes this water to flow?", we could reasonably answer, "a certain head of water, that is, a pressure difference". The pressure difference can, of course, be understood in terms of forces; the energy exchange theorist, however, will have to weave some implausible story about energy flowing from the potential state to the kinetic state. There are also conditions such as the length and diameter of the piping, and the temperature of the water. All these determinate conditions combine to produce the determinate effect. The absence of a block at a certain point in the pipe (i.e. the absence of a restraining

---

48 Cf. Kant, *Critique of Pure Reason,* B 248ff., and Thomas Aquinas, *Summa Theologica,* Part I, Q. 46, A. 2, ad 1um.

force, such as that provided by a closed tap) is certainly one of those conditions. The absence of restraints – that is, that other things are indeed equal – is a condition for all causal situations, but not always one we draw attention to. On the other hand, it is better to regard the determinate structure that actually exists as what is relevant for causality.

We could try saying that the cause of the water *beginning* to flow is the tap being turned on, and that the cause of it *continuing* to flow is the head of water. But this will not do, since if there were no head of water, it would not have begun to flow, and if the tap were not on, it would not continue to flow. Perhaps, then, what counts as a cause depends on what aspect of the situation we are interested in.

There are two possible resolutions of this problem. One is to focus on the intuitive notion of "instigate", and regard the active factor as the cause, and to regard the static, passive factors as mere conditions. This is, I believe, the approach of ordinary language and common sense, and I think there is something to be said for it. The other approach is to regard all the prior conditions that are required for the effect as the cause – quite a mixed bag as we have pointed out. This is the approach of the philosophers. It regards the highlighting of one factor as the instigator of the effect as somewhat subjective.

In static causal situations like the concrete ball on top of a building, it is implausible to pick out one factor. On the other hand, in causal situations where something happens, it often does make sense to pick out one factor. Although I sympathize with the common-sense habit of picking out one active factor, it is not an issue I have much interest in resolving.[49]

Information trigger

The fourth type of causality is that of information trigger. If the president presses a button in order to send up a missile, then it is possible that his pressing the button completes a circuit that starts the rocket motor, and that is all there is to it. It would be an example of a mechanical trigger – for our purposes electricity is part of mechanics. On the other hand, the link between pressing the button and

---

49 Cf. G. E. M. Anscombe, "Causality and Determination". Anscombe emphasizes the intuitive notion of the cause being productive of the effect, and at the end she says, "The most neglected of the key topics in this subject are: interference and prevention."

the missile's being launched could involve the sending and reading of messages, either using human agents or using machines. Strictly speaking such a message is a command, but it is a command that involves information. Reading a message does not usually or necessarily involve the transfer of energy from the message writer to the message reader. Nor does it involve a force relation: The reader's new informational state does not come about because the message writer exerted a force on him. Nor does it involve a mechanical trigger – at least this is not the interaction between message writer and message reader. An information trigger is plausible as a causal relation as it not only instigates something to happen, but can also transfer the specification of what should happen.

Information triggers are interesting on account of the possibility that neither energy nor momentum need be transferred from message writer to message reader, and also because of the way in which this comes about. It is true that when a message is written (with pen and ink or using a computer) forces are exerted and energy is transmitted and dispersed. It is also true that when a message is read energy is transmitted and dispersed and forces are exerted. But it does not follow that any of the energy or momentum put forth in the writing of the message is transmitted to the reader. A written message is quite static and inactive; it may contain potential energy locked up, but there is no reason why that potential energy should be unlocked in the reading of it. It follows that we can have two "circuits", each of which is closed under the conservation laws, but which nevertheless interact causally with each other, and this is a physical possibility, not a mere logical possibility.

An information trigger is very similar to a mechanical trigger; they are both triggers – they are species of the same genus. A mechanical trigger contributes no energy or force (or momentum) to the effect, and the same can be said for an information trigger. But there are differences. A mechanical trigger does not contribute to the nature of what is going to happen; it simply makes it happen at that time, unleashing powers and forces that determine what should happen. An information trigger, on the other hand, can be the main determining factor governing the nature of what happens. Also, information triggers admit of time lags; the information can remain unread for an indefinite period of time. For a mechanical trigger time is of the essence: A mechanical trigger simply determines *when* those powers and forces should be unleashed.

The four previous types of causality were all mechanical or physical; in other words, they did not involve anything unknown to physics. On the face of it, however, the world we live in is a world in which there is also human agency. I suggest that our habitual way of understanding human agency, metaphysically speaking, amounts to free-will initiative. It is of course controversial whether there is any such thing, as there are those who contend that a human person is simply an overcomplicated mechanical system. In which case, human agency only *appears* to be a distinct type of causality; it is in reality reducible to various physical types of causality.[50] This is, of course, not an issue we can resolve here. There is no doubting, however, that human agency understood as a matter of free-will is one of our important "types" of causality, so that to omit it in a catalogue of types of causality would seem strange.[51]

In the natural world where everything is governed by natural laws, no thing ever takes any initiative. If a stream is made to flow in a new channel because of a landslide, that landslide is causally related to something else, and so back and back. Everything that happens has a cause sufficient to make it happen, a cause adequate to the effect. If something happens in a way that is not precisely determined, then which of the possible alternatives comes about is a matter of chance. Even information systems such as computers do not initiate anything; their method of working is purely deterministic, except if you are unlucky. Now the human mind, as conceived of by those who believe in free-will, is capable of initiative; it does things without adequate prior cause. The mind possesses a self-determining power – a self-determining power to opposites, as Scotus and Ockham would put it. Choice is not to be understood as chance; chance is blind, but choice is deliberate. For humans there

50 It is possible to be a substance dualist or a property dualist and still be a determinist; on those views it is usually the physical aspect that determines what happens, with the mental aspect merely following along.
51 Cf. H. L. A. Hart and A. M. Honoré, *Causation in the Law,* Chapter 3; they discuss human agency in terms of voluntary acts but do not raise the metaphysical issue of free-will. Cf. the comments of Colin McGinn on pp. 121 and 122 of *The Character of Mind.* Freedom seems to presuppose some sort of independence of the mind from the machine; for recent comments on this issue from the point of view of causality see Mark Bedau, "Cartesian Interaction", and R. C. Richardson, "The 'Scandal' of Cartesian Interactionism".

does not exist an adequate set of causal conditions for our choices; for God, there are presumably no causal conditions whatsoever behind his decisions.

It may be that some of our intuitions concerning cause and effect are essentially anthropomorphic, that when we look for the cause we are looking for the "who" that initiated the matter and is therefore responsible. The "who" that initiates something is an object, if a somewhat exalted type of object. We naturally think of such an initiator as the cause, and clearly this "cause" is an object that persists through time and not an event.[52]

The aim in describing these types of causal relation was to set forth a broad and representative set of fundamental causal relations. And as far as the natural world goes it seems very likely that the relations we have described are fundamental. The study of the natural world has not revealed any other sorts of causal relations to which our five types can be reduced, so that our five types of causal relation represent the ways in which the natural world is connected together.

All these examples of causal relations are productive relations: They make things happen. They are also relations that involve dependency in accordance with our intuition about causality. If, then, we wanted to explain what is meant by a causal relation, we could point to these five types as exemplars. Causal relations are relations that do what these relations do. But we can improve on that explanation. We have explained a causal relation as a relation that can make a particular change its basic attributes. Basic attributes are attributes that are causally significant, and which we have recognized to be so *a posteriori*. We may add that the causal relations that are to be found in the world as real constituents of the world are fully determinate relations and are examples of basic universals. Only determinate relations make determinate things happen.

In none of these examples do we find events or things like events as the terms of the causal relations. It is physical objects, such as the things Newtonians refer to as bodies, that enter into force relations

---

52 Armstrong uses the term 'Singularist' for Anscombe's account of causality: "In a causal sequence it is a particular event *qua* particular which brings about a further particular event" (Volume I, p. 23). For the first four types of causality I agree with Armstrong that it is properties as repeatable things that are what is significant for causality. For the fifth type the character of the cause is significant for causality, but it is not the only thing that is significant.

with each other; an event is simply not the sort of thing that can exert a force. Similarly, it is bodies or fields that possess energy, and therefore it is bodies or fields that transmit energy to each other. Events, as such, do not possess energy, and therefore they do not, as such, exchange energy with each other. The only way in which an event could be said to possess energy is on account of a body that is a component of the event. Similar conclusions can be drawn for the other three types of causal relations. Later it will be argued in more detail that events cannot be the terms of causal relations.

7

Arbitrary particulars and unified particulars

1. THE DISTINCTION

There are two sorts of particular, those that have a natural principle of unity and those that do not. The principle of unity is whatever it is that gives us a reason for thinking we have a single particular. It is a natural principle of unity if the principle of unity is there in the world independently of human thought, human conceptualization, or human decisions. It is, of course, controversial whether there are in fact natural principles of unity. With respect to this issue Michael Ayers uses the word 'realist' for those who support his position, as I do, that there are particulars with natural principles of unity, and the word 'conceptualist' for those who oppose it: "Adopting, then, a 'realist' tone of voice, let me say first that physical objects are natural unities or natural structures which come into existence, continue to exist and cease to exist quite independently of any conceptualizing on our part."[1] It is difficult to know what picture of reality conceptualists are presenting us with; they seem to see reality itself as something obscure or unknowable: "The picture of reality as an amorphous lump, not yet articulated into discrete objects, thus proves to be the correct one, so long as we make the right use of it."[2] It is also very difficult to argue against this position in general terms. Perhaps the easiest answer is simply to point out that we do have knowledge of naturally occurring species, such as atomic species and animal species, and that our conception of these species is fairly insensitive to changes of theory. In fact, there is no scientific reason to believe that reality is entirely amorphous. Dummett's views are based on language, and we have already argued in Chap-

---

1 Michael R. Ayers, "Individuals without Sortals", p. 114; cf. David Wiggins, *Identity and Spatio-Temporal Continuity*, p. 42, where he quotes Hobbes, and *Sameness and Substance*, Chapter 5, which is entitled "Conceptualism and Realism".
2 Dummett, *Frege*, p. 577.

ter 2 that language is not much of a guide to the nature of the world, and certainly not the only guide.

The realist does not have to be certain in every case as to whether a particular has a natural principle of unity or not. For example, it is often not clear whether we have one mountain or two.[3] It is sufficient that there be particulars that have a natural principle of unity, and we do have examples of these. The alternative to a particular having a natural principle of unity is for it to have a principle of unity that depends, at least in part, on human thought, that is, on human conceptualization and human decisions. We shall call such particulars arbitrary particulars.

Sets of particulars are a good example of arbitrary particulars. Even if the members are particulars that have most things in common, an intuitive case can be made for regarding sets of such things as arbitrary. Intuitively it seems that there is something arbitrary about the set of all tigers in a certain cage and the set of all tigers in India, though these sets do not appear to be as arbitrary as some. Equally, there is something arbitrary about the set of all tigers unqualified, as it must be the set of all tigers existing now, and that is just as much an arbitrary collection as the other sets of tigers. Things exist "now" if they are simultaneous with us in our inertial frame, but that is an arbitrary way of slicing up space-time.

What makes a set to be a unit is the fact that some person insists on taking it to be a unit. A set can be specified in one of two ways: either by listing the elements or by stipulating that all the elements fall under a certain concept. In a sense the concept provides a natural principle of unity for its extension; it appears to be a natural collection of things, in some appropriate sense of the word 'collection'. But considered as a set it is still something arbitrary. The principle of unity for a set, which is whatever it is that makes it to be an individual thing, is the same whether the elements have nothing in common or whether they have everything in common. If the members have nothing in common, then the principle of unity is arbitrary, and therefore it is arbitrary if they have many things in common, despite the appearance of degrees of arbitrariness.[4]

It is true that sets can be constructed out of nothing – for example, by starting with the empty set and then forming sets of sets in

3 Cf. Lowe, "What Is a Criterion of Identity?", pp. 20 and 10.
4 See Chapter 9, Section 1, for a more detailed discussion of the view that sets are arbitrary particulars.

various ways. There are also sets in mathematics that have abstract objects as their members – it is in mathematics where the notion of set seems most appropriate. However, we are interested in sets, which if they do not have a claim to be real constituents of the world, are at least related to the real spatio-temporal world. To form first-order sets, we need individuals that are not themselves sets. They must have a principle of unity different from the principle of unity of a set. In most cases then, sets of particulars in the real world have as their elements particulars with a natural principle of unity, such as physical objects. In most cases, then, sets are ontologically subordinate to unified particulars, though it is possible that there be others sorts of arbitrary particulars besides sets, which could be the elements of first-order sets.

As is well known, and often stressed, the criterion of identity for a set is clear and simple: If x and y are sets, then x is identical with y if and only if x and y have the same members. The criterion of identity for a set depends on the criteria of identity for the members of the set, since we need to know what it is for the members to be the same. The criterial condition, "x is identical with y if and only if x and y have the same members", does not tell us what a set is, though it is partly constitutive of the meaning of the term 'set'.[5]

Given certain individuals we can "construct" from them either a set or an ordered set. Ordered sets are like sets in that they too have members, but if we tried to apply the criterion of identity for sets to ordered sets, it would not work, since ordered sets and sets are different sorts of things. Sets and ordered sets have different principles of unity; whatever makes certain things to constitute a set is different from what makes them to constitute an ordered set. But whatever makes those things to be a set, or from another point of view, an ordered set, is nothing in the objects themselves, but lies entirely in the choices of some human being.[6]

Because of the criterion of identity for sets, the set of chairs in a room remains the same set however the chairs are rearranged; indeed it is the same set however widely they are scattered. When you interact with the chairs you change their positions and perhaps their shapes (slightly) and other attributes. Nothing about the set *qua* set is changed, however. It seems that sets as such are inert to causal

5 Cf. Lowe, *Kinds of Being*, p. 17.
6 Lowe argues that Kuratowski's definition of ordered sets is just a way of representing ordered sets and is not a true definition; see *Kinds of Being*, p. 18.

interaction; it is not possible to interact causally with a set.[7] The only way to affect a set is to destroy one of its members, and then the set simply ceases to exist, since what then exists fails to meet the stipulated conditions. That you cannot interact causally with a set underlines the fact that a set is ontologically subordinate to its members.

This argument makes it seem unlikely that any arbitrary particular, as such, is something that could enter into a causal relation. Causality has to do with what is physically real, so it seems unlikely, to put it mildly, that entities that depend for their existence on human choices would be significant in causality. If it can also be shown that events are arbitrary particulars, then it seems that events, as such, are not the sort of thing with which you could interact causally. In what follows we shall try to show that events are arbitrary particulars and by focussing on their arbitrary nature show that they cannot be the terms of causal relations.

2. EVENTS

Davidson, in company with others, thinks it is events that are the terms of causal relations, and that events are ontologically significant in an important way:[8] "But the assumption, ontological and metaphysical, that there are events, is one without which we cannot make sense of much of our most common talk; or so, at any rate, I have been arguing. I do not know of any better, *or further,* way of showing what there is."[9] In order to show that there are events and that they are significant for causality, Davidson is in effect applying the syntactic priority thesis. He is inferring the properties of the world from the properties of language.

Despite the title of his article, Davidson does not tell us anything about the nature of causal relations. All that we can assume about them is that they relate events and are the means whereby one event "produces" another. They seem very obscure for such important relations.

7 Cf. Armstrong, Volume I, p. 31.
8 Cf. Bigelow et al., "Forces", and Bas van Fraassen, *An Introduction to the Philosophy of Time and Space.*
9 Donald Davidson, "Causal Relations", p. 162; my italics. See also John Watling, "Are Causes Events or Facts?"

It has also been noted that Davidson's account of the nature of events is obscure.[10] Given a true affirmative sentence about something that has happened, such as 'Caesar was killed', then, according to Davidson, there is an entity out there in the world corresponding to it, called an event. For Davidson states of things do not count as events. He gives us one additional piece of information to explain what an event is, and that is his criterion of identity for events in terms of causality: If x and y are events, then "($x = y$ if and only if ((z)(z caused x ↔ z caused y) and (z)(x caused z ↔ y caused z)))."[11] In other words, two events are the same if and only if they have the same causes and the same effects. Davidson does not claim that it is the only way of establishing that two supposedly distinct events are identical, though he claims that the criterion based on causality is comprehensive and always usable. His assessment of its importance is contained in these words: "It is one thing for a criterion to be correct, another for it to be useful. But there are certainly important classes of cases at least where the causal criterion appears to be the best we have."[12]

Davidson's criterion of identity for events has been accused several times of circularity; he himself merely claims that it is not formally circular. It is all very well to say that x and y are the same events if and only if they have the same causes and the same effects. But if we say x and y are the same event if and only if the *same events* caused x as caused y, and the *same events* were caused by x as were caused by y, then the circularity is evident.[13] Moreover, as Lowe has pointed out, a criterion of identity for a type of thing is only partly constitutive of the meaning of the corresponding term.[14]

So if we want an explanation of what an event is we have to return to the notion of some entity that corresponds to a true affirmative sentence that says that something happens. It is true that there can be more to an event than is expressed by the given sentence, but how much more we cannot say; to do that we would need to understand the principle of unity of events. If an event were just what was ex-

---

10 See J. E. Tiles, *Things That Happen*, p. 17.
11 Davidson, "The Individuation of Events", p. 179.
12 Ibid.
13 Cf. Lowe, "What Is a Criterion of Identity?", p. 8; for a longer discussion see Tiles, *Things That Happen*, pp. 3–7.
14 Lowe, *Kinds of Being*, p. 17.

pressed by a given sentence, then events would be facts, but on the other hand there is no reason why the whole event cannot be expressed by a more complicated sentence.

3. ARGUMENTS AGAINST EVENTS

If a physical object acquires a property, then its acquiring of the property is an event – an event is something that happens. If a physical object possesses a property, then its possessing the property is a state of affairs – a state of affairs is something that continues. According to Hamlyn, an event corresponds to a non-continuous-tensed verb, and a process or state corresponds to a continuous-tensed verb.[15] What is it then that is caused? Is it the something that happens, the event, or is it the new state, the state of affairs?

Change of position is the most easily understood form of change; and on some views of the world all changes can be analysed in terms of change of position. Change of position appears never to be instantaneous, and physics gives us some reason to think that no changes are in fact instantaneous.[16] If a change takes time, then the physical object concerned is in a state of change during that period of time. If a body acquires a new position, it must possess a velocity in order to do so. What from one point of view is an event, a changing of position, is from another point of view a state of affairs, the possessing of a velocity.[17] Something that happens can therefore also be described by a continuous-tensed verb. We can, therefore, combine the categories of event and state of affairs, since we have one ontological category, not two. We shall use the term 'event' for the new combined category.

15 Hamlyn, *Metaphysics,* p. 56.
16 Quantum jumps are sometimes thought of as instantaneous, but it is quite possible for an atom to go from one excited state to another without the electrons changing position at all, given that electrons have positions. It is the probability densities for position that change. Under a perturbation the wave function evolves continuously; it is only when a measurement is made that the wave function collapses into a definite state – and that change defies description or explanation even by standard quantum theory. J. L. Martin's comments about continuous trajectories being ruled out strike me as rash; see *Basic Quantum Mechanics,* p. 34. There are serious problems associated with a particle disappearing at a certain position at one point in time and reappearing in a different position at a later time – or is it at the same time?
17 For an excellent defence of velocity as a property in its own right, see Bigelow and Pargetter, *Science and Necessity,* pp. 62–74.

If an object changes shape or colour, or acquires a new position, velocity, or acceleration, that is an event, in the old sense of the word and in our new sense. It is described by a true affirmative sentence that says that something happens. When we think of an event we think of a particular that has many properties, and we highlight one of those properties. Which property we highlight depends on what we are interested in, or on what sort of interaction the particular is participating in, though of course it may be participating in several.

When we refer to an event, we have to specify a time, as a time index is essential to an event. It should be remembered that a sentence about the natural world has to include a time index if it is to be regarded as timelessly true. We can distinguish a "point event" from an "interval event": A point event involves only one instant of time, whereas an interval event involves a finite period of time. Consider a simple event such as "object a's having property P at time t"; it is a point event, and we can write it: $E_t(a; P)$.[18] On the other hand, "Object a's having property P during time interval t_1-t_2" is an interval event, and it can be written: $E_{t_1-t_2}(a; P)$. These are both simple events, where a simple event can be defined as one that involves only one property of one object.[19] To regard events (i.e. things that happen or states of affairs, as entities) is in effect to reify what is asserted, or could be asserted, by true affirmative sentences. The sentence 'a has P' is supposed to correspond to an entity "a's having P", and the sentence 'a becomes blue' is supposed to correspond to the entity "a's becoming blue". It follows that this notion of event, and therefore our conclusions, include such things as Wittgenstein's facts.

In ordinary language one event can be described in a number of different ways. What from one point of view is "a killing" is from a more discriminating point of view "a stabbing". But from our point of view, there is a preferred way of describing the world that reflects how it really is – namely, a description in terms of basic attributes. It follows that there is a preferred way of describing an event, so that a certain event either involves a certain basic attribute

18 Cf. Tiles, *Things That Happen*, Section 3. For the event of a's having relation R to b we could write $E_t(a, b; R)$, where the order of a and b is significant. There could be many relations between a and b and we have chosen to highlight R.
19 It will be necessary to consider events such as $E_{t_1-t_2}(a; P_1 \rightarrow P_2)$, where object "$a$" divests itself of property P_1 and acquires property P_2. Such an event has to be an interval event.

that occurs at a certain time or it does not. It is because basic attributes are constituents of events that it is sometimes possible to refer to events successfully using higher-level attributes.

Unlike a physical object an interval event does not as such persist through time. A physical object may exist only for a short interval of time, but the object that exists at the beginning of the interval is the same object that exists at the end of the interval; the interval is accidental to what the object is. The same cannot be said for an interval event; it can no more be said to persist through its time interval than the time interval itself can be said to so persist.

At time t object a has many properties: P_1, P_2, P_3, . . . , and to each there must correspond a different simple point event. Causal theory requires them to be different events, since the properties P_2 and P_3, for example, may have nothing to do with the causal interaction P_1 figures in. If we are given a physical object and a time, we can select events simply by selecting different properties of the object, taking them one at a time, or two at a time and so on. Selecting an event in this way by arbitrarily choosing properties is like selecting a set by arbitrarily choosing objects. If we are led to choose a particular event it is on account of that property of that physical object being relevant to a certain causal interaction, though it is the object and its properties that come first. If we can select any number of properties, then we can select all the properties of the object to give the event $E_t(a; P_1 . . . P_n)$. We can call this event the maximal point event relative to that object at that time, though how it differs from the object itself is obscure. Perhaps the difference is analogous to the difference between an object and the singleton set of that object. If a particular is somehow constituted out of its properties as in certain theories about the nature of particulars associated with immanent realism,[20] then an event somehow involves one of those properties twice.

A simple event, such as $E_t(a; P)$, does not have a natural principle of unity in the way a physical object does, since which property is selected to be included in the event is arbitrary; the property P is highlighted merely because someone insists on highlighting it. If a simple event appears to have a principle of unity, it is probably associated with the principle of unity of the object concerned. More-

---

20 See Hamlyn, *Metaphysics*, p. 57, and Armstrong, Volume II, Chapters 9 and 11.

over, reference to that event is always via the object concerned. For events in general it seems that they have a criterion of identity partly analogous to that for sets, but not exactly: Two events are the same event if they have the same components – that is, if the specification of the events involves the same time interval, the same physical objects, and the same properties and relations, *and* the same properties must be exemplified by the same objects. This criterion of identity for events, though not circular, depends on criteria of identity for physical objects and universals.[21]

The principle of unity for sets or for ordered sets is only partly expressed by the corresponding criteria of identity; whatever makes those things to be a set, or ordered set, lies entirely in the choices of some human being, so that they are arbitrary objects.[22] Something similar is true for events. Although events are in a sense a collection of things, they are not sets because of the constraints that are placed on those things. The things can include a particular and certain properties, but the properties cannot be just any properties; they have to be properties of the particular at the given time. The very same things can be looked on at the same time as an event, as a set of things, and as an ordered set; it all depends on the point of view of some human being, that is to say on his or her choices.

It might be possible to define a type of event in terms of the state of all the things at a certain space-time location. Such an event would have a principle of unity similar to that of a spatial collection or crowd, but such events will not do for causal theory. Not every aspect of that space-time location will be relevant to a given causal interaction, since for a given causal interaction only a few properties will be relevant.

A collision is a paradigmatic example of cause and effect. If the cause of what happens is to be an event, then two objects and several properties have to be mentioned. That event has no spatio-temporal unity, since the two objects can be any distance apart and yet be bent on a collision. We can call an event involving more than one object a 'separated event'. There is really only one principle of unity for such an event: It is the event that will lead to the effect we are interested in assigning a cause to. There is also the further problem

---

21 Cf. Jaegwon Kim, "Events as Property Exemplifications".
22 Cf. note 6, this chapter.

that there is no unique cause, but rather a continuum of events that lead to the effect.

If an event that is supposed to be a cause involves two or more physical objects separated by some distance, then there are problems associated with the relativity of simultaneity. Two states of separated objects are only simultaneous according to a certain inertial frame; they are not simultaneous according to all inertial frames. Not only is there a continuum of causes as we trace worldlines backwards, there is no unique cause corresponding to a given point on a worldline.

Consider the event $E_t(a; v)$, which is "a's having velocity v at time t". Let us try to assign a cause to this event – for every event has a cause. Suppose a force acted from time t_0 to time t and brought the body's velocity up from u to v. The interval event of the force acting for time to t is part of the cause. But whatever caused the body to have the initial velocity u is also part of the cause, and that could have been a very long time ago. The cause of the event $E_t(a; v)$ has at least two parts and would have to be thought of as a complex separated event with no conceivable principle of unity, except that it leads to the event $E_t(a; v)$. There is no reason for saying that we have one event rather than two events, or vice versa; whether there are two events or just one is entirely a matter of preference. As was explained earlier, $E_t(a; P_1)$ and $E_t(a; P_2)$ are two different simple events, whereas $E_t(a; P_1, P_2)$ is one event, a complex event. If we insist on talking about *the event* that is the cause of $E_t(a; v)$, then that event is a collection of complex events whose only principle of unity is that of being the cause of $E_t(a; v)$. It seems that the events needed for causal theory have no natural principles of unity; they can only be understood as arbitrary objects.

To underline this point, consider interval events. Only rarely is a natural time interval given us; usually the choice of end points for the time interval is arbitrary. Moreover, events of this type can overlap; for example, $E_{t_1 - t_2}(a; P)$, $E_{t_1 - t_3}(a; P)$, and $E_{t_1 - t_4}(a; P)$ overlap. It would seem unreasonable to regard them all as equally elements of reality. However, the view that events are the terms of the causal relation seems to demand this, since a cause might be capable of producing $E_{t_1 - t_2}(a; P)$ but not $E_{t_1 - t_3}(a; P)$. It is, however, not possible to regard two overlapping interval events as distinct elements of reality, since where they overlap we would have two elements of reality, a difference without a distinction.

174

For Davidson, it is the event in all its fullness that does the causing. It does not matter that we do not know, or simply do not supply, the full details of the event that is the cause. Since an event is an object, it is enough that we refer to it successfully, which we can do by means of partial descriptions: "But they share Mill's confusion if they think every deletion from the description of an event represents something deleted from the event described."[23]

But the events that we need for causes are complex events involving more than one physical object; their principle of unity is not spatio-temporal location. Like simple events they are reality sliced in a certain way, that is, looked at from a certain point of view, with only certain properties highlighted. These considerations raise serious problems about how to refer to events. It is not clear that a partial description, by itself, succeeds in referring to the event being thought of, since for reference to be successful there must be some way of finding out what the rest of the event is. For a physical object the natural principle of unity will enable you, in principle, to discover the things about the object not given by the referring description. Referring to a physical object involves grasping what kind of thing it is, and therefore understanding something about its principle of unity. Referring to an event does involve understanding that it is an event, but the notion of "event" is more like a category than a sortal. For events there is no principle of unity that enables us to determine what else is included in the event.

The only ways to refer successfully to an event are either to specify the objects and properties completely or to refer to it as the event that caused such and such an effect. And we have already shown that it is not possible to pick out a unique event by referring to it as the cause of a certain event.

We conclude that events are arbitrary particulars, and from the preceding discussion it appears that events are unsuited to be the terms of causal relations, in the same way that sets are unsuited to be the terms of causal relations. Given an event that is taken to be "the effect" it is very difficult to find another event that can be identified as "the cause". This failure is related to the fact that events lack a natural principle of unity.

Arbitrary particulars have to be constructed out of something, and events as arbitrary objects are constructed out of physical objects

23 Davidson, *Essays on Actions and Events,* p. 157.

and their properties Events are therefore subordinate to physical objects and their properties. If it can be shown that there are relations between physical objects that have a good claim to be called causal relations (see Chapter 6), then any relations between events that were candidates for being causal relations would be subordinate to them. I suspect, though, that there are no relations that are even candidates for that position. It is physical objects and their properties that are significant for causality; arbitrary groupings of those objects and properties are not, as such, going to enter into causal relations with each other.

In answer to the question "Are there events?" or "Do events exist?" it is possible to say yes, provided it is added that events exist in the same way that sets of physical objects exist. Events also exist with the same sort of abundance as first-order sets of physical objects. To admit that in some sense sets and events exist is not to admit that they are real constituents of the world, or that they are real in the same way that physical objects and their properties are physically real. It can be said of a set that it has been given existence by human choice, and exactly the same thing can be said of an event. However, to admit that in some sense events exist is not to admit that events as arbitrary particulars have any significance for the ontology of causality. In some contexts it might be useful and convenient to talk about events in the same way that it is useful and convenient to talk about sets. But what we frequently talk about, and even what is useful and convenient to talk about, is not by itself a guide to what is real.

A point event such as $E_t(a; P)$ is simply the property P being instanced by the object a at time t, or the act of a's having property P at time t. How does it help to say that we have a special sort of entity here? What reason is there to say that there is a special sort of entity? Is not ontology as well served by physical objects and their properties? If the event is a change in properties, which is an interval event such as $E_{t_1-t_2}(a; P_1 \rightarrow P_2)$, how is ontology served by reifying *the changing* of properties, thereby making the act of changing an entity in its own right? To argue that there is an object that is "a changing of properties" from the fact that we talk about "the changing of properties" is like taking that theory of meaning that is naturally and usefully discussed in terms of truth conditions and then turning "truth conditions" into a special sort of object:

Such a move would indicate a lack of understanding of that theory of meaning.[24]

Are events always associated with physical objects? Could it not be that what really exists are *bare events* out of which we construct physical objects? Now the sort of object that is being contrasted with an event is an object with a principle of unity, a unified object. Physical objects include not only material objects but also objects not made of matter, such as fields. It is possible for unified objects to persist through time, since it is possible for their principles of unity (for example, their structures) to persist through time; events, by their very nature, do not persist through time.

It is possible to obtain events from a unified object by arbitrarily dividing the worldline of the unified object, though it is not possible to obtain a unified object from events unless a principle of unity is recognized as persisting through time. Unified objects are, therefore, in some way prior to events. If there are unified objects, then it is not the case that the world is a world of bare events, where a bare event is an event that does not involve a unified object, or any sort of object. It does not follow that there are no bare events, but I suspect it would be very difficult to find any examples.

Strawson argues that there *are* bare events: "But that a flash or a bang occurred does not entail that anything flashed or banged. 'Let there be light' does not mean 'Let something shine'."[25] As far as "entailment" and "meaning" go, no doubt Strawson is right. Suppose a flash were followed by a bang, and that such flashes were always followed by such bangs. Would we conclude that the bangs were caused by the flashes? Hume might, but most people, particularly physicists, would not. Flashes and bangs have a phenomenal sort of existence and are caused by something else, that is to say, by some physical object. Similarly, if someone says "Let there be light" and there is light, we would expect it to have a source. If it had no source, then as an oscillating electromagnetic field it would be a physical object in its own right, something that persists through time.

If a bare event is a point event, then that event and its properties exist only at that time, and in fact exist for no time at all. There is

24 It is considered an advantage of that theory that it does not multiply kinds of entity; cf. Mark Platts, *Ways of Meaning*, p. 35.
25 Strawson, *Individuals*, p. 46, but cf. p. 53.

something problematic about something existing only at a point in time – in fact, for no time at all. If a point event were ontologically dependent on something else such as an interval event, or a physical object, then the notion of point event can be allowed as being a limit of something.[26] But the very idea of a bare event is that it should stand alone, as something ontologically self-subsistent.

If a bare event is to be understood as an interval event, then what is the rationale for choosing that particular segment of worldline? If it is the persistence of a property or a group of properties occurring together, is not that grounds for asserting the existence of a persisting physical object? If it is not the persistence of properties, then what is it?

The problem of the existence of bare events is closely related to the problem of the existence of bare isolated properties, that is, properties that are not the property of any object. Only if there can exist a single bare isolated property is it reasonable to suppose there are bare simple events, whether point events or interval events. A bare complex event would then have to be some sort of collection of bare simple events. It is generally assumed, however, or argued, in the theory of universals that a single property cannot exist alone but must be the property of some object.[27] If this is right, then it follows that there are no such things as bare events.

Finally, consider the basic attributes that we know to be real constituents of the world, such as shape attributes, masses, quantities of energy, and velocities. These are the properties of physical objects; they are not the properties of events, and they certainly do not hang there in space by themselves belonging to no physical object. In Chapter 9, Section 5, I argue in detail that physical properties do not enter into causal relations or act as isolated properties.

4. CAUSALITY AND CONTINUITY

If the physical world were such that bodies did not move in continuous paths and interactions between bodies did not involve contiguity of some sort, we would have difficulty understanding how

26 For a discussion of points of space and points of matter as limits see Newman, "A Metaphysical Introduction to a Relational Theory of Space".
27 Cf. Armstrong, Volume I, Chapter 11.

178

causality worked. Nevertheless, as Russell has pointed out, continuity does itself present certain difficulties for causality.[28]

Consider two events E_{t_1} and E_{t_2} linked by a common worldline but separated by a finite distance and existing at different times. How could E_{t_1} be a cause of E_{t_2}? We have it on the authority of David Hume and Max Born that cause and effect must be contiguous, and indeed it does seem reasonable that if one thing is to act on another, then those two things must in some way make contact.[29] Here, however, there is no possibility of any interaction between E_{t_1} and E_{t_2}, let alone contiguous interaction, unless it is that E_t emits something that is subsequently received by E_{t_2}. But events as such are not emitters and receivers; it is not events as such that emit and receive energy, as Quine seems to think.

The ideal of contiguity seems to require a chain of cause and effect linking E_{t_1} and E_{t_2}. Newton's cradle is a good illustration of what is normally thought of as a chain of cause and effect. Five steel balls are hung in a row (by bifilar suspension) touching each other; one is swung out and allowed to collide into the others. The impulse is wholly imparted to the next ball, and so on until the last ball swings outwards. If the balls were separated slightly from each other you could see it all happening, though the impulse would no longer be totally transmitted. This is a paradigmatic example of the contiguity of cause and effect; it involves objects moving continuously and then interacting by contact.

There is, however, no possibility of regarding a chain of events such as those between E_{t_1} and E_{t_2} as a chain of contiguous causes and effects. Given any two distinct events between E_{t_1} and E_{t_2}, however close together, they still exist at different times and are separated by a finite distance. There is no more possibility of their interacting than there is for E_{t_1} and E_{t_2} themselves. The events that we are considering lie on a worldline and are indexed by time, and therefore are in one-to-one correspondence with the real numbers. It follows that event E_{t_1} has no immediate successor with which to interact. Any event after E_{t_1}, however close to E_{t_1}, exists at a different time and a different place from E_{t_1}. Events are not, and cannot, be the sort of

28 Russell, "On the Notion of Cause".
29 David Hume, *An Abstract of a Treatise on Human Nature,* and Max Born, *The Natural Philosophy of Cause and Chance,* Chapter 2.

things that interact with each other. Therefore they cannot be the terms of the causal relation.

Similar difficulties afflict all theories that posit independently existing point entities. For example, a theory that dealt with material points would face the dilemma that two material points were either separated by a finite distance or coincided: As Leibniz wrote to de Volder, "One unit is not touched by another."[30] On the other hand, extended bodies can touch at a point if a point is regarded ontologically in the Leibnizian manner as a limit of something with finite extension.[31] Similarly, there is no problem with the interaction of extended bodies that persist through a finite period of time, whether the interaction is a force relation, which is simultaneous, or an energy exchange, where energy is transmitted continuously at finite speed.

Interval events also face problems. Two interval events cannot interact if they are separated. If they exist at different times and in different places, something would have to be sent from one to the other; but interval events are no more the sort of things that send and receive things than point events are. If two interval events overlap we have the problem of individuation that was mentioned in Section 3 of this chapter. If one interval event stops at the same point that the other begins, it is likely that the distinction between them is arbitrary – why are there two interval events and not one? – and we shall look in vain for an interaction between them.

Russell suggests that the old notion of causality has been replaced in modern science by the uniformity of nature, in particular by the deterministic evolution of a system as governed by physical law.[32] A physical system, which is assumed to be isolated, evolves from a certain definite state at time t_1, to another definite state at the later time t_2. The deterministic evolution considered by physics is usu-

---

30 On 11 October 1705; C. I. Gerhardt, *Die philosophischen Schriften von G. W. Leibniz*, Volume II, p. 279; translated by Bertrand Russell, *A Critical Exposition of the Philosophy of Leibniz*, p. 247.

31 Leibniz illustrates his view by considering a triangle with a broad base being divided into several triangles by lines drawn from the vertex to different points on the base. When separated the triangles each have a point that is their top vertex; when joined together again all those vertices coincide in one point. So any number of extended objects can meet at one point, provided points are understood as limits of extended objects. Letter to des Bosses, 24 April 1709, Gerhardt, *Shriften*, p. 370, translated by L. E. Loemker, *G. W. Leibniz: Philosophical Papers and Letters*, p. 597.

32 Russell, "On the Notion of Cause", pp. 196–9.

ally thought of as continuous and therefore describable by continuous mathematical functions. If events are causes and effects, then the event that is the state of the system at t_1 could be regarded as a cause of the event that is the state of the system at t_2. It would be far-fetched to say that there was a causal relation between these events, and in fact neither Russell nor Lucas suggests this.[33] The notion of causal relation and of distinct causes and effects has been replaced by that of the continuous development of an isolated system. Lucas regards this development as causal development, and he uses the term 'causal cord' for segments of the causal development of a system.

But it does not follow that because a system is evolving deterministically it is evolving causally. An isolated body moving uniformly in a straight line according to Newton's first law is a counter-example. The motion is deterministic but not causal, since uniform motion in a straight line is not caused by anything. The basis of the Newtonian point of view is that uniform straight-line motion is one of the things that can happen when there are no causes. Leibniz could not accept this and posited an internal power responsible for the continued motion. But what if the internal power stopped working, would the body cease to move – and is that with respect to absolute space? The notion of an internal causal power making a body move in a straight line is difficult to make any sense of, particularly for a relationist.

Suppose that a body moving in a straight line begins to interact with a field that causes it to deviate from straight-line motion and to adopt some sort of curved path. We can say that the change in path is caused by the field, or that the new curved path is caused by whatever is responsible for the field. There is no reason to say that events on the path are causally related, nor to say that a segment of the path is a causal cord. Neither would Russell or Lucas have us say such things. The system that evolves deterministically is an isolated one, and our body, which is now in a field, is no longer isolated. The isolated system is the body, the field, and whatever is responsible for the field.

Let us suppose that we have two bodies with a Newtonian gravitational field acting between them. The state of this system at time

---

33 J. R. Lucas, *Space, Time and Causality*, Chapter 10.

t_1 involves two positions and two velocities. In the Lagrangian formulation of Newtonian mechanics the development of this combined system is dealt with by considering the motion of a representative point in a six-dimensional space, called configuration space. The coordinates of the representative point are a combination of the three spatial coordinates of the first body and the three spatial coordinates of the second body. The development from the "position" at time t_1 to that at time t_2 is represented by a segment of a path in configuration space. In the Hamiltonian formulation the state of the system as opposed to its "position" is represented by a point in phase space or state space. A state of the system is given by all the independent positions and momenta. The development of the system from its state at t_1 to its state at t_2 is represented by a segment of a path in its phase space, and it is this segment that Lucas would call a causal cord. The state of the system at a time is an event, so a causal cord is something that connects events. It follows that if the causal cord is to be of any metaphysical significance it will be in terms of events, with all the problems associated with events that we raised earlier.

The Lagrangian and Hamiltonian formulations are excellent formalisms for representing the deterministic nature of certain systems that can be dealt with by Newtonian mechanics. Apart from that it is questionable how metaphysically illuminating they are. Causality has to do with interaction, with one thing acting on another, whereas causal cords as dealt with by these more advanced formulations of Newtonian mechanics involve seeing a system as an isolated whole.[34] Consequently the Lagrangian, Hamiltonian, or similar formulations neither replace nor undermine our ideals of causality.

My earlier appeal to the authority of Hume and Born that cause and effect must be contiguous was, I am afraid, not entirely serious. Born is of course thinking of special relativity, where all disturbances are propagated at finite speed. Special relativity was discovered by considering electromagnetism, which sees space as filled by fields that are physical entities that propagate at finite speed. Special relativity is an important part of modern physics and its natural

---

34 It should be noted, however, that perturbation theory had its origin in these formulations of classical mechanics. Perturbation theory is an approximation method that deals with an interaction as a small energy increase contributed from the outside.

metaphysics is an important ideal of causality. I do not believe, however, that all examples of causality need meet a contiguity requirement in exactly the sense of special relativity.

In Bohm's hidden-variable theory, for example, one of the hidden variables propagates in a way quite different from the way a relativistic field propagates, though the change is continuous and there is contact of a sort. It is based ultimately on the way in which the wave field itself changes as governed by wave equations. Some idea of the nature of this change can be understood from Dirac's method of variation of constants used in perturbation theory. And in fact the non-locality of Bohm's hidden variables arises from reifying the wave function, and so there may be general lessons to be learnt here.[35] It must not be assumed, however, that I am a believer in Bohm's hidden variables; it is merely that his theory is metaphysically very different from what we are used to and therefore interesting. Without a number of different sorts of natural philosophy to survey it is difficult for us to understand what is possible.

However, I find true action at a distance where there is nothing intervening disturbing. Newton may have been right to have put forward his theory of gravitation in the way he did, but it was something crying out for explanation, as he himself was aware.

5. SUMMARY OF WHY EVENTS ARE NOT TERMS OF CAUSAL RELATIONS

My strategy for showing that events are not the terms of causal relations involves five main groups of arguments:[36]

1. The collection of arguments in Section 3 of this chapter, which maintain that events are arbitrary particulars and which, by focussing on their arbitrary nature, show that they cannot be the terms of causal relations.
2. The arguments about continuity in Section 4 of this chapter, which show that two events connected by a worldline cannot interact causally with each other.
3. The observation that the five main, representative types of causal relation described in Chapter 6, Section 4, do not have events as their terms. Instead, they have unified objects that persist through time as

---

35 My view is that there is a case for regarding the phase of the wave function as physically real.
36 In Chapter 3, Section 5, I mention certain considerations that count against reifying Wittgenstein's states of affairs. At the beginning of this chapter, I gave reasons for thinking that states of affairs and events were in the same category.

their terms. Since two of those causal relations are the causal relations known to physics, it appears that physics does not recognize events as the terms of causal relations.

4. The argument that basic attributes are attributes of unified particulars, not events. For example, in Chapter 6, Section 3, in the discussion of energy flow I argue that quantity of energy is an attribute of physical objects, not of events. It also seems fairly clear, for example, that events as such do not possess mass; only things that persist through time possess mass. According to my account of causality, a causal relation is a relation that can make a particular change its basic attributes, so that causal relations have possessors of basic attributes as their terms. An event may "include" a basic attribute, but that attribute is first possessed by a unified particular.

5. Finally, the problem of finding the causal relations that the event theorist suggests relate events. I discuss this problem in Section 1 of Chapter 8 and show it to be serious.

These arguments strongly recommend the conclusion that it is not events that are the terms of causal relations. The terms of causal relations appear to be particulars with a natural principle of unity that persists through time.[37]

37 See Section 3 of this chapter for a discussion of the distinction between an interval event and an object that persists through time.

8

Further considerations concerning the causal relation

1. THE LOGICAL FORM OF SENTENCES ABOUT CAUSALITY

One reason the problem of causality is difficult is that language and ordinary thought appear to presuppose what we can call the linguistically natural picture of causality. It appears to suppose that there are objects such as a, b, c, d, . . . that are causes and effects, *and* that there are relations between them that are causal relations. If there is a causal relation between a and b, then that causal relation is a matter of a's producing b, or a's being responsible for b, though these phrases merely further express our intuition. It is further supposed that causes and effects occur in causal chains: a causes b, b causes c, and so on. Russell ascribes this view to Mill.

Events are appealing as causes and effects, since they are at least particulars and are easily arranged into chains. They seem to fit the linguistically natural picture of causality. The main problem with events is that of finding a causal relation to link one event with another. This is a serious problem for events, as without causal relations to link them together events cannot be taken seriously as causes and effects. Physical objects, as we have shown, can enter into causal relations; but the problem with physical objects is that it is difficult to see them as causes and effects in the hoped for chain of causes and effects. Neither events nor physical objects really fit the linguistically natural picture of causality.

Suppose that two physical objects a and b interact by means of a force relation, R_F, so that the physical object b is caused to change direction. The situation can be looked at from both the point of view of physical objects and from the point of view of events. We can represent these two points of view by the following diagram:

185

$$\text{Events:} \quad E_a\text{------}R_e\text{------}E_b$$
$$\text{Objects:} \quad a\text{-------}R_F\text{------}b$$

where E_a is "a's having P_1, etc." (i.e. the event of a's having all the relevant properties it does in fact have), and E_b is "b's changing direction".

The metaphysical issues are these: Which is the more fundamental level, the level of events or the level of physical objects, and what is the relationship between the two levels? This latter issue would become important if there were in fact a causal relation between events.

This causal situation we have been considering can be described by a number of different causal statements involving both levels:

1. "There is a force relation R_F between object a and object b."
2. "Object a causes b's changing of direction."
3. "The force relation, R_F, causes b's changing of direction."
4. "a's having P_1, etc., causes b's changing of direction."

Language seems to allow for all these forms, which is not insignificant since event theorists such as Davidson think the structure of language shows us that events are fundamental.

Let us consider the first form of causal statement:

1. "There is a force relation R_F between object a and object b."

If there were no force relation between objects a and b there would be no change in direction. And moreover, there is no other relation known to physics that is relevant to the change in direction. No object is going to induce another to change direction unless there is some sort of causal relation, such as a force relation, holding between them. Form (1) is a statement about causality, and it does have the simple, easy-to-handle form, aRb, but it does not say anything about effects or what happens.

Consider the third type of causal statement:

3. "The force relation, R_F, causes b's changing of direction."

We have a choice: We can say either that the horse caused the cart to move or that the force in the traces caused the cart to move. If you allow one sort of statement, then you must allow the other, since clearly the two sorts of statement are closely related.

The third type is an example of a perfectly good sentence about causality that cannot be understood as being of the form aRb. If it were of that form there would have to be a "causal relation" between the force relation on the one hand, and "b's changing of direction" on the other hand. To look for an ontologically significant relation between a force relation and a changing of direction is the same sort of thing – nay, worse – as looking for an ontologically significant relation to connect a force relation to the object that is one of its terms. Relations simply relate two particulars; they are doubly unsaturated as Frege would put it. To posit further relations relating relations to their terms, or anything else, brings in those infinite regresses Bradley made so much of. Such a "relation", though, is what the event theorist is looking for, since for an event theorist it is the causal relation that interacts directly with the event E_b.

If the event theorist is unhappy about introducing a "causal relation" to connect the force relation and the event of b's changing of direction, then he should be even more unhappy about introducing a "causal relation" to connect the object a with the event of b's changing of direction. In other words, he should be more unhappy about understanding the statement:

2. "Object a causes b's changing of direction"

as having the form aRb. Although statements of type (2) are as acceptable as any other type of causal statement, it seems very far-fetched to understand them as being of the form aRb.

Consider the fourth type of causal statement:

4. "a's having P_1, etc., causes b's changing of direction."

What is problematic about (4) is supposing that there is an ontologically significant relation corresponding to the verb 'causes'. In fact, there is no more reason here to make the supposition that there is a causal relation with events as its terms – in other words, that (4) has the form aRb – than there was with types (2) and (3). Although (4) may be his ideal, the event theorist cannot really rule out types (2) and (3), since they are in most circumstances linguistically more natural.

My suggestion is that there are basically two sorts of statements about causality: ones that assert there is a causal relation between two objects and ones that say what the effects of that causal relation are. The first sort can be analysed in terms of aRb, but the second sort cannot; in my view nothing more can be said about their logical form.

If there were no causal relation between the objects a and b of our example, there would be no change in direction. And moreover, there is no other relation that is relevant to the change in direction. The statement "object a causes b's changing of direction" has to be left as it is. It cannot be analysed as a statement about a special sort of object such as a "changing of direction".

There is here an analogy with statements about truth conditions in certain theories of meaning, which are also not to be analysed as statements about special sorts of objects.[1] Truth is not to be understood as a relation between two objects: the sentence and the "truth conditions". Truth conditions are not even to be understood as being arbitrary objects, in the way that sets are arbitrary objects; such an analysis would do nothing to help a theory of meaning. Similarly, to introduce events as special sorts of objects (even as arbitrary objects), such as "the event of b's changing of direction", does not help our understanding of such statements from an ontological point of view. What is significant ontologically are physical objects, their properties, and causal relations between objects.

In our example the only relation that is significant as far as causality goes is the force relation between a and b. It would not make any sense to say that there was an additional causal relation between the object a, which is a fairly ordinary sort of object, and an object that is a "changing of direction", which is a rather strange sort of object. What sort of causal relation is it anyway that relates a physical object to an event?

Some people such as Bennett think that events are supervenient on physical objects.[2] The event theorist has to hold a position something like this. But to say that the relation between events is supervenient on the force relation not only heightens the sense of mystery but also concedes that it is the force relation that is really important for causality.

Our previous arguments have ruled out any diagonal relations between R_F and E_b, and between a and E_b. The only way for an event theorist to introduce a causal relation is to try to link E_a and E_b by a relation such as R_e, which has events as its terms. But it is difficult to understand what R_e is, or how it is related to R_F, or how we can have two productive relations working in parallel. It is via R_F

1 It is considered an advantage of that theory that it does not multiply kinds of entity; cf. Platts, *Ways of Meaning*, p. 35.
2 Jonathan Bennett, *Events and Their Names*, pp. 12–18.

that the physical object *a* interacts with the physical object *b*, and it is that causal relation that is responsible for the changes in *b*. Why should there be a need for another relation? Moreover R_F is what the physicist knows about and must therefore be regarded as having primary ontological significance. R_e is unknown to physics.

2. THE ONTOLOGY OF CAUSALITY

The traditional ontology of causality is one of events linked by causal relations, so that it is certain events and causal relations that are ontologically significant. They are the real constituents of the world. On this view, events have properties or involve properties, depending on whether the properties are ascribed to unified particulars, or to the events themselves, or are just regarded as free-standing properties belonging to nothing in particular. In one sense properties themselves do not figure in this ontology of causality, since the having of properties and the changing of properties are events. On the other hand, it seems that there would first need to be an ontology of properties out of which the ontology of events could be constructed. How could events be real unless there were real properties? The identification of which properties to regard as real is not difficult. What is difficult for the event ontology of causality is the identification of which events are ontologically significant, and the identification of the causal relations that are supposed to relate them.

On our view, which excludes events, there are three categories of things that are significant for causality: unified particulars, basic attributes, and causal relations. There is no problem with where the basic attributes belong; they are the properties of unified particulars. And there is no problem with the identification of the terms of causal relations, or with the identification of the causal relations that connect them.[3]

Unified particulars, basic attributes, and causal relations have primary ontological significance, and each figures in causality in a different way. Unified particulars are the particulars that enter into causal relations; they are the terms of those relations. When unified particulars enter into causal relations with each other, they do so on account of their basic attributes. We could say that the basic

3 See Chapter 9 for a discussion of unified particulars.

attributes of unified particulars give rise to causal relations. Causal relations are basic relations and like basic attributes are real constituents of the world. Causal relations and basic attributes are both examples of basic universals. What makes a relation to be a causal relation is that it is possible for a particular to change its basic attributes on account of the fact that the particular is a term of that causal relation. It does not follow that its basic attributes will always change when that causal relation obtains, since where there is a network of causal relations a static causal situation is possible.

It is only for unified particulars that we can say that entering into causal relations is a necessary condition for their being real. It must not be thought that basic attributes themselves enter into causal relations, either with other basic attributes or with anything else. Concerning basic attributes, we can say that they are significant for causality, or that they figure in causality, or that when unified particulars take part in causal interactions they do so on account of their basic attributes. Basic attributes are significant for causality in two ways: They give rise to causal relations, and a particular's basic attributes are changed by causal relations. Basic attributes are therefore our starting point.

My account of which things are real, and the criteria for their being real, follows this order: First, certain universals that satisfy the criteria for basic attributes given in Chapter 4 are chosen *a posteriori* to be basic attributes. Science tells us about universals, such as the determinate shapes and certain determinate quantities, which are causally significant and are real if anything is; we merely have to show that they satisfy the criteria. They are taken to be real constituents of the world, and they form a base for what follows. Monadic universals are chosen first because the natures of unified particulars depend on their monadic properties. There is no reason in principle why relational properties of unified particulars should not both give rise to causal relations and be changed by them. (Distance relations are an example.)

Next, causal relations are understood to be basic relational universals that can make a particular change its basic attributes. Basic attributes need particulars to possess them, and causal relations also need particulars to be their terms. It can be shown that it is certain unified particulars that fill both roles. So the possibility of entering into causal relations is a necessary and sufficient condition for a particular to be a real constituent of the world. It follows that the pos-

190

session of basic attributes is also a necessary and sufficient condition for a particular to be real, since a particular enters into causal relations only on account of its basic attributes.

Because these three different types of things – unified particulars, basic attributes, and causal relations – figure in causal situations in different ways it is not possible to give a single criterion for being a real constituent of the world, though I would claim that what is given is a unified account.

Looking at the issue from the point of view of particulars, we can say that unified particulars possess basic attributes and enter into causal relations on account of them, and that causal relations are the sort of relation that can bring about changes in unified particulars by changing their basic attributes.

If there is any circularity in this account of causality and reality, it is a form of conceptual circularity in that the idea of a particular's changing its basic attributes *on account of* causal relations is essentially causal. I doubt, however, whether an account of causality can be given in non-causal terms. There is also circularity in the *a posteriori* choice of certain basic attributes, since that choice is founded on things already understood to be causally significant, which is an appeal to our scientifically educated intuition. I think, however, that it can be safely asserted that those scientific properties would be understood to be causally significant in any reasonable account of causality, even ones with different starting points. My aim is to give an account of which things are real, not to explain what causality is in terms of something else.

Although we can maintain a large part of our causal intuition, there is a sense in which my account splits our causal intuition. Take the notion of one thing *producing* another. Causal relations can be said to *produce* changes in a particular by changing its basic attributes; these are the effects of causal relations. And then particulars and their basic attributes can be said to "produce" causal relations. Hitherto I have used the form of words "basic attributes *give rise to* causal relations", but the word 'produce' seems intuitively acceptable. Now, if it is possible that basic attributes should produce causal relations, then it is equally possible that if a particular changes its basic attributes, then this should make the two particulars change the causal relation between them.

There is no going back to events for the fundamental reason that there is no causal relation between the event that is a particular changing its basic attributes and the event that is two particulars changing the causal relation between them. There are two primitive notions corresponding to our intuitive notion of "produce" that we need to distinguish. Basic attributes of particulars can be said to "give rise" to causal relations, and causal relations can be said to "cause" particulars to change their basic attributes, though both types of action are in a very general sense causal.[4]

Causality is essentially relational in the sense that it is one particular that acts on another. An attribute does not itself act on another attribute, whether that attribute belongs to a different body or to the same body. If there is any interaction within a body, it is that of one part acting on another part. There is very little difficulty involved in recognizing the existence of basic attributes, or in recognizing the existence of causal relations, relations that can produce ontologically significant changes. Therefore, when there is a change of a particular's basic attributes so that the causal relation between two particulars is changed, that change is causally significant precisely because it is one productive causal relation that is exchanged for another.

Having admitted basic attributes and causal relations as being real constituents of the world, we need an account of how other universals can be determined to be real constituents of the world. The original set of basic universals is the standard against which the reality of other things is measured. Now the only way to interact with a basic attribute is via a causal relation between particulars. So the criterion for some other universal being causally significant is that it contributes to giving rise to a causal relation, a causal relation of course being one that can make a particular change its basic attributes. If the universal is also perfectly determinate (i.e. does not classify other universals and cannot be construed as a conjunction of universals of the same level), then it is a real constituent of the world and we shall call it a basic universal. There may still, however, be

4 For the event theorist one event causes another event, but it is not clear whether he regards the causal relation between as being given rise to by anything. In the event ontology causal relations are nameless and amorphous, and seem to be of one type. If nothing gives rise to them, then causal relations just occur, determined by nothing in particular. If not, then it could be that the two events that are the terms of the causal relation give rise to the causal relation, or that the event that is the cause gives rise both to the effect and to the causal relation. There are difficulties both ways. Although the event theorist tends to ignore causal relations, he cannot really deny that they exist and that they are ontologically significant.

the need for some *a posteriori* considerations to be taken into account in the determination.

If distance relations are real constituents of the world, then it follows that relative velocity and relative acceleration are real constituents of the world. Now, the point of view of Newtonian mechanics and special relativity is that uniform changes in distance relations between bodies are not the result of causal relations, any more than a state of constant-distance relations is the result of causal relations. From this point of view it is changes in velocity that require the intervention of a causal relation. But this is not relevant to the status of distance relations and relative velocities. A causal relation is merely one that can make a particular change its basic attributes; and a basic universal is one that can contribute to giving rise to a causal relation. It does not follow from any of this that when a basic universal or one of the original basic attributes changes, it *always* does so as a result of the action of a causal relation. A distance relation can change as a result of the action of a force relation – for example, the distance relation between the extremities of an elastic material object; or a distance relation can change by itself without the intervention of a causal relation – for example, the distance between two bodies that do not interact but that possess a relative velocity.

This of course leaves open the possibility of any basic universal changing by itself, under its own steam. This sort of behaviour is a logical possibility, since it is consistent with our abstract schema that describes causality. However, from the point of view of that schema it is not causal activity, since it is not the result of a causal relation. The abstract schema is the account of causality presented above with the *a posteriori* choice of basic attributes left open. It appears that distance relations are the only type of basic attributes among the ones we have chosen that has this characteristic of changing in a way that is not due to a causal relation. If the phase of the wave function is physically real, it may be another example.

Relations such as distance relations and more complex spatial relations are basic universals without being causal relations. Proportion and other relations between particulars, such as "being heavier than" or "being ten times heavier than", are not themselves basic universals though the monadic attributes of particulars that are their foundations are basic universals. Proportion and order relations between particulars are explained by internal relations between basic attributes, which are second-order universals. The proportion relations between particulars and the proportion relations between basic attributes have a secondary ontological significance, as do the the relations between basic universals that explain natural laws.

Shapes, distance relations, and relative velocities are not relativistic invariants. According to special relativity two different observers in different inertial frames will agree that two bodies are the same, but will describe their spatial separation with different distance universals and will disagree about the appropriate relative velocity universals. Causal relations also differ for different observers; the direction of energy flow is relative to the frame of reference, as can be seen from considering a simple collision between billiard balls.[5] A change in frame of reference that reverses the direction of the velocities of the balls also reverses the direction of energy flow on collision. The observers will agree that a causal interaction is taking place and will agree on the type of interaction, but they will not agree on its exact nature, though, in a sense, it is the same interaction. On the other hand, if body A emits something that is absorbed by body B, the direction of the exchange is the same for all observers.

It follows then that some real constituents of the world are not the same for all observers. This is true for shape attributes, which are basic attributes. It is not possible to exclude from our ontology quantities that depend on the inertial frame, since you cannot do physics with relativistic invariants alone. In relativistic physics bodies possess determinate properties and interact on account of them, so there are no grounds here for doubting their reality. The details of a causal interaction are not relativistically invariant,[6] so that the attributes and relations that are ontologically significant are in most cases not relativistically invariant.

If this is considered to be a problem, then one solution would be to regard the shape in the rest frame as the true shape of a physical object that does not interact. This could be extended to distance relations, relative velocities, and causal relations by taking the inertial frame defined by the centre of mass of the two bodies in question as the rest frame of the combined system. The true basic universals would be the ones relative to that frame. This is a natural approach for a philosophical point of view that emphasizes physical objects.

5 Cf. David Fair, "Causation and the Flow of Energy", p. 240.   6 Ibid.

It should be noted that the analysis of causation given in this book does not say that certain things are causes and other effects and that the cause always *precedes* the effect. Instead, it focusses on causal relations between physical objects and on physical objects changing their properties as a consequence of those relations. Unlike the theories of Quine and David Fair, this analysis does not identify the causal relation with a flow of something, though sometimes the causal relation does amount to a flow of something with an invariant direction.

3. CAUSAL RELATIONS AND NATURAL LAWS

It is basic attributes that give rise to force relations, energy exchanges, and so on, as governed by simple scientific laws. If scientific properties are to be understood as basic attributes (i.e. as universals), then it appears that scientific laws should be understood as relations between universals. Understood in this way, there is a close connection between the logical form of statements about causality and the logical form of basic natural laws.

Statements that assert scientific laws are therefore similar to statements that assert essential subordination, in that both are about relations between universals and both require the immanent realists' second interpretation of predicate calculus. The difference arises from the fact that essential subordination is a necessary relation between universals, where the necessity arises from the nature of the universals, whereas scientific laws are not necessary in the same way.

Armstrong's view is that the necessity of natural laws does indeed have its basis in the nature of the universals: "But what is the basis in reality, the truth-maker, the ontological ground, of such necessity? I suggest that it can be found in *what it is to be an F* and *what it is to be a G*."[7] If natural laws are fixed by the nature of universals, then it seems to follow that, as far as necessity goes, natural laws are similar to statements about essential subordination between attributes and statements about proportion relations between determinate quantities. This does not seem to allow for the logical possibility that different natural laws may link the same universals.[8] On the other hand, Armstrong is right in a sense that the ontological

7 Armstrong, *What Is a Law of Nature?*, p. 77.
8 But cf. ibid., Chapter 11.

ground of natural laws does lie in the nature of universals. It lies in the nature of the basic universals *and* in the nature of the second-order relation that relates them. But the second-order relation is not an internal relation; it is not something that is essential to the nature of the basic universals, so that it is not like essential subordination or proportion relations.

Scientific laws, however, do determine a form of necessity. Not only do scientific laws say what has happened and what will happen, they say what *can* happen and what *cannot* happen, and what *would* happen under certain circumstances. Statements asserting relations between universals are true whether the universals are instanced or not, or whether they ever have been, or ever will be instanced. It follows that we should expect statements about relations between universals to be saying something about possibility, about what could happen and what could not happen. Scientific laws therefore determine a form of necessity, which is narrower than logical necessity.

To get an intuitive idea of the difference, consider two material objects with different masses. The material objects have a proportion relation between them in that one is so many times heavier than the other, but this relation has no primary ontological significance beyond that of the determinate mass attributes that can be said to determine it. The corresponding relation between the determinate mass attributes is an internal relation and a logically necessary relation. The material objects also have a gravitational force relation between them that does have ontological significance beyond that of the determinate mass attributes that give rise to it. The corresponding relation between the determinate mass attributes (the natural law universal) is not an internal relation and it is not logically necessary.

According to Armstrong natural laws are dyadic relations between universals such as $N(F, G)$. They entail extensional formulas but are not entailed by them:[9]

$$N(F, G) \Rightarrow (x)(Fx \rightarrow Gx)$$
$$(x)(Fx \rightarrow Gx) \not\Rightarrow N(F, G).$$

This is not surprising as natural law second-order universals are merely about the order and arrangement of basic universals that must occur together.

9 Ibid., p. 85.

From our point of view one of the archetypal forms of natural laws is a relation between basic attributes and basic relations, where at least one of them is a causal relation. For example, gravitational force is given by the equation:

$$F = GM^k M^l / r^2.$$

It tells us about the force relation that holds between physical objects that have certain basic attributes and a certain basic relation between them. As a relation between universals we can write the law as:

$$N(M^k, M^l, r; R_F).$$

R_F is a two-place force relation; it is not the force that appears in the equations of physics, which is a monadic reduction of the force relation – in other words, a one-sided way of looking at the force relation itself.

The universals that are related by the second-order natural law universal fall into two classes. There are the universals that are given – namely, M^k, M^l, and r – and there is the universal that is given rise to – namely, R_F. The natural law understood as a relation between universals can be interpreted as saying that certain determinate attributes give rise to a determinate relation. It would be wrong to say that this "giving rise to" was itself a causal relation, since it would be wrong to say that certain universals caused a causal relation; they might be said to explain why the causal relation occurred, but they do not "cause" it. It would be a mistake to look for a relation, in the sense of another causal relation, linking R_F to M^k, M^l, and r. It would be a mistake, that is, to look for a relation other than N itself. N is a different sort of relation. It is a relation between universals, a second-order universal, whereas causal relations are relations between particulars. There is a distinction between causal statements such as $aR_F b$, which says that a causal relation holds between two objects, and natural laws, which are about the general conditions under which causal relations arise – because they relate universals.

Looked at from the point of view of causality natural laws can be divided into those that govern how causal relations are given rise to or determined, which correspond to causal statements of type (1) of Section 1 of this chapter, and those that govern the effects causal relations have, which correspond to causal statements of types (2) and

(3). These latter inevitably portray causal relations from a one-sided point of view, for example:

$$F = ma,$$

or

$$dQ = mC_v \, dT + PdV,$$

which says how an input of heat causes an increase in internal energy and the doing of external work. The equation shows how basic attributes change when there is an energy exchange. Laws of this type give the general conditions under which causal statements of types (2) and (3) are true. The application of laws of this type is preceded by a process of combining the causal relations that act on the object. The rules that govern the combination of causal relations represent a third type of natural law.

If all states and changes in the natural world are causal in nature, then whenever there are states and changes these are to be explained in terms of causal relations. It follows that the ultimate basis for the assertion of natural laws, including Armstrong's dyadic examples, are relations between universals of the three types we have described: those that govern the setting up of causal relations, those that govern the effects of causal relations, and those that govern how causal relations combine.

Let us go back to the comparison of laws of nature with proportion relations between determinate quantities. If a material object a has mass M^k and material object b has mass M^l then *as a consequence* object a is so many times heavier than object b. This implication could be understood as being due to the following law:

(a) $(x)(y)(M^k x \ \& \ M^l y \rightarrow x R_h^M y)$

where R_h^M is the relation of "being h times heavier than", which is not topic neutral. Although this law is true and logically necessarily true, it does not explain the implication; it merely generalizes it. The implication is explained by the topic-neutral proportion relation between the determinate masses, $M^k R_h M^l$, and therefore by the following implication:

(b) $M^k R_h M^l \ \& \ M^k a \ \& \ M^l b \rightarrow a R_h^M b.$

The conclusion $a R_h^M a$ is a contingent truth as are two of the antecedents, $M^k a$ and $M^l b$. But one of the antecedents, $M^k R_h M^l$, is a logically necessary truth, which explains why the implication is necessary and in what way it is necessary. (b) could also be generalized.

The material objects a and b also have a gravitational force relation between them *as a consequence* of their masses and the distance between them. This implication could be understood as being due to the following law:

(c) $(x)(y)(M^k x \ \& \ M^l y \ \& \ (x)r(y) \to xR_F y)$

where R_F is a force relation and $(\ )r(\ )$ a distance relation as before. Although this law is true and physically necessarily true, it does not explain the implication; it merely generalizes it. The implication is explained by the relation between the determinate masses and distance relation, $N(M^k, M^l, r; R_F)$, and therefore by the following implication:

(d) $N(M^k, M^l, r; R_F) \ \& \ M^k a \ \& \ M^l b \ \& \ (a)r(b) \to aR_F b.$

The conclusion, $aR_F b$, is a contingent truth as are three of the antecedents, $M^k a$, $M^l b$, and $(a)r(b)$. But one of the antecedents, $N(M^k, M^l, r; R_F)$, is a physically necessary truth that explains why the implication is necessary and in what way it is necessary. If N were founded on the natures of M^k, M^l, and r, as Armstrong supposed in *What is a Law of Nature?*, then it would be an internal relation, but it is unlikely that there would be internal relations between determinate universals of totally different types such as masses and distances.

(c) can be expressed in conditional terms. If object a were to have mass M^k and object b were to have mass M^l, and the distance between were r, then there would be a force relation R_F between a and b. The implication expressed by (c) is not a simple material implication; it involves a form of necessity, and it may well be a counterfactual conditional. However, (c) is explained by the generalization of (d), which is itself explained by the second-order relational universal $N(M^k, M^l, r; R_F)$. It follows that it is causal laws that explain counterfactual conditionals, and not the other way round. We can say that causal laws imply counterfactual conditionals.[10]

In the first type of causal law, which governs how causal relations are given rise to, there is no possibility of interference or prevention

10 Goodman, Quine, and Ayer say that laws "sustain" counterfactual conditionals.

for force relations. If the basic attributes are there then all the law-
fully determined force relations will be there also. This is also true
for some types of energy exchanges and for some of the other types
of causal relations as well. It is the third type of law that governs
how causal relations are combined that deals with interference and
prevention – an issue Anscombe drew attention to.[11] Before the effect of a network of force relations can be worked out, it has to be
determined how they combine, which is easily done by the paral-
lelogram law. Only then can the law that gives the effects of forces
be used. Forces are easy because there is only one type of force. Energy exchange relations are more difficult because of the different
types of energy exchanges such as the exchange of radiation energy,
the exchange of particles and the exchanges of energy in collisions,
and so on. Nevertheless there are ways of combining these relations,
and this must be done before the law governing effects can be used;
this is where inference and prevention are dealt with. It follows that
causal laws of the second type in combination with laws of the third
type can also imply counterfactual conditionals: They enable us to
infer what would happen given certain circumstances.

4. CAUSALITY AND COUNTERFACTUAL CONDITIONALS

Among event theorists the counterfactual analysis of causality is often regarded as the fundamental explanation of what causality is. I
argue that it is not, even for an event ontology. There are a number
of different counterfactual accounts of causality varying in sophis-
tication. Although no one presents it precisely like this, the basic
form that underlies these accounts is as follows: If X and Y are two
events that may occur, then X causes Y if and only if it is true to say
that if X were to occur, then Y would occur, and if X were not to
occur, then Y would not have occurred.[12] Lewis, for example, has a
sophisticated possible-worlds account of the counterfactual – "If X
were to occur then Y would occur" – as well as other refinements.
I shall consider Mackie's account because it is closely related to our
intuitive understanding of causation.

11 See Chapter 6, note 49.
12 Cf. David Lewis, "Causation", p. 563; J. L. Mackie, *The Cement of the Universe*,
   Chapter 2, and John Earman, "Causation: A Matter of Life and Death", p. 9.

The cause is a *sine qua non* for the occurrence of the effect, or necessary for the effect in the counterfactual sense: If X were not to occur, then Y would not have occurred. Let X be the event of a certain ball being thrown in a certain direction at time t_1 and let Y be the event of the breaking of a certain window at time t_2. The throwing of the ball at time t_1 is necessary for the breaking of the window at time t_2 in the sense that if the ball had not been thrown, then the window would not have been broken. But it does seem *prima facie* possible that something else might break that window at time t_2 and so cause the specified effect. Even if the ball had in fact been thrown at time t_1, then it still seems true to say counterfactually that the window could have been broken by something else.

Consider an experiment on the breaking of windows where the experimenter decides to throw a brick at time t_1 instead of a ball; in this case the specified event that is the effect would still occur. Now Mackie tells us that in order to understand how the throwing of the ball is necessary for the breaking of the window at time t_2 we have to take into account the circumstances. In order for the window to break, the mere throwing of the ball is not enough; other conditions that are also causally relevant would have to hold.[13] We have to say that *given certain circumstances,* the window would not have broken if the ball had not been thrown; those circumstances include a number of things, but they exclude bricks being thrown.

Mackie is thinking then of a bundle of causal factors, one of which could plausibly be highlighted as the cause. These factors are regarded as forming a sort of closed system, where, ideally, all the factors are severally necessary and jointly sufficient; given that closed system, were one of the factors absent, the effect would not occur. But this is a relative type of necessity; it is relative to the bundle of factors, not to the world at large. X, the cause, is necessary in the circumstances for Y. On the other hand, if the cause is taken to be the bundle of factors, then the cause is not necessary for the effect, since some other bundle of factors could have caused it.

Necessary in the circumstances seems to be a rather arbitrary limitation. What is it about that bundle of factors that necessity relative to it should be so significant, other than that they were the factors present? The restriction to *necessary in certain circumstances* makes us focus on the bundle of factors as metaphysically significant. But the

13 Mackie, *The Cement of the Universe,* p. 31.

most we can say about that bundle is that it is sufficient for the effect in a counterfactual sense, providing, that is, that no other factors operate – which is also an appeal to circumstances. But even this is not true in general, since in an indeterministic situation, even the bundle of factors is not a sufficient condition.

Mackie's approach isolates one factor as the cause that stands out against a background of circumstances or conditions or the causal field. "There are no firm rules governing this selection, but there are some fairly systematic tendencies."[14] Causes generally involve changes rather than static conditions; causes are intrusive rather than things that are normal. He is aware that this is not a very fundamental distinction, since he gives an example involving three factors: (A) an electric current, (B) decayed insulation, (C) inflammable material, with a causal field consisting of the presence of oxygen, absence of fire extinguishers, and so on.[15] Someone who took either (A), (B), or (C) as the cause would regard the other two as the circumstance, but which he chose would depend on his interests, not upon fundamental, metaphysical considerations. But then Mackie admits that his aim is "not so much to give a logically neat account as to analyse our ordinary thinking about causal sequences".[16] He is right, of course, that ordinary thinking does tend to highlight one factor as the cause.

In his discussion of overdetermination Mackie seems to suggest a way in which the cause *as a bundle of factors* could be necessary for the effect.[17] This is how Earman interprets him.[18] Mackie does this by emphasizing that it is the "concrete event effect" – that which actually happened – that is in fact caused. The effect considered as "concrete event effect" brings out the nature of events as against facts. An event is something that is supposed to be fully determined though not fully known, whereas a fact, though also fully determined, is something that is only determined by a proposition such as "the window broke at time t_2". A fact corresponds to many possible events.

14 Ibid., p. 34.   15 Ibid., p. 37.   16 Ibid., p. 36.
17 Ibid., p. 46. In our example, if the brick and the ball were thrown together, then the effect would be overdetermined. They would be joint coincident causes either of which would be sufficient, but in the circumstances neither is a *sine qua non*. Mackie considers the case of a desert traveller whose water is poisoned and whose water bottle has a hole. Neither is a *sine qua non* for his death, which is overdetermined. Here, one event is a backup cause, as opposed to a coincident cause.
18 John Earman, Review of J. L. Mackie, *The Cement of the Universe*.

Using this notion of "concrete event effect" there are two ways of arguing that the cause is necessary for the effect. If X, the cause as bundle of factors, had not occurred, then Y would not have occurred, because another event, X', however similar, would have produced a slightly different effect event. Therefore X is counterfactually necessary for Y. The other way is this: Suppose an event, X', had occurred that differed from X only in causally irrelevant details; an effect, Y', would then be produced that was exactly like Y in every respect, only we would not call it Y because it had a different cause. Therefore X is counterfactually necessary for Y – but it is a Kripke-type necessity of origin.[19] This approach implies that events are individuated by their causes, and we have already discussed the problems of circularity that accompany individuating events by their causes.[20] It also implies that Mackie's counterfactual account of causality employs two notions of necessity: In one sense a factor is necessary for the effect relative to the circumstances (i.e. relative to the bundle of factors that make up the cause in question), and in another sense the bundle of factors is necessary for the effect. The second type relies on dubious metaphysics of one type or another; the first type appeals to our intuitive understanding of counterfactuals.

Events cannot be individuated by their causes, and it is not clear that they can be individuated by the exact nature of the factors that constitute them. It could be argued that the breaking of a certain window at a certain time was one event, which could have happened in a number of different ways. The exact pattern of the breaking could happen in any number of ways, each way corresponding to different numbers and shapes of the pieces of glass produced. Clearly, slight variations are possible. On the other hand, as far as logical possibility goes, or indeed physical possibility, there is no reason why exactly the same pattern of breaking could not be caused by the throwing of several different objects.[21]

19 Ibid., p. 391.   20 See Chapter 7, Section 3.
21 Chapter 3 of *The Cement of the Universe* is about lawlike regularities, and the terms 'necessary' and 'sufficient' in that context have to do with forms of regularity. Regularities sustain counterfactuals, but the meaning of causal statements is still given by the conditionals, though their grounds may well include the corresponding regularities. Mackie says that the *full cause* of a certain effect is a disjunction of bundles of factors (*ABC* or *DGH* or *JKL*). Since several different bundles could precede any given effect ia a way governed by a law, the disjunction of those bundles is necessary and sufficient for the effect. The *full cause*, however, cannot be regarded as anything of ontological significance, since it is a disjunction. Each factor of each bundle is an *insufficient* but *nonredundant* part of an

203

Mackie also considers whether a cause is sufficient for the effect, that is, sufficient in the counterfactual sense and of course relative to the circumstances. To illustrate the place of sufficient conditions in causality Mackie considers three different vending machines that deliver bars of chocolate operating in different ways. K: This machine normally delivers a bar of chocolate whenever a coin is put in the slot. If it does not, it is because of some easily discovered fault. It will also deliver if certain foreign coins are put in or if the mechanism is tampered with. This machine is deterministic, and *in normal circumstances* the insertion of the correct coin is a necessary and sufficient condition for the effect – namely, the delivery of a bar of chocolate. However, in non-normal circumstances the insertion of the right type of coin is not necessary for the effect.

Note that it is not some particular event that is necessary for the effect but rather a narrow event type. Examples like this show that the way in which a cause can be necessary for its effect has to do with event type, not the concrete event. Therefore it also shows that the type of necessity cannot be the Kripke-type necessity of origin.

L: This machine is indeterministic. In normal circumstances it only delivers a bar of chocolate when a coin is put in the slot, so the event of putting a coin in the slot is necessary in the circumstances for the effect. But sometimes, as a matter of pure chance, it does not deliver the expected result on the insertion of the coin. So even in normal circumstances the cause is not sufficient for the effect.

M: The third machine is also indeterministic. In normal circumstances it delivers a bar of chocolate whenever a coin is put in. But the machine has the peculiarity of sometimes delivering bars of chocolate by chance, purely on its own initiative, whether a coin is put in or not. So in normal circumstances the insertion of a coin is sufficient for the effect, but not necessary. This machine is unusual in that sometimes it acts in a causal fashion and sometimes in a non-causal fashion. Mackie suggests that it may be possible to decide which way the machine is acting by examining the mechanism; we could look to see, for example, whether both the earlier and later

---

unnecessary but *sufficient* condition – an inus condition. The inus condition as an analysis of what it means for a factor to be a cause only applies to deterministic situations. If events were causes, then it could be plausibly maintained that all deterministic causes were inus conditions for their effects. But the conclusions of the section on causality and continuity (Chapter 7, Section 4) show that not all inus conditions are causes.

stages of the mechanism were operating. From the point of view of what is going on in reality, we may say that in any particular act of delivering a bar of chocolate the machine acts either causally or non-causally; it cannot act in both modes at once. This will be true regardless of whether we are able to discover which mode it is operating in.

Mackie says that the cause is necessary in the circumstances for the effect: X caused Y entails that X was necessary in the circumstances for Y. In the case of machine M the insertion of the coin is not in general necessary for the effect, but if the effect occurs without the insertion of a coin, then the machine is acting non-causally and presumably the circumstances are different. Either Mackie is appealing here to the concrete event circumstances, or he is simply requiring that circumstances be causal circumstances. Either way there are problems. What is at issue is the operating of the machine. Is it causal or not? The mode of operation of the machine is not "circumstances" in the usual sense of passive, stable factors that nevertheless have to be there, though they could be replaced by other factors. The original idea was to explain causality in terms of counterfactuals; here, in order to make his counterfactual analysis fit Mackie has to appeal to an understanding of when the machine is operating causally or non-causally.

Mackie is aware that in many cases the cause is not sufficient in the counterfactual sense for the effect; his machines show that "this is not required, though in general it holds for what we regard as causes, at least in the physical sphere. Indeterministic machines are pretty rare."[22] By the 'physical sphere', Mackie probably means the world of large material objects that are discussed by ordinary language and considered by ordinary thought, hence the expression 'what we regard as causes'. On the other hand, for physics indeterministic machines are an important paradigm.

Whether in ordinary thought we think of the cause as normally necessary and sufficient in the circumstances for the effect, I cannot say. It seems clear, however, that Mackie has himself shown that there are examples of causality where the cause is not sufficient for the effect, and to my mind his examples show that strictly speaking it is not necessary either. His machine K shows that. It is a defect of his theory that there is some ambiguity and obscurity surrounding

---

22 Mackie, *The Cement of the Universe*, p. 43.

the appropriate sense of "necessary". What is more, it seems that ordinary thought is quite able to recognize those examples of causal situations where the cause is not necessary or is not sufficient. There is no reason to think that within "ordinary thought" there is a single coherent notion of causality, nor is there any reason to think that if there were that it would be metaphysically significant.

The picture of a cause as a bundle of factors where all the factors are severally necessary and jointly sufficient is appealing from an empirical point of view, since we can imagine varying each factor with the others held constant to see which factors are necessary for a certain effect. It is a theory of causality that appears to mirror the epistemology of the sciences. On the other hand, we are not usually so much interested in whether the ball is thrown or not, but in what happens when the speed is varied continuously. Presumably the cause is an event that is made up of a number of factors, including there being a ball with a certain velocity as the main factor. What we are being told is that if that main factor is absent, then the event would not take place; not that if the velocity were different, the event would not take place, but simply if the whole ball-with-velocity factor were absent. This may be true. But the effect would still take place if the ball had any number of velocities. This view takes each event as individuated by a velocity even when considered counterfactually. If person A throws a certain ball at time t, he could throw it at any number of velocities, but each constitutes a different event. Many different but very similar events could then be the cause of the given effect. The counterfactual approach considers only the presence or absence of each factor within each finely individuated event.

Metaphysically, it appears that the counterfactual approach presupposes that there are individual factors that conform to a type, and that each type can figure in many different causal situations. Each event that is regarded as a cause has to be a collection of such factors. Presumably each factor, considered as a type, acts in the same way in each causal situation. Counterfactual theorists acknowledge that a cause consists of factors, but have no explanation of how they are put together. There cannot be counterfactual propositions about the component factors, since they cannot act alone; and even if there were, there would be no way of putting counterfactual propositions about individual factors together to get a counterfactual proposition about the whole situation. To understand how the factors combine one has to consider causal relations.

The metaphysics of causality concerns those factors, the causal relations they give rise to, and how they combine in causal situations:

What *is* an ideal situation for studying a particular factor? It is a situation in which all other 'disturbing' factors are missing. And what is special about that? *When all other disturbances are absent, the factor manifests its power explicitly in its behaviour.* When nothing else is going on, you can see what tendencies a factor has by looking at what it does. This tells you something about what will happen in very different mixed circumstances – but only if you assume that the factor has a fixed capacity that it carries with it from situation to situation.[23]

Cartwright's 'factors' correspond to my 'basic attributes'. I understand the "powers" and "tendencies" of basic attributes as the causal relations they can give rise to, and the changes the causal relations can produce – corresponding to two different types of natural law. These types of law arise from looking at natural laws from the point of view of causality, and I understand both as relations between universals. They say what would happen if a certain kind of attribute acted alone, or at least with a minimal number of other factors, and in theory they allow us to work out what would happen when many bodies and their attributes act together. At the end of the preceding section I showed how the first two types of causal law as well as the laws that govern the combination of causal relations enabled us to determine how a network of causal relations implied counterfactual conditionals.[24]

23 Nancy Cartwright, *Nature's Capacities and Their Measurement*, pp. 190–1.
24 There are also counterfactuals that do not correspond to causality, such as the proposition that if the birth of a certain individual had not occurred, his death would not have occurred. Mackie says that it is among the condition or field; it is not the highlighted cause. Kim gives other examples.

9

Arbitrary particulars and physical objects

1. SETS AS ARBITRARY PARTICULARS

Although the criterion of identity for a set may be clear, it is not clear what a set is. It is not clear in what sense a set is one thing, or what it is that binds its elements together to make it one thing. A number of attempts have been made to answer this question, but unfortunately none of them appears to be very satisfactory. By reviewing some of these answers I shall try to show that sets of particulars deserve to be called arbitrary particulars. The basis of my discussion will be Max Black's discussion of the nature of sets as collections, as abstract objects, and as examples of plural reference.[1]

The elements of a set have to be sharply demarcated things. It has to be made clear that it is the copse that is to be the element of the set, and not the five trees as trees that make up the copse; and it has to be made clear that it is the material object as such and not its constituent parcel of matter that is to be the element of the set. Each element must therefore have associated with it an unambiguous criterion of identity. And since each type of particular has its own criterion of identity, if follows that an element of a set enters into membership only as a particular of a certain type. Of course other things besides particulars can be elements of sets, but for the purposes of this work I am only interested in sets of particulars, because I am only interested in things that could be real constituents of the spatio-temporal world.

Collecting particulars together to form the sort of whole relevant to a set does not make any difference to them physically, either to their natures or to the relations between them. Even for physical objects, the relevant sort of collecting together is not a matter of putting them together in one spatial location. The spatial proximity that

1 Cf. Max Black, "The Elusiveness of Sets", and Eric Stenius, "Sets".

has everything to do with forming of packs, bunches, and flocks is irrelevant to sets. It is even more obvious with numbers that when they are "collected" together to form a set they are not moved together spatially and their natures are not changed.[2]

If a set is understood as certain things collected together, then the word 'collect' is not being used in the literal sense of collecting things together spatially, which means putting them within a certain boundary. The word 'collect', then, must be used in some figurative sense. If the elements are not collected spatially, perhaps they are collected in thought: "But so long as no sense has been supplied for 'assembling' or 'collecting,' the expression 'assembling *in thought*' is a *flatus vocis*: what makes no sense in reality, the mysterious conversion of several things into one, makes no sense 'in thought' either."[3] Still it seems very difficult to avoid the notion of collecting altogether. If certain physical objects are elements of a set, then their location is irrelevant to the set; the nature of the set is unaffected by how closely they are packed together or how far apart they are scattered. Nevertheless, when we think of a set we do think of the elements as collected together; otherwise all those explanations of sets in terms of packs, bunches, and flocks would not help us to understand what a set is, whereas it seems that they are not completely misleading. There may, perhaps, be a difference between things *collected in thought* and things *thought of as collected*.

If sheep are collected together spatially so that they lie within one boundary, then the result is a spatial collection of particulars; it is called a 'flock of sheep' in one use of the term 'flock'. What is the criterion of identity for this spatial collection of sheep? The essential features of a spatial collection in this sense are a spatial boundary and a type of particular so that the criterion of identity should be as follows: If x and y are spatial collections of sheep, then x is identical with y if and only if they can be regarded as having the same closed convex spatial boundary and they contain the same sheep. The type of particular has to be mentioned, because there may be other things within the same boundary. Those other things within the boundary are not relevant – this form of abstraction is already reminiscent of a set.

When a sheep leaves the boundary one spatial collection is simply replaced by another, different spatial collection, though this is not

---

2 Black, "The Elusiveness of Sets", pp. 620–2.   3 Ibid., p. 620.

the case for a flock of sheep in the usual sense of the word 'flock'. There will still be a spatial collection when only one sheep is left, but when that one leaves there will cease to be a spatial collection. This is not dictated by the criterion of identity as we have given it, and our intuitions about collections of objects might lead us to reject collections with one or two members as not being flocks. The notion of a singleton spatial collection can be maintained formally, but perhaps not the fiction of a null spatial collection.

In fact, two spatial collections of sheep can be the same even though the boundaries are different. It depends, of course, on how the boundary is to be specified, since, though the sheep really are collected together, they are within many closed convex boundaries, which are imaginary anyway. The criterion of identity has to specify that it is *possible* to regard the spatial collections x and y as having the same spatial boundary. Apart from the mention of the boundary the criterion of identity for a spatial collection is the same as that for a set. An explanation of the notion of a spatial collection, which is not the same as a criterion of identity, is that it is a set of particulars within a closed convex boundary. 'The sheep' in 'the sheep within the boundary' could be understood as a term with plural reference, but a spatial collection is something singular, so in fact it has to be understood as an example of singular reference. It appears then that our attempt to explain the notion of "spatial collection" depends on the notion of set.

If a spatial collection is to be explained as a collection of sheep in the literal sense of the word 'collection', then the process of forming the collection has to start with collecting sheep together and putting them within a boundary, but that is not precise enough. You have to collect together certain sheep, and there may already be sheep within your boundary and you will need to get rid of those sheep. Therefore to form a spatial collection certain sheep have to be collected together spatially within a boundary so that no other sheep lie within that boundary. But by now the dependence of the notion of "collection", in the literal sense, on the notion of "set" should be clear. If a spatial collection is not certain sheep within a spatial boundary, then it is *whatever* sheep may be within a certain boundary, which is a different notion altogether and of doubtful usefulness.

There is indeed something mysterious about regarding a set as certain things collected in thought so that the resulting whole is a mental construct. A set is something objective; it remains what it is whether anyone is thinking about it or not, and there are sets no one

210

has thought about and whose elements have therefore not been through the process of mental construction. Besides, the mind does not make any difference to the things it supposedly collects together into a whole.

As Max Black puts it, the line around the things so collected is as imaginary as the equator.[4] But though the equator may be imaginary, it is in a sense objective, and the boundary around a spatial, or literal, collection is just as imaginary or objective.[5] Think of a sculptor inspecting a block of marble. He sees in it, in a figurative sense, a large number of shapes, any one of which he could realize by cutting the marble. Those shapes are not instanced, so they are not real constituents of the world, but in a sense they are objective. Those shapes collect quantities of marble, which can be thought of either as continuously divisible wholes or as spatial collections of molecules, and providing the shapes are simply connected the collection of molecules is a collection in the literal sense. The difference between a set and a collection of physical objects in the literal sense is that for a set the spatial boundary is disconnected whereas for a spatial collection the spatial boundary is simply connected.

This does not explain the nature of sets, because a disconnected spatial boundary has to be explained as a set of connected boundaries. George Bealer criticizes the ontological significance of sets by saying that sooner or later explanations of the concept of set fall back on the "invisible plastic bag" conception.[6] We should add that those plastic bags will have to carry labels and be capable of intersecting each other. Nevertheless these considerations show how an "imaginary" boundary can collect, and how that collection is in a sense objective. The collection is not a mental construct in the sense that it depends on the mind; it is, however, things *thought of as collected*. A set is an arbitrary particular in the sense that it is things thought of as collected.

The notion of spatial collection is a formal version of our ordinary ideas of flocks, groups, and bunches. The criterion of identity allows for a unit spatial collection, showing its formal nature, but it seems unreasonable to legislate that there should be a null spatial collection. A spatial collection is a collection of things that actually

4 Ibid., p. 621.
5 In Frege's sense of *objective* as opposed to *real* or *actual*; cf. Frege, *Foundations of Arithmetic*, Section 26.
6 Bealer, *Quality and Concept*, p. 106.

exist, so that if the members of a spatial collection are particulars, as we assume they must be, then a spatial collection must itself be a particular – something that inhabits the spatio-temporal world.

If we ignore for the moment the dependence of the notion of spatial collection on the notion of set, we can form a notion of set by modifying the notion of spatial collection: Drop the reference to spatial boundaries in the criterion of identity and legislate that there shall be a null set. The criterion of identity is silent on the issue of a null collection or null set, so it is permissible to legislate it into existence; all that is required is that the notion so formed be consistent. A set of this type would have particulars that actually exist as members and would itself be a particular, and like a spatial collection it would have persistence conditions.

This is not, however, the notion of set that is always employed when talking about sets of particulars. There appears to be a notion of set according to which a set can have as members any particulars that did at one time exist. The ancient library at Alexandria could be included in the set of libraries, even though there is no longer any such library. Such a set does not have persistence conditions, and it is not a particular in the usual sense. It might be regarded as a particular in the sense that the library at Alexandria is still a particular, although I cannot understand the metaphysical significance of that claim. The notion of a set that can include past particulars needs clarifying.

There appear to be three notions of "set of particulars": (1) where the members have to be particulars that actually exist in the present; (2) where the members exist in a four-dimensional sense of "existence", so that past, present, and future libraries are included in the set of all libraries; and (3) where the members are particulars that can be successfully referred to, so that future members are excluded. The last two correspond to two different ways of accounting for the inclusion of past particulars.

If the universe of discourse is determined by (1), then it appears that a set is a particular in the same way that its members are particulars. If it is determined by (2), then it could be claimed that a set has four-dimensional "existence", although this is not the same as existence as an abstract object. If it is determined by (3), the ontological status of sets of particulars is not clear – the problems raised are simply passed on to the theory of reference. Whichever notion of set of particulars we choose there are problems arising from the ontological status of the members. (1) has problems arising from

212

the fact that according to special relativity simultaneity is relative to the frame of reference, so that which sheep exist now depends on the frame of reference. (2) has associated with it all the problems of the notion of four-dimensional "existence". (3) is not based on an ontological notion at all; it is based on the semantic notion of reference.

A set of particulars, then, is merely something that satisfies the following conditions: It has the well-known criterion of identity; the members are selected from a universe of discourse given by (1), (2), or (3); the members have clear criteria of identity; and there is a null set. These notions of set can presumably be used consistently, but each notion is something of a construction and has serious ontological problems associated with it. My claim is that sets are arbitrary objects as opposed to naturally given objects. Not only are the members arbitrarily chosen, but it appears that the notion itself is not a naturally given notion.

The view that a set is an abstract object is founded on the view that a concept itself is something abstract; in other words, a concept is an inhabitant of Frege's third realm. It starts by considering the extensions of concepts. If a concept is something abstract, it follows that a feature of a concept will itself be something abstract; the extension of a concept is a feature of the concept and hence something abstract.[7] Since an extension is something abstract, there is no reason why concepts with no instances or only one instance should not have extensions in the same sense other concepts do. What collects together the members of an extension is that they all possess something in common – namely, they all fall under the same concept. So the extension of a concept is an abstract object with which the particulars that fall under the concept have a relation, a relation that for some reason is called 'membership'.

7 Cf. Black, "The Elusiveness of Sets", pp 622–4. Frege denies that extensions are collections: "The extension of a concept does not consist of objects falling under the concept, in the way, e.g., that a wood consists of trees; it attaches to the concept and to this alone. The concept takes logical precedence of its extension" (Frege, "A Critical Elucidation of Some Points in E. Schröder, *Vorlesungen über die Algebra der Logik*", p. 228). "I move on to the extension of a concept. The word itself indicates that we are not dealing with something spatial and physical, but something logical" (*Posthumous Writings*, p. 181). "The extension of a concept simply has its being in the concept, not in the objects which belong to it; these are not its parts" (ibid., p. 183). For Frege both a concept (reference of a predicate) and its extension are extensional, though the concept is unsaturated, whereas its extension is saturated. Both are abstract.

Unfortunately this view that sets are abstract objects sheds little light on the nature of sets. It assumes that we both understand and accept the view that concepts are abstract things. For Frege a concept is something unsaturated but extensional, differing from the extension itself only in that it is unsaturated. Although the extension is saturated, the concept is prior to the extension – you have to grasp the concept first.[8] In fact Fregean concepts seem more obscure than sets themselves. And it is difficult to see how this view could transfer to other ontological theories about what predicates refer to. It would not make any sense, for example, to understand an extension as a feature of one of the universals of immanent realism. It is difficult to understand what feature of a universal could be its extension. A feature of a universal would be a second-order universal and a necessary property of a universal, and something similar should be true for Fregean concepts. Perhaps the view that an extension is a feature of a concept gains such plausibility as it has from the obscurity of the notion of Fregean concept.

The view that sets are abstract objects has to assume that concepts that apply to particulars determine a well-defined collection – in the figurative sense. In fact, physical spatio-temporal considerations are important in considering whether a well-defined collection corresponds to such a concept even though it is supposed to be abstract. Take "sheep" as an example of a concept. It is all very well saying that its extension is an abstract object, but it is not clear that there is an extension until it is determined whether there is a well-defined membership – in other words, a well-defined collection of animals. My point is that our search is a search for a well-defined membership, that is, a well-defined collection; we are not searching for a well-defined feature of an abstract object.

As it stands the abstract objects view of sets leaves many sets unaccounted for, including subsets of extensions and sets of arbitrarily chosen things – unless, that is, a concept can be found to cover virtually any list of diverse, but well-demarcated, things. Recently John Bigelow has suggested a device to do just this, only he regards a set as a universal, not as a feature of an abstract object.[9]

8 Cf. Frege's letter to Husserl of 24 May 1891: Gottlob Frege, *Philosophical and Mathematical Correspondence*, p. 63.
9 Bigelow, *The Reality of Numbers*, pp. 103–9; cf. Bigelow and Pargetter, *Science and Necessity*, pp. 366–76.

Consider the open sentence

$$(x_1 = a_1) \ \& \ (x_2 = a_2) \ \& \ . \ . \ . \ \& \ (x_n = a_n).$$

It corresponds to a certain n–place relation that holds between the individuals $a_1, a_2, \ . \ . \ . \ , a_n$ and between no other things. Bigelow regards this relation as the same thing as the set $\{a_1, a_2, \ . \ . \ . \ , a_n\}$.

Bigelow also observes that all universals can be divided into equivalence classes by the relation of coextensiveness, though the notion of equivalence class cannot be used to explain what a set is. A set can then be explained as something shared in common by each coextensive universal.[10] This, of course, does not define the notion of set or explain the nature of sets; it merely gives a criterion of identity. Bigelow appears to identify what coextensive universals have in common with his n–place relation, though it is not a matter of the universals' having something in common in the sense of having a common feature, which would be a second–order universal.

Bigelow has indeed found a method for constructing a predicate that corresponds to one and only one set. Whether there is a universal corresponding to it is an ontological issue, and it is only if there is a universal corresponding that he can be said to have explained the nature of sets. His n–place predicate is a universal only if predicates such as ' $= a_1$' correspond to universals and if conjunctions of universals are also universals. Having no reason to believe either, I cannot accept that the n–place predicate corresponds to a universal.[11] In any event it is difficult to see how a conjunction could be a relation in any ontologically significant sense.[12]

Black himself thinks that the nature of sets can be explained in terms of the ordinary language phenomenon of plural reference.[13] Referring to a set is simply a matter of referring to several things at

---

10 Ibid., Bigelow, *The Reality of Numbers*, p. 104. This was also Frege's view; see Black, "The Elusiveness of Sets", p. 627.

11 See Chapter 1, Section 2, note 25. In Chapter 4, Section 3, I argued that conjunctions of universals are not themselves universals.

12 He also suggests that a set is plural essence, since a set as a universal is a conjunction of individual essences, each expressed by 'being a'. Some things that are elements of sets may have individual essences, but it seems that particulars do not. Even if a particular had an individual essence it would not be expressed by 'being a '. If it could be so expressed everything that could be named would have an individual essence.

13 See Black, "The Elusiveness of Sets", pp. 628–31, and cf. Peter Simons, *Parts: A Study in Ontology*, pp. 141–8.

the same time. Referring to two things at the same time is no more mysterious than pointing to two things at the same time, and pointing to two things at the same time is no more mysterious than touching two things at the same time, which is obviously possible. This shows the possibility of plural reference.

Plural reference occurs when there is plural predication, such as *a* and *b* and *c* are *F*, and it has to be understood in terms of plural predication. For example, in ordinary language it is possible to say that Tom, Dick, and Harry are Corsicans. But plural reference is just a convenient way of combining singular reference. The explanation of what is meant by '*a* and *b* and *c* are *F*' is that *a* is *F* and *b* is *F* and *c* is *F*. What combines *a* and *b* and *c* together is that they are each individually *F*, and so the three statements can be conveniently combined. There is thus no explanation of singular reference to a set as a set, or of why a set is an individual. And there is nothing here that explains singular predication of the set itself.[14]

It does appear very difficult to say what a set is without making use of the notion of set. Although it is not possible to explain the nature of sets of particulars in terms of literal collections of particulars, it is difficult to exclude altogether the notion of collection from the notion of set. A set is an arbitrary particular in the sense that it is things *thought of as collected* in some way. There is certainly nothing given to us that binds the elements together to make them a set; the imaginary boundaries and invisible plastic bags have no ontological significance. Whatever principle it is that binds a randomly chosen number of things together to form a single set is exactly the same as whatever principle it is that binds all the things of a certain type together to form a set. They are both equally sets, and they both are sets in the same way.

David Lewis understands a many-membered set as a mereological fusion of unit sets.[15] In general a mereological fusion can be arbitrarily divided into parts in any number of different ways; the role of unit sets as atomic parts is to restrict the number of ways the fusion can be partitioned. Nevertheless the many-membered sets are still arbitrary selections. Although a many-membered set is explained as a mereological fusion of unit sets, we will only know

14 Cf. Armstrong's comments on numbers, Volume II, p. 74.
15 See David Lewis, *Parts of Classes,* and Armstrong, "Classes Are States of Affairs".

what sort of thing a set is, and what sort of fusion is involved, when we know what a unit set is.

In his paper "Classes Are States of Affairs" Armstrong provides an interpretation of Lewis's theory. A unit set is the state of affairs of the individual concerned possessing the property of unithood, which is the property of having some unit-making property. The type of fusion involved in constructing a many-membered set is conjunction of states of affairs. For Armstrong the set $\{a, b\}$ is the state of affairs of a's having unithood and b's having unithood. But it is not clear what binds the two distinct states of affairs together to make a unit. To say that the two states of affairs are conjoined, or indeed that the two unit sets are mereologically fused, adds nothing about what makes them a unit. There is nothing in reality that makes the unit sets a combined unit; they are only conjoined or mereologically fused in someone's thought.

Although we know what a conjunction of propositions is, it is not clear what a conjunction of states of affairs is. A conjunction binds two propositions together to make a single proposition in the well-known truth-functional way, whereas "conjunction" for states of affairs is not truth-functional. Since a state of affairs is supposed to be an entity, a particular according to Armstrong, its existing is what corresponds to a proposition's being true. But although propositions can easily be false, it does not make any sense to talk about entities not existing, even if those entities are states of affairs. There is a "conjunction" of two states of affairs when both exist together. A "conjunction" of two entities existing together is apparently a collection, or set, of the two entities; the notion of set is explained in terms of the notion of set. If not, then the notion of conjunction of states of affairs is too obscure to explain the notion of set.

A member of a set is a unit on account of a unit-making property that will be ontologically significant in some way if the member of the set is. Although the actual unit-making property is ontologically significant, the property of unithood, which is the property of having some unit-making property, is not. Consequently there is no reason for taking the state of affairs of something's having the property of unithood, which is Armstrong's unit set, as ontologically significant. It follows that many-membered sets are not ontologically significant either.

It is also not clear whether Armstrong is saying that sets and certain states of affairs have the same properties and therefore the notion of set can be replaced by that of state of affairs, or whether the notion of set has all along been nothing other than that of state of affairs.

2. PARCELS OF MATTER

A physical object is a spatio-temporal particular that has its shape or structure as a natural principle of unity and that is causally significant. A material object is a physical object that is made out of matter such that the matter is topologically connected. Material objects are the "bodies" of classical physics. Physical objects also include particulars that have structure in which the matter is disconnected (as is the case with the solar system or a gas) or that are not made of matter at all (as is the case with classical fields). Shape or structure can persist through time, so a physical object is something that can persist through time. All the macroscopic physical objects we know about, except for fields, are thought of as composed of matter.

If a material object is something that has its shape or structure and the cohesion of its components as a natural principle of unity, then there is a distinction between the material object itself and the matter the material object is made of. The relationship between the two is the "is" of constitution.[16]

If all the gold of a gold coin is used to form a gold ring, then there is something that persists through the change; that something is the gold, or some gold, or what some people call a quantity of gold. It is what I shall call a parcel of gold.[17] The change from coin to ring is a change of shape and therefore a change of the relative distribution of the matter. It is also a topological change in that the coin, which was simply connected, is replaced by the ring, which is multiply connected with one hole. If the ring were now melted down and the gold used to form two gold rings, or several gold earrings, then the gold as gold would still persist; it is the same parcel of matter de-

---

16 Cf. Wiggins, *Sameness and Substance*, p. 30, and Lowe, *Kinds of Being*, pp. 3–4.
17 Cf. Helen Cartwright, "Quantities", and "Heraclitus and the Bath Water", where she emphasizes the expression 'some water'; V. C. Chappell, "Stuff and Things", uses 'parcel' as a technical term. Locke talks about "masses of matter" and "parcels of matters"; *An Essay concerning Human Understanding*, II, xvii, 3. I prefer the term 'parcel' because I have already used the term 'quantity' for universals such as determinate masses.

spite the fact that the gold has been divided and separated. In fact, provided that no gold is destroyed, and that all the matter of the parcel continues to be gold, then we still have the same parcel of matter, however much the gold is divided or scattered.

The story of the gold and the changes it undergoes shows that we have a conception of matter as something that persists through time independently of the persistence through time of material objects. The criterion of identity for a parcel of matter is different from that for a material object.[18] Similar stories have been told about "some coffee" that goes from pot to cup and is then drunk. Liquids are easier to understand in terms of parcels of matter and less naturally understood as material objects with a shape or structure, though there is cohesion between their component parts. The matter that persists through time and that I have called a parcel of matter is a particular, since it occurs only once.

There are two conceptions of matter corresponding to two ways matter could be: Either matter is continuously divisible or it is atomic. Atomic matter: Anything that is made of gold is made of atoms that are gold atoms, but the atoms themselves are not made of gold. The atoms have components and structure, and that structure may explain the nature of gold – but that is another story. Traditionally atoms are thought of as indivisible particles, though this conception is not necessary for our purposes. Continuously divisible matter: Anything that is made of gold, whatever its size, can be divided into pieces that are also made of gold, and made of gold in the same way.

If matter is atomic, then the criterion of identity for a parcel of matter is this: If m and n are parcels of matter, then m is identical with n if and only if the atoms that make up m are the same atoms as those that make up n. This criterion depends on the criterion of identity for the atoms that make up a parcel. The persistence conditions for a parcel of matter similarly depend on the persistence conditions for the atoms: If the component atoms each persist through time, so does the parcel.[19]

18 Cf. Lowe, *Kinds of Being*, pp. 97ff.
19 Atoms obey the quantum mechanical principle of indistinguishability, which implies that they are in some ways similar to fields. In ordinary quantum mechanics there are at any given time a fixed number of atoms that are presumably distinct from each other; indistinguishability presents a difficulty for their persistence as individuals.

A parcel of matter understood in this way is a collection of atoms that is indifferent to how the component atoms are arranged together or how far apart they are scattered. It is therefore very similar to a first-order set[20] with the atoms as elements, particularly if parcels can overlap so that an atom can belong to more than one parcel, though it is not necessary to make this assumption about parcels. The main differences are that there are no parcels of parcels analogous to sets of sets; a parcel of parcels would not be a parcel of matter, because material objects could not be made out of it. And it could be argued that there is no null parcel corresponding to the null set. There would be no reason to understand a null parcel as specifically a parcel of matter; it would just be the null set.

The denial of a null parcel stands in the way of parcels being understood as first-order sets of atoms. However, if an atomic parcel is a collection of atoms, in the figurative sense of 'collection', then there is no more reason to deny the existence of a null parcel than there is to deny the existence of a null set; a null collection is as acceptable or as unacceptable as a null set. Introducing a null collection is not like introducing a null object like a null atom.[21]

Alternatively an atomic parcel could be regarded as an *aggregate* of its atoms in George Bealer's sense.[22] Bealer argues that a collection, according to our ordinary understanding of the term, is more like an aggregate than a set. In set theory the membership relation is not transitive, and a distinction is made between membership and set inclusion. Aggregates, on the other hand, obey a transitivity principle: If an individual, x, is a member of an aggregate, y, and the aggregate y is a member of another aggregate, z, then the individual x is also a member of the aggregate z.[23] In effect, theories of aggregates start with first-order sets of basic individuals and then impose restrictions, such as no null aggregate and no distinction between an individual and the aggregate that contains only it.

Armstrong uses the term 'aggregate' in a similar way. The example he gives is that the aggregate of armies is the same as the aggregate of soldiers. Soldiers are the basic sort of individual, and if an army is an aggregate of soldiers Armstrong's aggregates obey the

---

20 See G. Boolos, "The Iterative Conception of Set".
21 Cf. P. T. Geach, "On Rigour in Semantics".
22 Bealer, *Quality and Concept*, p.105.
23 Ibid., p. 103. Bealer also gives a "power principle", p. 104. Cf. Tyler Burge, "A Theory of Aggregates", p. 106.

transitivity principle.[24] Frege, on the other hand, uses the term 'aggregate' for anything in which we can distinguish parts.[25] However, it is not clear exactly what he means, since parts must be considered under some determination. Either it is an aggregate consisting of certain basic individuals, each enrolled as an individual of a certain kind, or else it is a parcel of matter consisting of matter of a certain kind.

Atomic parcels can be understood as obeying the transitivity principle: If a certain atom, x, is a member of a parcel, y, which is a subparcel of a parcel, z, then x is a member of the parcel z. The relation between subparcel and parcel is a spatial part–whole relation and an example of the part–whole relation of mereology. If the membership relation between atom and parcel were also to be understood as the same spatial part–whole relation, and the parts of the atoms were not taken into account, then the theory of parcels restricted to a given time is formally similar to mereology. And in fact it should be a model of mereology.[26] It would also have to be assumed that an atom can be a part of more than one parcel. It is an advantage that there is normally no null individual in mereology.[27]

If matter is continuous, then it is more difficult to formulate a criterion of identity for parcels. Material points are not ontologically significant entities and so cannot be regarded as the atomic components of continuous parcels, though in a sense the subparcels of continuous parcels are their components. Consider the following criterion of identity: If m and n are parcels of matter, then m is identical with n if and only if the subparcels of m are the same as the subparcels of n. It is essential to a continuous parcel that it can be divided into subparcels, either by physical division and separation or by imaginary cuts. Although it is true that identical parcels will have the same subparcels, the criterion of identity is of no value because it depends on the criterion of identity for subparcels that have the same criterion of identity as parcels themselves.

---

24 Armstrong, Volume I, pp. 29–31. According to Tyler Burge, "Since aggregates are individuated by their member-components and the member-components differ, the aggregate of molecules and the aggregate of atoms would not be the same" (ibid., p. 113). The reason is that a molecule is an individual and not an aggregate of atoms.

25 Frege, *Posthumous Writings*, p. 181.

26 It appears that mereological concepts are tenseless or eternal; Simons, *Parts: A Study in Ontology*, p. 105. For comments on mereology that I sympathize with, see Lowe, *Kinds of Being*, pp. 89–96.

27 Ibid. Simons, *Parts: A Study in Ontology.*, p. 13.

Although a parcel of matter can be divided into separate pieces again and again, at any given time there are certain pieces of matter that are natural components of the parcel – namely, the pieces of matter that are connected. These pieces of matter can be called 'connected parcels'. Consider then the following criterion of identity: If *m* and *n* are parcels of matter, then *m* is identical with *n* if and only if *m* and *n* have the same component connected parcels. This depends on the criterion of identity for connected parcels. Two connected parcels are the same if they are made of the same type of matter and occupy the same space. Combining the criteria of identity we obtain: If *m* and *n* are parcels of matter, then *m* is identical with *n* if and only if the connected subparcels of *m* are made of the same type of matter and occupy the same regions of space as the connected subparcels of *n*. The regions of space occupied by the connected subparcels will also be connected because a connected parcel has to occupy a connected region of space.

This criterion of identity also applies to mixed parcels, which contain matter of different types. There are always sufficiently small connected subparcels that are made of one type of matter, though in this case two different connected subparcels of different types of matter need not be physically separate from each other; it is sufficient that there be a boundary between the different types of matter.

Two disjoint connected parcels of classical matter, whether atomic or continuous, cannot occupy the same place at the same time, so it seems that true mixtures are impossible.[28] Impenetrability, or solidity, for classical, continuous matter can be defined as follows: Two disjoint parcels of matter do not interpenetrate, because when they are combined together there always remain sufficiently small connected subparcels such that each belongs to one parcel or the other. Impenetrability implies that there can be no true mixtures in which two disjoint, connected parcels of matter occupy the same region of space at the same.[29] Any attempt at blending simply results in smaller and smaller connected subparcels.[30]

A necessary condition for a mixture is that the combination be *homoeomerous* – in other words, the same in every part. To understand

---

28 True mixtures are different from the mixed parcels discussed in the previous paragraph. I am thinking of solids and liquids rather than gases because solids and liquids can form connected parcels.
29 See Richard Sharvy, "Aristotle on Mixtures".
30 Cf. Sharvy on Zeno's blender; ibid., p. 444.

the concept of a mixture it is best to think of classical, continuous matter. If *a* is a connected parcel of water and *b* is a connected parcel of alcohol and *a* and *b* are combined together, then the combination is *water and alcohol;* it would be a homoeomerous mixture if every connected subparcel were also *water and alcohol* and in the same way. If there were such a thing as a homoeomerous mixture of water and alcohol, then in a sense the water would be part of the whole and so would the alcohol, but it would not be the spatial sense of the word 'part'. The water would have to remain water and the alcohol would have to remain alcohol and both occupy the same volume, in the way that two gases are said to occupy the same volume in the theory of partial pressures. On the other hand, any account of the notion of "homoeomerous" has to be in terms of spatial parts.

Unlike classical matter, classical fields can occupy the same region of space at the same time, and unlike real matter they are continuous. They come nearest to providing examples of mixtures. If two fields of different types (say, electrostatic and gravitational) occupy the same region of space, they do so independently of each other and they do not form a whole of any kind. If the two fields are of the same type they form a whole by the principle of superposition, and they act as a whole. The components of a field can be regarded as non-spatial parts of the whole, and the combination is indeed homoeomerous. It is not clear, however, that the components retain their identity, so that it makes sense to claim that the same components can be separated out again, and it appears that the whole can be resolved into components in arbitrarily many ways.[31]

A connected parcel is similar to a material object in having a spatial principle of unity, though it is topological rather than geometrical. In real life the connectedness will be due to the cohesion of its parts, though connectedness and cohesion are conceptually distinct. Because of its principle of unity a connected parcel of matter is not a parcel in the usual sense. The notion of connected parcel cannot replace that of parcel. A connected parcel is constituted out of a parcel of matter in the usual sense, and the usual notion of parcel is needed to explain the division and fusion of connected parcels. It is also usually assumed that parcels can overlap like sets, whereas connected parcels cannot be regarded as overlapping.

31 See Neil A. Sheldon, "One Wave or Three? A Problem for Realism", and the discussion of force relations in Chapter 6, Section 4.

The persistence conditions for a material object depend on its continuing to fall under the same covering concept and following a continuous trajectory. Similarly the persistence conditions for a connected parcel depend on its remaining the same type of matter and on its following a continuous trajectory that cannot branch, and it also has to remain the same matter or made out of the same matter. Unlike some material objects the persistence conditions for connected parcels depend on the persistence conditions for parcels of matter.

The criterion of identity for a parcel of continuous matter given earlier provides no help in formulating the persistence conditions for parcels of matter. If a parcel of matter is to persist through time it has to remain the same matter – which can be taken as entailing that it remain the same type of matter. All that is required is that none of the matter be destroyed. There is no need for it to have the same connected subparcels; they can be quite different owing to any number of processes of division and fusion.

There are two theories of the persistence of continuous matter through time. Eli Hirsch's view is that the identity of matter is an ultimate form of identity that explains other sorts of identity, but is not itself explained by the persistence of anything else:

> Our concept of persisting matter, even at the most commonsense level, incorporates something in the way of a theoretical-explanatory posit of an underlying mode of physical persistence which ultimately accounts for the observed behaviour of ordinary articulated objects.[32]

> The unity through time of matter, in contrast to that of familiar articulated objects, is in a sense *ultimate*.[33]

On this view it is the persistence of matter as matter that explains the persistence of properties.

Robinson's view is that the identity of matter through time is explained by the trajectories of instantiated properties.[34] A property is said to *propagate* if the present spatial distribution of the points at which it is instanced depends in a lawlike way on its preceding distribution.[35] There are groups of properties that normally propagate together such that it is not physically possible for one to split off by itself; these properties are said to be *coupled*. They are in some

32 Hirsch, *The Concept of Identity*, p. 121.
33 Ibid., p. 123.
34 Denis Robinson, "Re-identifying Matter".
35 Ibid., p. 333.

way dependent on each other but independent of other properties. These properties, I take it, are the properties associated with types of matter that are also natural kinds. They are intensive properties like density, rather than extensive properties like mass. Robinson's view is that our concept of *some matter,* or of a parcel of matter, persisting through time is the concept of such properties propagating together.[36]

As we have seen, it is essential to the persistence of a parcel of matter through time that the matter persist through any amount of fusion, division, and scattering. Robinson's theory will have to understand the continuous trajectories as ones that can split and come together again. After all, our conception of a parcel of matter persisting through time involves the imaginary tracing of the same type of matter along continuous trajectories that split and join, and something is only the same type of matter if it possesses the same properties essential to being that type of matter. Such a view is consistent with the bundle theory of particulars that is defended later in this chapter. Hirsch's alternative view seems to posit a substratum that persists through time, and we have no conception of what the persistence of a substratum amounts to.

Like a parcel of atomic matter a parcel of continuous matter is also similar to a set. And again the similarity is strengthened if the components of a parcel can be components of several parcels at the same time, as is usually assumed. A set of particulars remains the same set through time if its elements persist through time; it is indifferent to how its elements are arranged or scattered. If the elements of a continuous parcel were taken to be its connected subparcels, then the persistence of the parcel through time is indifferent to how those elements are arranged or scattered, and it is indifferent to their division or fusion.

For any given parcel there is a set of its connected subparcels, and there is also an aggregate of its connected subparcels in Bealer's sense; but neither of these is a parcel of matter. A continuous parcel does not have elements in the way that a set does, or in the way that I assume an aggregate does; its components are best thought of as parts.[37] The parts of a continuous parcel include its connected sub-

36 Ibid., p. 334.
37 In mereology an atom is an individual without proper parts; whether there are atoms is an unresolved question for mereology. See Simons, *Parts: A Study in Ontology,* pp. 16 and 41.

parcels, and it includes collections of those subparcels. Natural parts of the connected subparcels are also parts of the whole parcel, as are parts marked out by arbitrarily chosen imaginary surfaces. And, of course, collections of parts of the connected subparcels are also parts of the whole parcel. A theory of continuous parcels that used this notion of part and the spatial part–whole relation would be like the theory of atomic parcels in being formally similar to mereology.

Parts of a continuous parcel can be chosen in an infinite number of different ways, and of course parts can overlap. Any division of a parcel into a set of parts, even a set of non–overlapping parts, is the result of an arbitrary choice. In general there is nothing naturally given about the parts of a parcel in the same way that there is nothing naturally given about the parcel as a whole. The material object a parcel constitutes may have a naturally given principle of unity, but a parcel considered as a parcel does not. We have called sets and parcels arbitrary particulars; they could equally well have been called formal particulars. In any event, recourse to sets and parcels is an artificial way of organizing the world.

On the other hand, the notion of parcel of matter is important to understanding the ontology of matter, particularly in understanding persistence through time and persistence through changes. It is difficult to describe the persistence of matter without making some use of the notion of parcel. The notion of parcel of atomic matter is something we cannot do without, and the notion of parcel of continuous matter is important for an understanding of continuous classical matter, which is an important metaphysical theory. Similarly, the notion of set or the notion of aggregate is important to understanding spatial collections and parcels of atomic matter.

3. PHYSICAL OBJECTS

Sets, aggregates, and parcels of matter as arbitrary particulars cannot be the terms of causal relations. For example, a volume of gas enters into causal relations as a whole, and a gas might be thought of as an aggregate of molecules or as a set of molecules – if sets of particulars are also particulars. But it is not *as* an aggregate, or *as* a set, that it enters into causal relations. It is as some sort of particular with a natural principle of unity that the gas enters into causal relations.

Occupying one region of space there is the gas, an aggregate of molecules, and the set of molecules as well. Each of these particulars has the same components, but they are distinct particulars, perhaps formally distinct, since they have different criteria of identity and different persistence conditions. This situation is analogous to a material object and its parcel of matter "occupying" the same region of space, or to a set and an ordered set having the same components.[38]

Whatever it is that enters into the causal relations described by thermodynamics is something that has volume. Let us assume, for the moment, that the gas considered as a spatial collection of molecules has a volume. I suggest that, unlike spatial collections, aggregates of molecules or sets of molecules, as such, do not have volume. Aggregates and sets remain the same, however much their members are scattered and dispersed among other things. When scattered, an aggregate or set of molecules does not have a volume in the way that a spatial collection of molecules does. It is true that each molecule has a volume, but the volume of a gas is not the sum of the volumes of its molecules; in fact, it is nowhere near it. It could be suggested that the aggregate or set acquires a volume at the moment it begins to constitute a spatial collection. If the aggregate or set did acquire a volume, then while it had that volume it would not be distinct from the physical object the gas is, and there cannot be a distinction without some sort of difference. But an aggregate or set cannot be identical to a spatial collection. The distinction between the spatial collection of molecules and an aggregate or set of molecules must be maintained, since they have different criteria of identity and different persistence conditions.[39] Therefore aggregates and sets as such cannot have volume.

A similar conclusion can be drawn for material objects and the parcels of matter that constitute them. If a parcel of matter could acquire a shape or structure, then while it had that shape or structure it would not be distinct from the material object, since there cannot be a distinction without some sort of difference. A material object

38 In fact, the material object, its connected parcel of matter, and the parcel of matter in the usual sense "occupy" the same region of space.
39 Bealer thinks that aggregates of physical objects have mass and volume; *Quality and Concept*, p. 102. Burge thinks that aggregates of physical objects exert forces; "A Theory of Aggregates", p. 102. It is true that the masses of objects separated from each other can be added together, but whether that sum has any ontological significance depends on whether the particulars can be regarded as acting together as a whole.

cannot be identical to a parcel of matter, since they have different criteria of identity and different persistence conditions. Therefore the shape or structure that is the principle of unity of a material object cannot be a property of the parcel of matter as such that constitutes it.

Our conclusion can be generalized as follows: The structure that is the basis for the principle of unity of some unified particular cannot be a property of an arbitrary particular that constitutes the unified particular, or that is formed in some way from the components of the unified particular.

In physical interactions the structure or spatial distribution is significant. It is not just the mass but also the distribution of the mass that is causally significant, and it is not just the charge but also the distribution of the charge that is causally significant. Similarly the quantum states of atomic systems, however they are to be understood, involve spatial distributions that underlie their structure. If the structure or spatial distribution is significant to the causal interaction, then whatever it is that enters into causal relations is something that possesses structure or spatial distribution. It is not parcels of matter or aggregates or sets of particulars that are the terms of causal interactions, but particulars with principles of unity based on some spatial structure.

It must not be assumed from this that all unified particulars have the sort of precise structure possessed by a simple atom or molecule, or possessed by a piece of apparatus produced by an engineer. A gas is a unified particular and as such it can go through many changes and still remain the same, such as change of shape and volume and loss of some of its constituent molecules. Similar things can be said about a lump of solid matter. Although the persistence conditions for arbitrary particulars are generally clear – that is their virtue – the same cannot be said for all unified particulars.

The principle of unity for a material object is based partly on the connectedness of the matter that constitutes it; in other words, its parts are contiguous. Connectedness for continuous matter is a clear and precise notion, but not for real atomic matter, at least not according to our current understanding of atoms. A collection of atoms forms a connected whole if the atoms are contiguous, and though it is true that atoms can get very close to each other, there are no clear conditions for whether they touch or not. On the other hand, there are short-range forces between molecules and there are situations when they clearly operate. We cannot do without the notion of connectedness; we simply have to recognize that connectedness is an imprecise concept and sometimes a matter of degree.

I claim that the principle of unity for a material object is based on the fact that it forms a connected whole due to cohesive forces between its parts, so that it moves as a whole. In particular, it accelerates as a whole, which is reason enough to think that it enters into causal relations as a whole. And it also exchanges energy as a whole. The principle of unity for a material object is also based on its shape or structure. It is the connectedness that distinguishes material objects from other physical objects. Other physical objects, such as volumes of gas, form wholes as a result of forces or constraints that maintain the spatial relations between the parts, so that it accelerates as a whole and exchanges energy as a whole.

This claim can be illustrated by answering Mark Heller's contention that such wholes are entirely conventional:

For instance, consider the very complex causal connections between the molecules which compose a table. Suppose that those connections break down. This is a purely physical, nonconventional occurrence. But why should this count as an object's ceasing to exist? Only our conventions can supply the persistence conditions of an object. It is because of our conventions that we count this as the temporal end of an object.[40]

It is interesting that Heller admits that the intermolecular forces can objectively break down. In fact, though the intermolecular forces are essentially short-range forces, they tail off to zero asymptotically, like most other physical forces. There is, therefore, no precise point at which the force relations are broken off. Nevertheless, it would be madness to say that the short-range forces are never broken off, and Heller is wisely not prepared to succumb to that form of madness.

In a continuous process of separation, there are times when the short-range forces definitely operate; there are times when they definitely do not operate; and there is a vague transition region. This is itself an objective fact and not a matter of convention. Someone might choose a point within the vague transition region to be *the point of transition*, but though the choice of the exact point is a matter of convention, the choice is guided by something objective; one

---

40 Mark Heller, *The Ontology of Physical Objects: Four-dimensional Hunks of Matter*, p. 52.

could not, for example, choose a point far removed from the transition region.[41]

The properties of a table are ontologically determinate in the sense explained in Chapter 4. Whether there is a table is ontologically determinate in another more limited sense; there are times when the table definitely exists and times when there is definitely no table, but there is also a transition region in which whether there is a table is not clearly determined.[42]

One important difference between the table and the scattered collection of molecules is that the scattered collection does not move as a whole whereas the table does. Of course the molecules could all have exactly the same velocity, but they would not behave like that without a reason. A table is something that in general accelerates as a whole and enters into force relations as a whole. A force relation between two macroscopic objects can be regarded as the resultant of force relations between the molecular components of those objects. But this resolution cannot go on indefinitely; at some stage there must be wholes with force relations between them. I see no reason why tables should not also be such wholes. In contrast, a scattered collection of molecules does not accelerate as a whole unless there is something that makes it to be a unity, such as being confined within an enclosed vessel or if there were sufficiently strong long-range forces between the molecules.

The table also exchanges energy with other things as a whole. Because of the close proximity of the molecules to each other, it comes to a more or less uniform temperature. And any energy it absorbs is spread throughout its parts. A collection of molecules contained in a closed vessel will do the same, but a scattered collection of molecules will not. In order for a collection of molecules to act as a whole the molecules must be continuously exchanging energy with each other in some way. This is the principle of unity of a gas considered as a physical object, and it is also a form of structure.

41 The Rayleigh criterion for resolution of optical images is a convention, but it is not arbitrary; it is true, however, that its precision arises from its conventionality. There are cases when two images are definitely resolved and cases when they are not, and there is a small range of cases when it is not clear. See R. S. Longhurst, *Geometrical and Physical Optics*, pp. 282–5 and 207–8. There are difficulties associated with things being imprecise, though there are also problems associated with things being precise as in the problem of the instant of change.

42 Cf. Roderick Chisholm, "Coming into Being and Passing Away"; for other approaches to destroying tables see Lowe, *Kinds of Being*, Chapters 5 and 6.

In a continuous process of separation the molecules of a table cease to exchange energy with each other by conduction at about the same time the short-range intermolecular forces are broken off. It therefore ceases to be a whole as far as motion and force relations go, at about the same time it ceases to be a whole for thermodynamic purposes. It could continue for a while to be a different sort of thermodynamic whole, a sort of gas, if the molecules continued to exchange energy by collision instead of by conduction.

At the other extreme from a table is a physical object like the solar system, which is a physical object whose parts are anything but contiguous. But from a sufficiently large-scale point of view it can be seen that the solar system also interacts causally as a whole, and moves as a whole because of the forces that hold it together. The solar system as a whole has a natural principle of unity that is related to its spatial distribution and the forces that hold it together and govern its motion.

Spatial contiguity and cohesion of parts are principles of unity because they are responsible for something interacting causally as a whole; they also have their limitations. A physical object does not always interact causally as a whole, since a part can always be pulled away from the whole, in which case the causal interaction was primarily with the part rather than with the whole. Although an atom moves as a single thing, emits energy as a single thing, and generally enters into force relation as a single thing, the same can also be said for the proper parts of an atom. There are then two classes of causal interaction, one for the whole and one for the parts. The class of causal interaction of the solar system as a whole is perhaps not so important relative to the class of causal interaction of the planets. But that the whole is causally significant is enough to justify regarding it as a natural whole.

A scattered object as usually discussed in philosophy is composed of objects that are not only spatially separate from each other but that have no connection with each other of any importance.[43] A scattered object therefore has no naturally given principle of unity; it is a unity merely because someone has chosen to regard it as a unity. There are, indeed, scattered particulars; they are parcels of matter, but as such they do not enter into causal relations. Of course any two bodies, however distant from each other, have a common centre

43 Cf. Richard Cartwright, "Scattered Objects".

of mass, but they do not enter into causal relations as a single thing. In theory they might have a slight interaction, but so slight as to make it relatively negligible.

A possible objection to the view that unified particulars are the terms of the causal relation is the fact that in physics what is taken to be a body often appears arbitrary. For example, when Newton wished to demonstrate (or was it illustrate) his third law of motion with a thought experiment, he imagined a body cut by an imaginary plane in an arbitrary way – it is essential to the demonstration that the cut be arbitrary. He then considered the forces acting on the two arbitrarily selected bodies so formed across the imaginary plane.

It is essential to Newton's thought experiment that the body cut by the imaginary plane be a cohesive body, since the argument is that the forces on each part are equal and opposite so that there is no net force on the body as a whole. We normally think of the shape of the bodies discussed in physics as their principle of unity, and then wonder how much the shape can change and the body remain the same. Whereas, in fact, simple cohesion is also an important natural principle of unity.[44] Because its parts stick together more than they stick to anything else the body moves as a whole and therefore should be regarded as entering into force relations and energy exchanges as a whole.

If a body is to stick together as a unity, then there must be forces between its atomic parts. It is these forces that we resolve in different ways when we cut the body with an arbitrarily chosen imaginary plane. I am not sure which forces we would combine together if matter were continuously divisible, since material points cannot be regarded as real units.

It also seems possible in physics to select some bodies in an arbitrary fashion and to regard them as one body from the point of view of their centre of mass. What is questionable is whether such a body would be ontologically significant. Consider two such "bodies" formed from the planets of the solar system, one of which includes Mercury and the alternate planets, while the other includes Venus and the remaining planets. These two bodies do have well-defined centres of mass, and perhaps some formalism could be worked out whereby it could be said that they interacted with each

44 Cf. Michael Ayers, "Individuals without Sortals", p. 115.

other. But they do not react to forces as a whole: It is either the solar system as a whole or the individual planets that accelerate.

I have, in effect, made a distinction that I have not drawn attention to, namely, that between structured unified particulars, which have their shape or structure as part of their principle of unity, and unified particulars such as connected parcels and spatial collections, which have a sort of topological principle of unity. Topological unified particulars are like arbitrary particulars in having precise criteria of identity, but the price paid for this precision is that they can lose a small part and become a different particular as a consequence. They can also undergo radical changes and remain the same. For example, a small lump of gold can be beaten into a single sheet of gold leaf of immense size, and yet remain the same connected parcel.

A physical object forms a whole on account of continuous energy exchange between its parts or on account of forces or constraints that maintain the spatial relations between the parts, so that it accelerates as a whole and exchanges energy as a whole. In the examples we have discussed it appears that the maintaining of spatial relations between the parts is also important for a physical object interacting as a whole, though they need not be exactly the same spatial relations but could be spatial relations of a certain type. Because topological unified particulars can change the spatial relations between their parts so radically, it appears that we must conclude that it is structured unified particulars that are the terms of causal relations and are therefore physical particulars.

The argument we used to show that arbitrary particulars could not as such possess a shape or structure also applies to topological unified particulars. If two different material objects, which are structured unified particulars, can be made out of the same connected parcel of matter at different times, then material objects have different persistence conditions from connected parcels of matter. If a connected parcel of matter could possess a shape or structure, then for a period of time it would not differ from the structured unified particular that it constituted. Since there cannot be a difference without out a distinction, it follows that a connected parcel of matter cannot, as such, possess a shape or structure. In this too it is like an arbitrary particular.

Similarly a gas – quantity of gas or volume of gas – should not be identified with the spatial collection of its molecules. It is the physical object that it is on account of the type of continuous energy exchanges between its molecules. It would remain the same spatial collection, because it would be within the same boundary, if it condensed into a liquid, which has a different way of exchanging energy between its molecules and is causally different.

It is easy to formulate a criterion of identity for physical objects except fields: If x and y are physical objects of type f, then x is identical with y if and only if their connected parts occupy the same places. The difficulty for structured unified particulars, particularly material objects, is that they lack precise persistence conditions. When they cease to exist, they do not do it cleanly; at best there is a vague transition period. However, I argued in the discussion of the example of the table that this need not be unacceptable. In causal interactions it is not persistence conditions that are significant; it is how one particular is marked off from another. Otherwise, I suggest that each type of structured unified particular has to be dealt with on its own terms, since each type will have its own persistence conditions. Our arguments have at least shown that these will differ from those for arbitrary particulars and topological unified particulars.

When I claim that it is physical objects that are the terms of causal relations I am not claiming that it is always easy to discern which things are physical objects. It may be that in a confused situation it is the atoms or molecules that are the relevant physical objects. I cannot see any reason for doubting that atoms or molecules are objective unified particulars, and it appears that some macroscopic objects have an equally strong claim to that title.

4. SUPERVENIENCE

A possible explanation for the relation between a material object and its atomic parts is that the relation is one of supervenience.

Supervenience is essentially an asymmetric relation between two families of properties: the supervenient properties and the properties that form the supervenience base. Properties in the supervenience base are said to "determine" supervenient properties, and a supervenient property is said to be "dependent" on a property in the supervenience base.

Taking his cue from Davidson's statement that "an object cannot alter in some mental respect without altering in some physical respect", Jaegwon Kim considers a type of particular that possesses two different sorts of properties, such as mental and physical properties, and gives a formal definition of strong supervenience as follows:

So let A and B be families of properties closed under Boolean operations as before: A *strongly supervenes* on B just in case, necessarily, for each x and each property F in A, if x has F, then there is a property G in B such that x has G, and *necessarily* if any y has G, it has F.[45]

A is the family of supervenient properties and B is the supervenience base. For strong supervenience the relation of determination is in some sense a necessary relation, with the exact nature of the necessity left open.

If we ignore whether both sorts of property belong to the same particular, the relation of strong supervenience between two families of properties can be summarized by four propositions:

1. A base property cannot occur without a unique supervenient property occurring that is determined by it.
2. A supervenient property cannot occur without some base property occurring to support it.
3. There can be changes of base properties without changes of supervenient properties.
4. There cannot be changes of supervenient properties without there being changes of base properties.

All that can be said about the notions of determination and dependence, in as much as they are explained by the concept of supervenience, is said by these four propositions. These propositions are best explained by taking the relation of determination to be a many-to-one function from the family of base properties to the family of supervenient properties.

The definition of supervenience provides no reason to regard the base properties as being more ontologically significant than the supervenient properties, since there is no reason why both sorts of property should not be causally significant. There is no more reason why a particular should enter into a causal relation on account of a base property than on account of a supervenient property. And there is no reason why both should not be changed by causal relations. If a particular enters into a causal relation that induces a change

45 Jaegwon Kim, "Concepts of Supervenience", p. 165. In this paper Kim also discusses the definition of weak supervenience and points out its inadequacies.

from one base property to another, then the change determines a corresponding change of supervenient properties. On the other hand, if a particular enters into a causal relation that induces a change from one supervenient property to another, the change might be accompanied by a change of base property, or it might not. This does not imply that an accompanying change in base properties is indeterminate, since it is possible that the change of base properties be determined by something other than the determination function of the supervenience relation.

It is Kim's belief that the macroscopic world is supervenient on, reducible to, and determined by its microscopic parts: "Thus, the microdeterminateness of this table amounts to the table's 'supervenience' upon microreducible physical properties. It is in this sense that this table is *nothing but* a microphysical structure."[46] If this is true, then the physical properties of a macroscopic material object, such as its shape and mass, should be supervenient on the physical properties of its atomic or molecular components. And relations between macroscopic material objects should be supervenient on relations between their atomic or molecular components. The most obvious departure from the formal definition of supervenience is that the properties belong to different particulars: Supervenient properties belong to macroscopic objects and the base properties belong to atoms or molecules.

The mass of a macroscopic object is obviously determined by the masses of its microscopic parts (proposition 1). There cannot be changes in the mass of the whole without changes in the masses of the parts (4), though usually the mass of the whole changes because it loses or gains parts. It is at least conceivable that there be changes in the masses of the parts without a change in the mass of the whole (3), though again microscopic changes are usually a matter of parts being added or lost. If matter is atomic, then a macroscopic object cannot have mass without having microscopic parts that have mass (2). But matter is not necessarily atomic; continuous matter is a logical possibility, and a macroscopic object made of continuous matter has mass independently of the masses of atoms.

46 Jaegwon Kim, "Supervenience and Nomological Incommensurables", p. 155. It is interesting that Bigelow et al. imagine that forces between objects are supervenient on forces between events ("Forces", p. 624), whereas Bennett imagines that events are supervenient on objects and their properties (*Events and Their Names*, pp. 12–15).

This is all very well, but in this case there are not two different families of properties as specified by the definition of supervenience; the macroscopic whole has exactly the same determinable property of mass as the microscopic parts. The determination function is merely summation, so it has to be the same property.

According to the usual accounts of supervenience, the families of properties should be not only different properties but different types of properties – so different in fact that "there is no relation of definability or entailment between the two families",[47] in which case it is unlikely that we would have a conception of what the determination function might be. This seems to be the price we pay for genuine supervenience.[48]

The shape of a connected material object depends on spatial relations between its atomic or molecular parts. Given that the microscopic parts are sufficiently close together, a set of relations between the parts determines a shape for the whole (1). There cannot be changes in the shape of the whole without changes in the relations between the parts (4), whereas there can be changes in the relations between the parts without changes in the shape of the whole (3). As with mass the possibility of continuous matter shows that macroscopic shapes can occur without benefit of spatial relations between microscopic parts (2). Unlike the determination function for mass, it is not clear what the determination function for shape is, though the type of necessity is clearer: It is the type of necessity relevant to geometry.

Each pair of microscopic parts, or atoms, has a two–place spatial relation between them. The set of such two–place relations determines the shape of the whole, but there are too many relations. It is enough to consider the set of two–place spatial relations, considered as vectors, that one atom has with all the other atoms. If this set of relations is considered as not picking out a particular atom, then it is equivalent to a multi–place arrangement relation of the sort discussed in Chapter 4, Section 4, except that this relation could have 10^{23} argument places. The determination function is then a matter of multi–place arrangement relations determining macroscopic shapes.

47 Ibid., pp. 149–50. Proportion and force relations are supervenient on basic attributes.
48 It has the advantage of keeping the levels distinct. They are not distinct with a property like mass, where the dependence of whole on parts applies to things of any size. I am ignoring binding energy.

In Chapter 4, Section 4, I suggested that the five-place arrangement relation that held between the parts of a cross-shaped particular was in effect equivalent to the shape of that particular; this cannot be right here, however, because there can be different multi-place arrangement relations that determine the same macroscopic shape. This may be simply due to the fact that a multi-place arrangement relation approximates to a macroscopic shape. There is also the possibility of permuting the atoms among the argument places, but we should ignore this since it does not affect the multi-place arrangement relation.

Ontologically there does not appear to be much difference between changing the shape of a material object and changing the multi-place arrangement relation between its component atoms. Admittedly, a causal relation can change the multi-place arrangement relation without changing the overall shape; it just does not seem very important.

The force between two macroscopic objects is determined by the set of force relations between its atomic parts. Each atom of one object has a set of force relations with all the atoms of the other object; these are summed vectorially and all such sums for all the atoms of the first object are also summed vectorially to give the total force. So a set of force relations between atoms determines a force relation between macroscopic objects (1).[49] As with "mass" and "shape", the possibility of continuous matter implies that forces can occur between macroscopic objects without there being any microscopic forces (2). And as with "mass", the macroscopic property is exactly the same property as the microscopic property.

These discussions of "mass", "shape", and "force" show that, according to the strict definition of supervenience, the macroscopic is not supervenient on the microscopic. It is logically possible that all the properties considered can occur without the support of microscopic properties, and in all the cases we considered the supervenient properties were not very different from the properties of the supervenience base; in fact, in two cases they were identical.[50]

49 It is easy to see that (3) and (4) are true.
50 One way out would be to claim that microscopic properties being governed by quantum mechanics are fundamentally different from macroscopic properties. This does not work because of the correspondence principle; see Feyerabend, "Problems of Empiricism, Part II", pp. 296–300.

On the other hand, all three examples conform to three of the four propositions we used to describe supervenience. These three properties are fundamental to our understanding of the physical world, so much so that we need not look to any further properties to decide whether the macroscopic is supervenient on or reducible to the microscopic.

5. THE CONSTRUCTION OF PARTICULARS

Particularists have an easy account of how an ordinary particular is constructed: It is simply a collection of compresent tropes with no need for any other factors. Particularists also have a straightforward account of causality: It is tropes that act on each other and that are therefore the terms of the causal relation. Although immanent realists may accept that an ordinary particular is a collection of properties in the sense of a bundle of universals, they cannot accept anything analogous to the particularist doctrine that it is tropes that are the terms of causal relations. Nevertheless, it is worthwhile to consider the particularist doctrine of causality, since criticism of that doctrine indicates that it is unified particulars that are the terms of causal relations, and it shows that they are unified in the sense that they involve many properties instanced together. In other words, those bundles or compresences of properties act and interact as wholes.

Tropes, which Keith Campbell sometimes calls 'abstract particulars', are abstract only in the sense that they normally occur in conjunction with many other tropes. The mind grasps a trope by a process of abstraction that is merely a matter of setting aside compresent tropes. A trope shares its place with many other tropes, whereas a concrete particular monopolizes its location.[51] Apart from the fact that a trope does not monopolize its location, there seems to be no reason why a trope could not occur alone, though for a lot of tropes, such as shapes, that does not seem possible.

According to Campbell's particularist theory of causality, a trope not only can *act* alone but in a sense always does:

Williams had little difficulty in showing that his abstract particulars needed to be given *some* place in everyone's ontological assays. If you are burnt by

51 Campbell, *Abstract Particulars*, p. 3.

a hot wire it is, after all, not heat in general, or wires in general, or other characteristics of this wire, but *the heat of this wire* which does the burning. If you fail to recognize this you will fail to take appropriate measures to stop this sort of thing happening again.[52]

Against Campbell and Williams we shall merely point out that from our understanding of the natural world it appears that a trope never acts alone. In fact, Williams is mistaken in thinking that only one property of the wire is relevant, and the words he uses, *the heat of this wire,* are from a physicist's point of view ambiguous. The relevant properties of the wire are its temperature, the quantity of heat energy it possesses, and its thermal capacity; these properties are not unrelated though they are different properties. The temperature of the wire could, perhaps, be said to cause burning in as much as the temperature, as a sort of heat potential, is one of the factors responsible for the transfer of a quantity of heat energy, but it is not the only factor that governs the transfer of energy.

The temperature difference between the two bodies together with the area of contact and conductivity governs the initial rate of flow of heat energy. But how fast the temperature of the wire drops depends on the thermal capacity of the wire, and the subsequent rate of flow of heat at any later time depends on the instantaneous temperature difference. Therefore the total quantity of heat energy transferred in the interaction depends on several factors, not merely on the initial temperature of the wire.[53]

The particularist will have to understand the quantity of energy transferred as a trope that separates itself from the quantity of energy of the wire and passes to the finger, adding itself to the quantity of energy already possessed by the finger. The immanent realist account of energy exchange that I discussed earlier does not say anything about the exact nature of what is passed in the interaction, whereas the particularist position seems to be that an energy exchange amounts to the transfer of a particular, albeit an abstract particular, and therefore of something that has identity through time,

---

52 Ibid., p. 4; cf. p. 113.
53 An extended object always has so much heat energy in the same way that it always has so much mass. But in general the temperature of an extended object will vary throughout it, in the same way that its density will vary. The corresponding properties of the object are the temperature distribution and the density distribution. It must not be thought that temperature and density are properties of points as distinct entities.

since energy transfer takes time.[54] Otherwise we cannot refer to something as *the cause* in the way Campbell appears to want to do. What causes the burning, then, is *this heat* in the sense of this particular quantity of energy. But giving energy an identity through time turns it into a sort of imponderable fluid, contrary to current ideas, and contrary to special relativity.

Strictly speaking, *this particular quantity of energy* is not a property of the wire, since it did its work as a cause when gone from the wire, and moreover it was only part of the energy of the wire, part of the trope that is a property of the wire.

Campbell is prepared to allow that several different kinds of things can be the terms of causal relations, such as events and states. They are, however, all particulars and, it seems, tropes.[55] But for him concrete particulars are not the terms of causal relations; in general it is only one characteristic of a concrete particular that does the causing: "Their other features have nothing to do with it."[56]

For the particularist causal relations hold between tropes and not between concrete particulars. Therefore if a quantity of heat energy is passed from one body to another it would be wrong, presumably, to say that it is emitted by one body as a whole and received by another body acting as a whole. If it is the temperature difference that is regarded as primarily responsible for the flow of heat, presumably then it is the temperature trope that causes the energy to be emitted – though as we saw in our previous discussion temperature does not act alone. But it seems strange to say that the temperature could possess energy so that it could pass it to something else.

If the temperature trope and the energy trope are independent particulars as Campbell suggests, they must interact and interact causally; perhaps the temperature trope kicks energy out of the energy trope. And when a body absorbs energy, presumably it is absorbed by the energy trope, which then kicks up the temperature. There is something strange about this way of talking, not least because it introduces unknown causal relations between tropes, and presumably unknown natural laws to govern those causal relations.

---

54 I am afraid that I am not clear as to whether Campbell regards his tropes as having identity through time. His aporetic approach counts against taking his comments on pp. 138–42 as a definitive pronouncement.
55 "And in a trope philosophy, all causes are, of course, tropes of one kind or another, since nothing else is available." *Abstract Particulars*, p. 140; cf. pp. 22–3.
56 Ibid., p. 122.

It also follows that if forces are causal relations, then they hold between tropes, not between concrete particulars. Electrostatic forces will hold between charge tropes, and gravitational forces will hold between mass tropes. On this view, a force cannot act on the body as a whole: "Strictly speaking, it is not the earth and the compass needle as entire complex wholes which are cause and effect in the compass's pointing north."[57]

Consider two charged bodies exerting a repulsive force on each other. The particularist must say that the force acts between the charge tropes. But it is not only the charge trope that accelerates, it is the charged body as a whole, and the amount of acceleration depends on the mass of the body. But if the force only acts on the charge trope, how did the mass trope get involved? If charge tropes and mass tropes are not the sort of thing that accelerates by itself, then how is it that forces act on them? It does not make much sense to say that the force acts on the charge trope, which in turn acts on the other tropes so that they accelerate together. But if tropes are particulars in their own right, and the terms of causal relations, then they must interact. The particularist cannot merely stipulate that a trope can interact with other tropes only if those other tropes do not belong to the same concrete particular.

Suppose the charge trope of a body is acted on by an electrostatic force and that the mass trope of the same body is acted on by a gravitational force so that they balance; in this situation the particularist has to introduce a force between the mass trope and the charge trope. But such internal forces between tropes are not known to science, and they are not the sort of force that could cause acceleration, since a charge trope cannot accelerate by itself, because by its nature it has no mass.

It is true that there will be features of a concrete particular that have nothing to do with a given causal interaction, but it is not true that in general only one characteristic of a concrete particular is relevant to a causal interaction. Typically, tropes do not act alone as Campbell suggests that they do. It is the body as a whole that emits energy and absorbs energy; it is the body as a whole that is acted on by a force; and it is the body as a whole that then accelerates. It is true that only one property of a concrete particular, such as its charge, may contribute to giving rise to a causal relation, but several are in-

57 Ibid., p. 122.

volved in determining the effect of that causal relation – though of course some of the properties of the particulars concerned will play no role.

These considerations do not by themselves tell us about the principles of unity of the particulars that are subject to the laws of physics, and they do not tell us that these bodies are merely bundles of properties as in Russell's bundle theory. They do tell us, however, that the particulars that are subject to the laws of physics and that interact causally with each other do at least involve properties instanced together and that it is the particular as a whole that acts and is acted on. And it seems reasonable to suppose that these particulars are the sort of thing that persists through time.

There do not seem to be cases where only one type of property of a concrete particular contributes to giving rise to a causal relation *and* where it is only a particular's properties of that type that are changed by that causal relation. Unfortunately I cannot give any reasons for regarding it as impossible. It does appear, however, that the natural laws that govern our world do not include causal interactions of this type; the basic attributes and the causal relations we know about do not behave in this manner. So it may be that it is a physical impossibility, assuming that the physical laws that govern our world cohere in some way, or conform to a type.

The particulars that are subject to the laws of physics and that are the terms of causal relations at least involve several properties instanced together that act as a whole. Some immanent realists, however, have gone further than this and have held Russell's bundle theory of particulars. In this theory a particular is understood as composed not of tropes but of universals instanced together *and* nothing else: "A thing is a complex of properties which all stand in some contingent relation, call it co–instantiation, to one another."[58]

There are a number of ideas contained in this theory, some of them fairly intuitive: (1) A particular is constituted out of its properties, in some sense of the word 'constitute'. There is an analogy here with a material object being constituted out of its proper parts. We expect the parts to have the same ontological status as the whole, and we expect the reality of the whole to depend on or to be derived in some sense from the reality of the components. So if a

58 Albert Casullo, "A Fourth Version of the Bundle Theory", p. 125.

243

particular is *constituted* out of its properties we expect the reality of the particular to depend on or to be derived from the reality of its constituents, but there is a problem in that a particular has a different ontological status from its constituent universals. We need to investigate what is meant by 'constitute'. (2) The bundle theory as usually stated makes a claim about what a particular is, as well as how it is put together, since it says that a particular is *identical* to a complex of co-instantiated properties. This identification leads to difficulties about criteria of identity for particulars, as we shall see. (3) At the very least, the bundle theory claims that there are no other factors besides universals that are to be found "within" a particular and that are relevant for explaining what a particular is. It is this minimal claim that we shall defend.

In his defence of the bundle theory Albert Casullo discusses three objections put forward by James Van Cleve. The first two, which he considers together, can be summarized as follows: If a particular is in fact identical to a complex of properties, then the particular, as a complex of properties (*FGH*), cannot change, since a change such as (*FGH*) → (*FGK*) is not a change in a particular, but the replacement of one particular by another (first objection). It follows that each property of a particular is an essential property (second objection).[59]

The bundle theory, which is the target of these criticisms, appears to understand a particular as a sort of set of properties, albeit with some sort of structure in that the universals are *co-instantiated* together in a certain way. The criterion of identity that seems to be presupposed in Van Cleve's objection is as follows: If x and y are bundles of properties (particulars), then x is identical with y if and only if x and y have the same component properties co-instantiated together. But there are many different sorts of particulars, and each sort has its own criterion of identity.

Casullo distinguishes two fundamental problems the bundle theory has to address.[60] The first problem is individuation: If a property as a universal is capable of occurring many times, then a complex of universals, being composed only of universals, is also capable of occurring many times. But a particular can only occur once, so how can a particular be a complex of properties, and how is it that two particulars with the same properties can differ? The

59 Ibid.   60 Ibid., pp. 126–7.

second problem concerns identity through time: Most enduring things are capable of change, meaning change of properties, but the identity of an enduring thing through time cannot be explained in terms of its maintaining exactly the same properties.

Casullo explains that the version of the bundle theory he accepts is a two-tier theory: Firstly properties are combined together by the relation of co-instantiation to form momentary particulars, and secondly momentary particulars are combined together in a different way to form enduring particulars. There is a special relation that binds together a series of momentary particulars to form an enduring particular, but it is clearly not the relation of co-instantiation. "Although momentary things are complexes of co-instantiated properties, enduring things are not. An enduring thing is a temporally extended series of momentary things."[61] The two-tier version of the bundle theory is therefore committed to a doctrine of temporal parts.

By means of this two-tier version of the bundle theory Casullo is able to answer Van Cleve's objections. The change $(FGH) \rightarrow (FGK)$ is merely the replacement of one momentary particular by another, but the two momentary particulars, (FGH) and (FGK), can still stand in the relation that binds momentary particulars together to form an enduring particular. The enduring particular has momentary particulars as temporal parts. The complex (FGH) considered as a momentary particular does have H as an essential property, but the enduring thing that has (FGH) as a temporal part does not have H as an essential property.[62]

The opponent of the bundle theory might now claim that the enduring particular has the complex (FGH) as an essential temporal part, and since the complex (FGH) does have H as an essential property, then the enduring particular must also have H as an essential property. Casullo merely suggests that the form of mereological essentialism on which this argument is based is unsubstantiated.[63] After all, the nature of the enduring particular concerned might have allowed it to have (FGI) as its temporal part at time t instead of (FGH).

Consider an enduring particular, a, which has a natural principle of unity. a possesses various properties and exists over a period of time; it therefore exists at many times, so "a at time t" can be re-

61 Ibid., p. 129.   62 Ibid., pp. 129–30.   63 Ibid., p. 130.

garded as a sort of particular simply because it only occurs once. However, it is not clear what sort of particular it is, though it bears some resemblance to a point event. Whatever principle of unity it has depends on the principle of unity of the enduring particular. So let us call it a time slice of the enduring particular a. Now, a's possessing the property F is not a matter of a's being composed, in the appropriate sense of the word 'composed', of certain time slices, and then the relevant time slices possessing F.[64] a possesses F directly, since time slices of a are constructed out of a, a particular that already possesses properties.

A time slice of an enduring particular is a very different sort of thing from the enduring particular itself; they are arguably both particulars, but they are very different sorts of particulars. A time slice of an enduring particular is not an enduring particular that just exists for an instant of time – strictly speaking there are no such things. The enduring particular will be an example of a sortal, f, but a time slice of the enduring particular cannot be an example of that sortal. A time slice of a horse is not a horse. An enduring particular, such as a horse, is something that by its very nature can exist through time, whereas the time slice by its very nature cannot.

A time slice is like a point event and a continuous series of time slices is like an interval event, and as we argued previously an interval event does not, as such, persist through time.[65] Consider an enduring particular that exists at time t_1 and at a later time t_2: The enduring particular that exists at time t_1 is numerically identical with that enduring particular at time t_2. In contrast, a time slice at time t_1 is numerically identical only with that time slice, and a continuous series of time slices from t_1 to t_2 is numerically identical only with that series of time slices. A series of time slices, as such, can no more be said to persist through its time interval than the time interval itself can be said to so persist. From a three-dimensional point of view the individual time slices of a continuous series come into existence and go out of existence instantaneously one after the other, so that the continuous series of time slices "unfolds". But if a continuous series of time slices were ontologically significant, then it would be as a four-dimensional entity, and it is that four-dimensional entity that would be numerically identical

64 Cf. Lowe, *Kinds of Being*, pp. 82–3.
65 See Chapter 7, Section 3.

with itself. According to the time slice ontology no particular persists through time.

Enduring particulars and continuous series of time slices have different characteristics with respect to numerical identity; they are therefore different kinds of thing. It follows that an enduring particular cannot be identical with a series of time slices.

The same point can be made by considering the criteria of identity for enduring particulars and continuous series of time slices. The criterion of identity for a time slice necessarily involves specifying a time, and the criterion of identity for a continuous series of time slices necessarily involves specifying a time interval. On the other hand, the criterion of identity for an enduring particular cannot involve any essential reference to a time interval; the period of time for which it exists is accidental to what an enduring particular is. Therefore enduring particulars and series of time slices have different criteria of identity. If they have different criteria of identity, then they are distinct kinds of thing, and therefore an enduring particular cannot be identical with a series of time slices.[66] Even the continuous series of time slices for the period for which an enduring particular actually exists cannot be identical with the enduring particular itself.

There may be those who think that there are no such things as enduring particulars – because the notion is incoherent perhaps – and wish to replace the notion of enduring particular with that of continuous series of time slices. They may even claim that it is a form of "reduction". I am not arguing here against that view, though my previous arguments show there are no reasons for such a view based on causality. I am claiming, given that the notion of enduring particular is coherent, that an enduring particular cannot be identical with a continuous series of time slices.

There is also a distinction between time slices of an enduring particular and the momentary particulars found in the first tier of Casullo's bundle theory. A momentary particular is understood as a complex of properties and appears to have this criterion of identity: If x and y are momentary particulars, then x is identical with y if and only if x and y have the same component properties co-instantiated together. Now the criterion of identity for an enduring particular with a natural principle of unity will not demand that the properties of x and y be exactly the same but will include the demand that x and

66 Cf. Lowe, *Kinds of Being*, p. 70.

y fall under the same sortal.[67] And a time slice of an enduring particular is understood by reference to the enduring particular, so that its criterion of identity has to be based on that of the enduring particular. It follows that we cannot even understand a time slice of an enduring particular as identical to a complex of co-instantiated properties with the criterion of identity as I have given it. The distinction between a time slice of an enduring particular and a complex of co-instantiated properties is a little like the distinction between a set and an ordered set: They have the same components but are looked at from a different point of view. According to the point of view developed in this book, neither momentary particulars nor time slices of enduring particulars are real constituents of the world.

The bundle theory can still be maintained, however, if it is the case that there is nothing more to an enduring particular at a certain time than certain universals. In other words, there are no factors present that are relevant to making the particular be what it is other than universals; there will be no non-universal individuating factors, for example. In this weak sense of the word 'constitute' universals constitute a unified particular. Those universals first include basic universals, including basic attributes and dyadic basic relations, and so on, though it does seem to me that relations are not among the constituents of particulars unless they are internal relations. Besides the basic universals there is also the sortal universal that the particular falls under. What makes the enduring particular to be the particular that it is, is not the possession of precisely the basic attributes it possesses at that time; in this sense the basic attributes alone do not *constitute* the enduring particular.

What makes an enduring particular to be the particular that it is, is some principle of unity that is nevertheless *based* on attributes. It is partly that it falls under a suitably fundamental sortal, but what makes it fall under a sortal is not the possession of precisely those basic attributes but how the particular is organized.[68] An enduring particular with a natural principle of unity is what it is on account of a certain structure, where its structure has to be understood as the general arrangement of proper spatial parts taking into account their

---

67 I am ignoring here the possibility of metamorphosis; cf. Lowe, *Kinds of Being*, p. 14. The sortal has to be a sufficiently fundamental sortal, perhaps the *substance concept*; it cannot be a *phased sortal*. See Wiggins, *Sameness and Substance*, p. 24.
68 See Chapter 4, Section 5.

allowed variation, together with the general type of basic attributes, taking into account *their* allowed variation. In a simple (idealized) case, for example, the sortal could be equivalent to a conjunction of determinables that the particular has to continue to fall under to remain what it is. Because the sortal universal is based on basic attributes the unified particular possesses, we can say that they *constitute* the particular in the weak sense of the term: No other factors are relevant for making the enduring particular to be the particular that it is.

The principle of unity determines the criterion of identity, and a criterion of identity for a unified particular will recognize that it is its structure that persists. It is not easy to explain what the principle of unity for a sortal is; it is usually easier to give the corresponding criterion of identity. Formulating the criterion of identity can itself be difficult, though where that is the case it may nevertheless be possible to show that two criteria of identity must differ and that therefore we are dealing with two different kinds of things. This is Lowe's strategy in Chapter 7 of *Kinds of Being*, and I am using the same form of argument.[69]

An enduring particular has a different sort of criterion of identity from a series of time slices of an enduring particular, and a time slice of an enduring particular has a different sort of criterion of identity from a momentary particular. Therefore an enduring particular has a different sort of criterion of identity from a series of momentary particulars. It follows that an enduring particular cannot be understood as constituted out of momentary particulars considered as temporal parts.[70]

Van Cleve's first two objections do not affect our version of the bundle theory, since we deny that an enduring particular is *identical* with a complex of co-instantiated properties or to a series of such complexes. They have different criteria of identity. The basic

---

69 See, for example, *Kinds of Being*, p. 121.
70 The temporal parts view has the consequence that there are, strictly speaking, no things that endure through time. The reasons I gave earlier for rejecting point entities such as point events also apply to temporal parts. Momentary particulars or time slices of enduring particulars being point particulars should not be regarded as real constituents of the world. If a so-called enduring particular is to be understood as a series of temporal parts, then there must be something that binds those temporal parts together, and it cannot be something that endures through time. It is not clear what it could be, though Armstrong thinks that causality is the required relation (private communication).

attributes an enduring particular possesses at a certain time only constitute the enduring particular in the weak sense of the word 'constitute'. The criterion of identity for an enduring particular determines its persistence conditions[71] and therefore determines which changes of the type $(FGH) \rightarrow (FGK)$ are changes in which the enduring particular remains the same enduring particular.

Van Cleve's third objection to the bundle theory is that if a particular were a complex of properties, it would be impossible for two particulars to have the same properties, for if they did they would be the same particular. This objection is also based on the identification of an enduring particular with a complex of co-instantiated properties, and on the implicit criterion of identity for complexes of co-instantiated properties: If x and y are complexes of co-instantiated properties, then x is identical with y if and only if they have the same component properties co-instantiated together.

Casullo avoids a direct identification by arguing that an enduring particular is not *identical* with a momentary complex of properties, but is constituted out of momentary complexes of co-instantiated properties, which are its temporal parts. And I have gone so far as to deny that an enduring particular is identical with the sum of its time slices, and also to deny that a time slice of an enduring particular is identical with a momentary complex of co-instantiated properties. The objection fails because an enduring particular as we understand it does not have the criterion of identity which the objection is based upon.

However, let us assume for a moment that all there is to a particular at a certain time is a number of basic attributes instanced together. We are therefore ignoring the structure. On this assumption there does seem to be a general problem of individuation for particulars. If all there is to a particular is basic attributes instanced together, how do we explain the difference between two particulars at the same time with exactly the same basic attributes?

There are two traditional answers to the general problem of individuation.[72] The first is to suppose that a particular must pos-

---

71 Cf. Lowe, *Kinds of Being*, pp. 57 and 71.
72 The theory of Aristotle and Aquinas that it is matter that individuates does not apply to all types of particular, as Aquinas was well aware. I do not know what to make of Scotus's theory of individuation by *haecceitas*, which is a sort of individual essence.

sess some factor, such as a substratum or bare particular, other than its properties that will *make it differ* from a particular with exactly the same properties. The second is to use a version of the principle of the identity of indiscernibles, either as a necessary truth or in some other way. The version of the identity of indiscernibles that will solve the general problem of individuation as we have just formulated it has to guarantee that there will never be two particulars with exactly the same basic attributes.

In Volume 1 of his work on universals Armstrong puts forward what can be understood as a general criterion of identity for particulars based partly on a version of the identity of indiscernibles: *"Sameness of total position AND sameness of nature do together guarantee sameness of particulars."*[73]

By this he means that sameness of place at the same time and sameness of all properties guarantee sameness of particulars. He denies that "sameness of total position guarantees sameness of particulars" and "sameness of nature guarantees sameness of particulars"[74] are necessary truths, but the combined version he has regarded as a necessary truth. Indeed, it does seem that for most types of particulars with natural principles of unity that we can think of, Armstrong's general criterion is right, but I draw the line at regarding it as a necessary truth.

A version of the identity of indiscernibles that was true for all types of particulars would be true for all types of arbitrary particulars as well as all types of particulars that are real constituents of the world. Even if we restricted ourselves to all types of particulars that are real constituents of the world it would be difficult to legislate in an *a priori* way for things like subatomic particles that obey the principle of indistinguishability, or for classical fields that can occupy the same place at the same time. If the relevant version of the identity of indiscernibles were a necessary truth it would be necessary in the sense of logically necessary, but there is no logical necessity about which things are real constituents of the world because their natures are associated with causal interactions and natural law.

Since there are different types of particular that do not have the same criterion of identity,[75] it follows that not all types of particular

73 Armstrong, Volume I, p. 123.
74 Armstrong calls this the identity of indiscernibles. But lately his inclination is to deny that the combined version is a necessary truth (private communication).
75 Lowe, *Kinds of Being*, pp. 24–5.

are individuated in the same way. There is no need, therefore, to explain how *any* two particulars differ from each other; all that is required is an explanation of how two particulars with the same basic attributes differ from each other. Clearly such particulars are of the same type, so that all we have to do is to explain how two particulars of the same type differ. All that is needed, then, is that each *bona fide* type of particular possess a criterion of identity.

By saying "All that is needed . . ." I do not claim to be able to provide such a criterion for all types of particulars, nor do I claim that such criteria always exist. There may be things that differ in an ultimate way that can be explained no further. Nevertheless, the manner of their ultimate difference is peculiar to that type of thing and not to be explained by reference to bare particulars or by appeal to the identity of indiscernibles. For example, two parcels of atomic matter differ because their constituent atoms differ, but two parcels of continuously divisible matter differ because however finely they are mixed there are always sufficiently small, connected subparcels that belong to one parcel or the other. For atomic matter we can refer to a different criterion of identity, namely, that appropriate to atoms; for continuously divisible matter we cannot refer to the criterion of identity for connected parcels.

Connected parcels of continuous matter may differ from each other in an ultimate sense – individuation by matter, or it could be suggested that connected parcels of matter differ because they always occupy different regions of space, and a criterion of identity could be formulated that referred us to the different regions of space occupied. Such a criterion of identity would then depend on a criterion of identity for regions of space. An absolutist about space would presumably claim that regions of space differed in an ultimate sense, while a relationist would claim that regions of space are individuated by the bodies that occupy space.[76] Both appear to claim that there is one type of particular the examples of which differ in an ultimate sense from one another.

Let us examine more closely the implicit criterion of identity for complexes of co-instantiated properties: If x and y are complexes of co-instantiated properties, x is identical with y if and only if they have the same properties co-instantiated. Whatever is meant by 'co-

---

76 For a discussion of the individuation of regions of space see Newman, "A Metaphysical Introduction to a Relational Theory of Space", Section III.

instantiated' it must at least entail that the properties are instanced at the same place, for if P_1 and P_2 are instanced at one place and P_3 and P_4 instanced at a distant place, then no one is going to say that we have only one particular.

'Co-instantiated' or 'instanced together' must also mean something like *mutually inhering*.[77] Suppose that two very different particulars occupy the same place at the same time, a gravitational field and an electric field, for example. The properties of the first particular and those of the second particular are instanced together in the sense that they are instanced at the same place at the same time, but they are not all instanced together in the sense we require. They are two independent particulars. The properties of the first particular mutually inhere, and the properties of the second particular mutually inhere, but they do it separately despite sameness of place.

Consider four properties, P_1, P_2, P_3, and P_4. Suppose that P_1 and P_2 mutually inhere and that P_3 and P_4 mutually inhere, and that only those two pairs mutually inhere. And suppose that we are dealing with a type of thing where two things can occupy the same place at the same time. There are two different particulars whether the complexes (P_1, P_2) and (P_3, P_4) occupy different spatial positions or the same spatial position, since spatial coincidence is not going to change facts about mutual inherence. Consider then two complexes with exactly the same properties: If they can occupy different positions they can also occupy the same position, since spatial coincidence is not going to change facts about mutual inherence.[78] Even when the two complexes are coincident in the sense of occupying the same place, the properties of the two complexes are not *co-instantiated*, and therefore the two complexes are not identical

77 There are two ways of looking at inherence. A number of properties can be said to mutually inhere, or one property can be said to inhere in the complex of properties. The relation is a formal relation and not a real constituent of the world. There is no such thing as inherence in the abstract.
78 Considerations like these might lie behind another approach to the problem of individuation: "From what has been said, 'tis easy to discover what is so much enquired after, the *principium individuationis;* and that 'tis plain is existence itself, which determines a being of any sort to a particular time and place incommunicable to two beings of the same kind." Locke, *An Essay concerning Human Understanding* II, xxvii, 3; cf. Leibniz, *New Essays concerning Human Understanding* II, xxvii, and also "de Principio Individui" (1663), where he says, "Every individual is individuated by its whole entity." This view probably derives from Suárez; see *Disputationes Metaphysicae,* Book V. These are probably the words of particularists, but I do not think that they arise consciously from particularism.

according to the criterion of identity as I have formulated it. Sometimes the metaphysical danger is held up before us of two things collapsing into one thing the instant their properties become identical; these considerations show that there is no such danger.

To get an intuitive grasp of what this means, consider two qualitatively identical wave packets merging for a short period of time before diverging, so that during that period they have everything in common including the same velocity, which is probably not physically possible. That there are two wave packets present is shown by the doubling of the amplitude. It certainly makes sense to say that they preserved distinct identities throughout the time when they occupied the same space, and so it seems that it is a logical possibility that they remained distinct. I am not claiming that this happens or that it is a physical possibility, merely that it is a logical possibility. There have been philosophers, such as Aquinas and Leibniz, who have appealed to history as an individuating factor, but that is outside our terms of reference; the problem we have been considering involves properties instanced together at a time.

It follows, therefore, that Armstrong's general criterion of identity for particulars (p. 251) should not be regarded as a necessary truth, since there is no *a priori* reason to think that it applies to all types of particulars. It is still possible, however, that it is true for all particulars that are real constituents of the world, and it may be possible to argue that it is physically necessary.

A complex of mutually inhering universals must not be thought of as a sort of conjunction of universals that exists in the abstract and needs something to tie it down to a place and a time. I argued in Chapter 4 that conjunctions of universals do not have any ontological significance. And according to the immanent realist theory of universals the only way in which a universal is found in any ontologically significant sense is if it is instanced by some particular. To say that *there is* a universal is to say something quite different.[79]

Suppose that a shape attribute, a mass attribute, and some other attributes mutually inhere to constitute, in the weak sense, a certain enduring particular. They will "fit together" in a certain way that is appropriate to attributes of that type. And it is only if the basic attributes fit together in the appropriate way that they can be said to

79 See Chapter 3 on the distinction between saying that there is a universal and saying that it is instanced.

be co-instantiated. For spatial objects, being instanced at the same place is a necessary condition for them to be co-instantiated, but not a sufficient condition as I have shown. Now I confess that the notion of mutual inherence is not a very clear one, but in fact we do not need a very clear understanding of mutual inherence. All we need is the acknowledgement that there is something like it that is distinct from spatial coincidence.

The previous arguments in defence of the bundle theory can be summarized by considering the argument that the bundle theory entails the identity of indiscernibles. Armstrong, for example, in order to discredit the bundle theory argues that the bundle theory of particulars entails that the identity of indiscernibles is a necessary truth.[80] The following is my reconstruction of his argument:
Necessarily, a particular is identical with a bundle of universals.
Necessarily, the criterion of identity for a bundle of universals is: If x and y are bundles of universals, then x is identical with y if and only if they have the same constituent universals co-instantiated together.
Therefore, particulars necessarily have the same criterion of identity as bundles of universals.
Therefore, two particulars are necessarily the same if and only if they have the same constituent universals.
Therefore, the identity of indiscernibles is a necessary truth for particulars.

The form of the principle of the identity of indiscernibles in the conclusion of this argument depends on the form of the bundle theory presupposed in the first premiss: If a particular is a bundle of relational as well as monadic universals, then the weak form of the identity of indiscernibles is necessarily true for particulars; if a particular is a bundle only of monadic universals, then the strong form is the appropriate one. Armstrong's point is that since the strong form cannot be a necessary truth (or any sort of truth), the bundle theory cannot be a necessary truth. It does seem more reasonable to suggest that the monadic properties of a particular "constitute" it. He thinks the weak form of the principle of the identity of indiscernibles might be true, but he argues that it cannot be a necessary truth and that as a consequence the bundle theory is not a necessary

80 Armstrong, Volume I, pp. 91–7.

truth. Since the only way the bundle theory can be true is as a necessary truth, it is not true.

The first premiss should be rejected, since it does not follow that because particulars have no constituents other than the universals instanced by them that particulars are identical with bundles of universals. In fact, enduring particulars have criteria of identity different from that appropriate to bundles of universals; and it is important to note that those criteria of identity do not require factors other than universals. If particulars were identical with bundles of universals, all types of particular would have the same criterion of identity. Our previous work in this chapter has shown that two particulars that are examples of different kinds of particular can have the same constituents and nevertheless be different particulars having different criteria of identity. The simplest example of this is a set and an ordered set; a number of other examples related to physical objects were discussed in Section 3. In this last section I have argued that momentary particulars (instantaneous bundles of properties), time slices of enduring particulars, and enduring particulars themselves all have different criteria of identity.

In order for the argument to work, the first premiss has to be true, and the criterion of identity of the second premiss has to be interpreted either as the criterion of identity for a set of universals or as that for some other type of combination of universals considered in the abstract. Although it is sometimes convenient to consider universals in the abstract, for the purposes of the bundle theory they must be considered as instanced together. A universal is something that can be instanced many times, and each instance is independent of the other instances. It follows that a certain set of universals can be instanced many times. A criterion of identity for bundles of universals must specify that they are co-instantiated, but 'co-instantiated' means more than instanced together in the same place, it must also mean mutually inhering. My previous discussion of co-instantiation in terms of mutual inherence shows that two particulars that instance the same universals can differ.

Bibliography

Aitchison, I. J. R. "Nothing's Plenty: The Vacuum in Modern Quantum Field Theory". *Contemporary Physics*, 26, pp. 333–91, 1985.

Alexander, Peter. "Incongruent Counterparts and Absolute Space". *Proceedings of the Aristotelian Society*, 1984–5.

Allaire, Edwin B. "*The Tractatus:* Nominalistic or Realistic?", in *Essays in Ontology*, Edwin B. Allaire (ed.). The Hague: Nijhoff, 1963.

"Tractatus 6.3751". *Analysis*, 19, pp. 100–5, 1959.

Anscombe, G. E. M. "Causality and Determination" (1971), in *The Collected Papers of G .E. M. Anscombe*, Volume Two. Minneapolis: University of Minnesota Press, 1981.

An Introduction to Wittgenstein's Tractatus. London: Hutchinson, 1959.

Armstrong, D. M. "Are Quantities Relations? A Reply to Bigelow and Pargetter". *Philosophical Studies*, 54, pp. 305–16, 1988.

"Classes Are States of Affairs". *Mind*, 100, pp. 189–200, 1991.

A Combinatorial Theory of Possibility. Cambridge: Cambridge University Press, 1989.

"In Defence of Structural Universals". *Australasian Journal of Philosophy*, 64, pp. 85–8, 1986.

"The Nature of Possibility". *Canadian Journal of Philosophy*, 16, pp. 575–94, 1986.

"Towards a Theory of Properties". *Philosophy*, 50, pp. 145–55, 1975.

Universals: An Opinionated Introduction. Boulder, Colo.: Westview Press, 1989.

Universals and Scientific Realism, Volumes I & II. Cambridge: Cambridge University Press, 1978.

What Is a Law of Nature? Cambridge: Cambridge University Press, 1983.

Ayer, A. J. *The Central Questions of Philosophy*. Harmondsworth: Penguin, 1976 (first published 1973).

"Individuals" (1952), in *Philosophical Essays*. London: Macmillan, 1954.

Ayers, Michael R. "Individuals without Sortals". *Canadian Journal of Philosophy*, 4, pp. 113–48, 1974.

Bealer, George. *Quality and Concept*. Oxford: Oxford University Press, 1982.

Bedau, Mark. "Cartesian Interaction", in *Midwest Studies in Philosophy, Volume X, Studies in the Philosophy of Mind*, Peter A. French (ed.). Minneapolis: University of Minnesota Press, 1986.

Bell, David. *Frege's Theory of Judgement*. Oxford: Oxford University Press, 1979.

Benacerraf, P. "What Numbers Could Not Be". *The Philosophical Review*, 74, pp. 47–73, 1965.

Bennett, Jonathan. *Events and Their Names*. Indianapolis: Hackett, 1988.

Bigelow, John. "Real Possibilities". *Philosophical Studies*, 53, pp. 37–64, 1988.

The Reality of Numbers. Oxford: Oxford University Press, 1988.

Bigelow, John, and Pargetter, Robert. "Quantities". *Philosophical Studies*, 54, pp. 287–304, 1988.

Science and Necessity. Cambridge: Cambridge University Press, 1990.

Bigelow, John, Ellis, Brian, and Pargetter, Robert. "Forces". *Philosophy of Science*, 55, pp. 614–30, 1988.

Black, Max. *A Companion to Wittgenstein's Tractatus*. Ithaca, N. Y.: Cornell University Press, 1964.

"The Elusiveness of Sets". *The Review of Metaphysics*, 24, pp. 614–36, 1971.

"Is Achilles Still Running?", in *Problems of Analysis*. Ithaca, N. Y.: Cornell University Press, 1954.

Bohm, David. *Causality and Chance in Modern Physics*. Princeton, N. J.: Van Nostrand, 1957.

"A Suggested Interpretation of the Quantum Theory in Terms of 'Hidden Variables', Part I". *Physical Review*, 85, pp. 166–79, 1952.

Boolos, G. "The Iterative Conception of Set". *The Journal of Philosophy*, 68, pp. 215–31, 1971.

Born, Max. *The Natural Philosophy of Cause and Chance*. Oxford: Oxford University Press, 1949.

Bradley, F. H. *Appearance and Reality*. Oxford: Oxford University Press, 1893.

Brillouin, L. *Tensors in Mechanics and Elasticity*. London: Academic Press, 1964.

Burge, Tyler. "A Theory of Aggregates". *Nous*, 11, pp. 97–117, 1977.

Butler, Ronald J. "*Distinctiones Rationis*, or the Cheshire Cat Which Left Its Smile Behind". *The Aristotelian Society*, suppl. vol. 49, 1975.

Campbell, Keith. *Abstract Particulars*. Oxford: Blackwell, 1990.

Carruthers, Peter. *The Metaphysics of the Tractatus*. Cambridge: Cambridge University Press, 1990.

Cartwright, Helen. "Heraclitus and the Bath Water". *The Philosophical Review*, 74, pp. 466–85, 1965.

"Quantities". *The Philosophical Review*, 79, pp. 25–42, 1970.

Cartwright, Nancy. "Do the Laws of Physics State the Facts?" *Pacific Philosophical Quarterly*, 1, pp. 75–84, 1980.

How the Laws of Physics Lie. Oxford: Oxford University Press, 1983.

Nature's Capacities and their Measurement. Oxford: Oxford University Press, 1989.

Cartwright, Richard. "Scattered Objects", in *Analysis and Metaphysics*, Keith Lehrer (ed.). Dordrecht: Reidel, 1975.

Casullo, Albert. "Conjunctive Properties Revisited". *Australasian Journal of Philosophy*, 62, pp. 289–91, 1984.

"A Fourth Version of the Bundle Theory". *Philosophical Studies*, 54, pp.125–39, 1988.

Chappell, V. C. "Stuff and Things". *Proceedings of the Aristotelian Society*, 1970–1.

Chisholm, Roderick M. "Coming into Being and Passing Away", in *On Metaphysics*. Minneapolis: University of Minnesota Press, 1989.

Coplestone, F. *A History of Philosophy*. New York: Image Books, 1950.

Creary, Lewis G. "Causal Explanations and the Reality of Natural Component Forces". *Pacific Philosophical Quarterly*, 62, pp. 148–57, 1981.

Davidson, Donald. "Causal Relations", in *Essays on Actions and Events*. Oxford: Oxford University Press, 1980.

"The Individuation of Events", in *Essays on Actions and Events*.

Donagan, Alan. "Universals and Metaphysical Realism", in *Universals and Particulars*, M. J. Loux (ed.). Notre Dame, Ind.: University of Notre Dame Press, 1976.

Dummett, Michael. *Frege: Philosophy of Language*. London: Duckworth, 1973.

"Frege", in *The Encyclopedia of Philosophy*, vol. 3, P. Edwards (ed.). London: Macmillan, 1967.

Earman, John. "Against Indeterminacy". *The Journal of Philosophy*, 74, pp. 535–8, 1977.

"Causation: A Matter of Life and Death". *The Journal of Philosophy*, 73, pp. 5–25, 1976.

Review of J. L. Mackie, *The Cement of the Universe*. *The Philosophical Review*, 85, pp. 390–4, 1976.

Ellis, Brian. "The Existence of Forces". *Studies in History and Philosophy of Science*, 7, pp. 171–85, 1976.

Fair, David. "Causation and the Flow of Energy". *Erkenntnis*, 14, pp. 219–50, 1979.

Feyerabend, Paul. "Problems of Empiricism, Part II", in *The Nature and Function of Scientific Theories*, Robert G. Colodny (ed.). Pittsburgh: University of Pittsburgh Press, 1970.

Field, Hartry. "Theory Change and Indeterminacy of Reference". *The Journal of Philosophy*, 70, pp. 462–81, 1973.

Forrest, Peter. "Ways Worlds Could Be". *Australasian Journal of Philosophy*, 64, pp. 15–24, 1986.

Forrest, Peter, and Armstrong, D. M. "The Nature of Number". *Philosophical Papers*, 16, pp. 165–86, 1987.

Franklin, James. "Mathematical Necessity and Reality". *Australasian Journal of Philosophy*, 67, pp. 286–94, 1989.

Frege, Gottlob. *The Basic Laws of Arithmetic*, M. Furth (trans.). Berkeley and Los Angeles: University of California Press, 1964.

"A Critical Elucidation of Some Points in E. Schröder, *Vorlesungen über die Algebra der Logik*", in *Collected Papers on Mathematics, Logic, and Philosophy*, Brian McGuinness (ed.). Oxford: Blackwell, 1984.

The Foundations of Arithmetic, J. L. Austin (trans.). Oxford: Blackwell, 1950.

"Function and Concept", in *Collected Papers*.

"On Concept and Object", in *Collected Papers*.
"On Sense and Reference", in *Collected Papers*.
"On the Foundations of Geometry: First Series", in *Collected Papers*.
"On the Foundations of Geometry: Second Series", in *Collected Papers*.
Philosophical and Mathematical Correspondence, Gottfried Gabriel *et al.* (eds.). Oxford: Blackwell, 1980.
Posthumous Writings, P. Long and R. White (trans.). Oxford: Blackwell, 1979.
"Thoughts", in *Collected Papers*.
"What Is a Function?", in *Collected Papers*.
Geach, Peter. "Form and Existence". *Proceedings of the Aristotelian Society*, 1954–5.
Mental Acts. London: Routledge & Kegan Paul, 1957.
"On Rigour in Semantics" (1949), in *Logic Matters*. Oxford: Blackwell, 1972.
Truth, Love and Immortality. London: Hutchinson, 1979.
Hamlyn, D. W. *Metaphysics*. Cambridge: Cambridge University Press, 1984.
Hardin, C. L. *Color for Philosophers*. Indianapolis: Hackett, 1990.
Hardy, G. H. *Pure Mathematics*. Cambridge: Cambridge University Press, 1908.
Harré, Rom. "Our Knowledge of Causality", in *An Encyclopedia of Philosophy*, G. H. R. Parkinson (ed.). London: Routledge, 1988.
Harré, Rom, and Madden, E. H. *Causal Powers: A Theory of Natural Necessity*. Oxford: Blackwell, 1975.
Hart, H. L. A., and Honoré, A. M. *Causation in the Law*. Oxford: Oxford University Press, 1959.
Hart, W. D. *The Engines of the Soul*. Cambridge: Cambridge University Press, 1988.
Heller, Mark. *The Ontology of Physical Objects: Four-dimensional Hunks of Matter*. Cambridge: Cambridge University Press, 1990.
Hertz, H. *The Principles of Mechanics* (1884), D. E. Jones and J. T. Walley (trans.). New York: Dover, 1956.
Hesse, M. *Forces and Fields*. New York: Philosophical Library, 1961.
Hilbert, D. *Foundations of Geometry*. LaSalle, Ill.: Open Court, 1971.
Hirsch, Eli. *The Concept of Identity*. Oxford: Oxford University Press, 1982.
Ishiguro, Hidé. *Leibniz's Philosophy of Logic and Language*. London: Duckworth, 1972.
Jackson, Frank. "Statements about Universals". *Mind*, 76, pp. 427–9, 1977.
Jammer, Max. *The Philosophy of Quantum Mechanics*. New York, Wiley, 1974.
Johnson, W. E. *Logic, Part I*. Cambridge: Cambridge University Press, 1921.
Kim, Jaegwon. "Concepts of Supervenience". *Philosophy and Phenomenological Research*, 45, pp. 153–76, 1984.
"Events as Property Exemplifications", in *Action Theory*, M. Brand and D. Walton (eds.). Dordrecht: Reidel, 1976
"Supervenience and Nomological Incommensurables". *American Philosophical Quarterly*, 15, pp. 149–56, 1978.

Koyré, Alexandre. *Galileo Studies*. Hassocks, Sussex: Harvester, 1978 (Etudes Galiléennes, 1939).

Krantz, David H., Luce, R. Duncan, Suppes, Patrick, and Tversky, Amos. *Foundations of Measurement,* vol. I. New York: Academic Press, 1971.

Leibniz, Gottfried. "de Principio Individui" (1663), in C. I. Gerhardt, *Die Philosophischen Schriften von G. W. Leibniz,* vol. 4. Berlin, 1875–90.

Fifth Paper, *The Leibniz-Clarke Correspondence,* H. G. Alexander (ed.). Manchester: Manchester University Press, 1956.

letter to de Volder, 11 October 1705, in C. I. Gerhardt, vol. 2.

letter to des Bosses, 24 April 1709, in C. I. Gerhardt, vol. 2.

"Meditations on Knowledge, Truth and Ideas" (1684), in G. W. Leibniz, *Philosophical Papers,* Roger Ariew and Daniel Garber (eds.). Indianapolis: Hackett, 1989.

Lemmon, E. J. *Beginning Logic*. Sunbury on Thames: Nelson, 1971.

Lewis, David. "Against Structural Universals". *Australasian Journal of Philosophy,* 64, pp. 25–46, 1986.

"Causation". *The Journal of Philosophy,* 70, pp. 556–72, 1973.

"New Work for a Theory of Universals". *Australasian Journal of Philosophy,* 4, pp. 343–77, 1983.

On the Plurality of Worlds. Oxford: Blackwell, 1986.

Parts of Classes. Oxford: Blackwell, 1991.

Linsky, Leonard. *Oblique Contexts*. Chicago: University of Chicago Press, 1983.

Loemker, L. E., *G. W. Leibniz: Philosophical Papers and Letters*. 2nd ed. Dordrecht: Reidel, 1976.

Long, Peter. "Possibility and Actuality". *Mind,* 70, pp. 187–200, 1961.

Longhurst, R. S. *Geometrical and Physical Optics*. London: Longmans, 1957.

Loux, Michael J. *Substance and Attribute*. Dordrecht: Reidel, 1978.

Lowe, E. J. *Kinds of Being*. Oxford: Blackwell, 1989.

"What Is a Criterion of Identity?" *The Philosophical Quarterly,* 39, pp. 1–21, 1989.

Lucas, J. R. *Space, Time and Causality*. Oxford: Oxford University Press, 1984.

Lycan, William. "The Trouble with Possible Worlds", in *The Possible and the Actual,* Michael J. Loux (ed.). Ithaca N.Y.: Cornell University Press, 1979.

Lycan, William, and Shapiro, Stewart. "Actuality and Essence". *Midwest Studies in Philosophy,* XI (1986), pp. 343–77.

McGinn, Colin. *The Character of Mind*. Oxford: Oxford Unversity Press, 1982.

Mackie, J. L. *The Cement of the Universe*. Oxford: Oxford University Press, 1974.

McPherran, Mark L. "Plato's Particulars". *The Southern Journal of Philosophy,* 26, pp. 527–53, 1988.

Martin, Gottfried. *Leibniz: Logic and Metaphysics*. Manchester: Manchester University Press, 1964.

Martin J. L. *Basic Quantum Mechanics.* Oxford: Oxford University Press, 1981.

Mayr, Ernst. *Animal Species and Evolution.* Cambridge, Mass.: Harvard University Press, 1963.

Miller, Richard. "Dog Bites Man: A Defence of Modal Realism". *Australasian Journal of Philosophy,* 67, pp. 476–8, 1989.

Moore, G. E. "Are the Characteristics of Particular Things Universal or Particular?" (1923), in *Philosophical Papers.* London: George Allen & Unwin, 1959.

"External and Internal Relations", in *Philosophical Studies.* London: Routledge & Kegan Paul, 1922.

Some Main Problems of Philosophy. London: Routledge & Kegan Paul, 1953.

Moreland, James Porter. *Universals, Qualities and Quality-Instances: A Defence of Realism.* Lanham, Md: University Press of America, 1985.

Morris, Thomas V. *Understanding Identity Statements.* Aberdeen: Aberdeen University Press, 1984.

Nagel, Thomas. *The Structure of Scientific Theories.* London: Routledge & Kegan Paul, 1961.

Nerlich, Graham. *The Shape of Space.* Cambridge: Cambridge University Press, 1976.

Newman, Andrew. "The Causal Relation and Its Terms". *Mind,* 97, pp. 529–50, 1988.

"The Material Basis of Predication and Other Concepts". *Australasian Journal of Philosophy,* 66, pp. 331–47, 1988.

"A Metaphysical Introduction to a Relational Theory of Space". *The Philosophical Quarterly,* 39, pp. 200–20, 1989.

Newton, I. "On the Gravity and Equilibrium of Fluids" (between 1664 and 1668), in *Unpublished Scientific Papers of Isaac Newton,* A. R. Hall and M. Boas Hall (eds. and trans.). Cambridge: Cambridge University Press, 1962.

Newton-Smith, W. H. *The Rationality of Science.* London: Routledge & Kegan Paul, 1981.

Ockham, William. *Summa Logicae,* Part I. See *Ockham's Theory of Terms,* Michael J. Loux (trans.). Notre Dame: University of Notre Dame Press, 1974.

Owens, Joseph. *The Doctrine of Being in the Aristotelian Metaphysics.* Toronto: Pontifical Institute, 1951.

Peterson, Donald. *Wittgenstein's Early Philosophy.* Toronto: University of Toronto Press, 1990.

Plantinga, Alvin. *The Nature of Necessity.* Oxford: Oxford University Press, 1974.

Platts, Mark. *Ways of Meaning.* London: Routledge & Kegan Paul, 1979.

Prior, A. N. "Determinables, Determinates and Determinants". *Mind,* 58, pp. 1–20, 178–94, 1949.

Putnam, Hilary. "The Meaning of Meaning", in *Mind, Language and Reality, Philosophical Papers,* vol. 2. Cambridge: Cambridge University Press, 1975.

Quine, W. V. *From a Logical Point of View*. 2nd ed. Cambridge, Mass.: Harvard University Press, 1961.

Ontological Relativity. New York: Columbia University Press, 1969.

The Roots of Reference. La Salle, Ill.: Open Court, 1973.

The Ways of Paradox. New York: Random House, 1966.

Word and Object. Cambridge, Mass: MIT Press, 1960.

Reichenbach, H. *The Philosophy of Space and Time*. New York: Dover, 1957.

Richardson, R. C. "The 'Scandal' of Cartesian Interactionism". *Mind*, 91, pp. 20–37, 1982.

Robinson, Denis. "Re-identifying Matter". *The Philosophical Review*, 91, pp. 317–41, 1982.

Russell, Bertrand. *A Critical Exposition of the Philosophy of Leibniz*. London: George Allen & Unwin, 1900.

An Inquiry into Meaning and Truth. London: George Allen & Unwin, 1940.

"Knowledge by Acquaintance and Knowledge by Description". *Proceedings of the Aristotelian Society*, 1910–11. Reprinted in *Mysticism and Logic*. London: George Allen & Unwin, 1917.

"On the Notion of Cause". *Proceedings of the Aristotelian Society*, 1912–13. Reprinted in *Mysticism and Logic*.

"On the Relations of Universals and Particulars" (1911), in *Logic and Knowledge*, R. C. Marsh (ed.). London: George Allen & Unwin, 1956.

"The Philosophy of Logical Atomism" (1918), in *Logic and Knowledge*.

The Principles of Mathematics. London: George Allen & Unwin, 1903.

The Problems of Philosophy, Oxford: Oxford University Press, 1912.

Searle, John R., "Determinables and Determinates", in *The Encyclopedia of Philosophy*, Vol. 2, pp. 357–9, Paul Edwards (ed.). London: Macmillan, 1967.

"Determinables and the Notion of Resemblance". *The Aristotelian Society*, suppl. vol. 33, 1959.

Sharvy, Richard. "Aristotle on Mixtures". *The Journal of Philosophy*, 80, pp. 439–57, 1983.

Sheldon, Neil A. "One Wave or Three? A Problem for Realism". *The British Journal for the Philosophy of Science*, 36, pp. 431–6, 1985.

Shoemaker, Sydney. "Causality and Properties", in *Time and Cause*, Peter van Inwagen (ed.). Dordrecht: Reidel, 1980.

Simons, Peter. *Parts: A Study in Ontology*. Oxford: Oxford University Press, 1987.

Skagestad, P. *The Road of Inquiry*. New York: Columbia University Press, 1981.

Sober, Elliot. "Evolutionary Theory and the Ontological Significance of Properties". *Philosophical Studies*, 40, pp. 147–76, 1981.

Sparnaay, M. J. "Measurements of Attractive Forces Between Flat Plates". *Physica*, 24, pp. 751–64, 1958.

Stein, Howard. "Newtonian Space-time". *Texas Quarterly*, 10, pp. 174–200, 1967.

Stenius, Erik. "Sets". *Synthese*, 27, pp. 161–88, 1974.

Wittgenstein's Tractatus. Oxford: Oxford University Press, 1960.

Strawson, P. F. "Concepts and Properties or Predication and Copulation". *The Philosophical Quarterly*, 37, pp. 402–6, 1987.

Individuals. London: Methuen, 1959.

Suárez, Francisco. *Disputationes Metaphysicae*, Book V. See *Suarez on Individuation: Metaphysical Disputation V, Individual Unity and Its Principle*, Jorge J. E. Gracía (trans.). Milwaukee, Wis.: Marquette University Press, 1982.

Disputationes Metaphysicae, Book VI. See *Suarez: Disputation VI, On Formal and Universal Unity*, James F. Ross (trans.). Milwaukee, Wis.: Marquette University Press, 1964.

Swoyer, Chris. "The Metaphysics of Measurement", in *Measurement, Realism and Objectivity*, J. Forge (ed.). Dordrecht: Reidel, 1987.

Teichman, Roger. "Three Kinds of Realism about Universals". *The Philosophical Quarterly*, 39, pp. 143–65, 1989.

Tiles, J. E. *Things That Happen*. Aberdeen: Aberdeen University Press, 1980.

van Fraassen, Bas. *An Introduction to the Philosophy of Time and Space*. New York: Random House, 1970.

Watling, John. "Are Causes Events or Facts?" *Proceedings of the Aristotelian Society*, 1973–4.

Weinberg, Julius. *Abstraction, Relation, and Induction*. Madison and Milwaukee: University of Wisconsin Press, 1965.

Wiggins, David. *Identity and Spatio-Temporal Continuity*. Oxford: Blackwell, 1967.

Sameness and Substance. Oxford: Blackwell, 1980.

"The Sense and Reference of Predicates: A Running Repair to Frege's Doctrine and a Plea for the Copula". *The Philosophical Quarterly*, 34, pp. 311–28, 1984.

Wilder, Raymond L. *The Foundations of Mathematics*. New York: Wiley, 1965.

Wiley, E. O. *Phylogenetics*. New York: Wiley, 1981.

Wittgenstein, Ludwig. *Letters to Russell, Keynes and Moore*, G. H. von Wright (ed.). Oxford: Blackwell, 1974.

"Some Remarks on Logical Form", *The Aristotelian Society*, suppl. vol. 9, 1929.

Tractatus Logico-Philosophicus, D. F. Pears and B. F. McGuinness (trans.). London: Routledge & Kegan Paul, 1971.

Wright, Crispin. *Frege's Conception of Numbers as Objects*. Aberdeen: Aberdeen University Press, 1983.

"On the Coherence of Vague Predicates". *Synthese*, 30, pp. 325–65, 1975.

Index

abstract objects, 28, 39–40, 213–14
abstraction, 104n
accessibility, 48, 70
actuality establishes possibility, 46
aggregates, 220, 221, 226–7
Aitchison, I. J. R., 78n, 151n
Alexander, Peter, 144n
Alexandria, library at, 212
alien individuals, 54–7, 58n, 67, 69
Allaire, Edwin B., 62n, 65n
Anscombe, G. E. M., 60n, 62n, 160n,
  163n, 200
anti-Haecceitism, weak, 55
Aristotle, 99, 136n, 137n, 250n
Armstrong, D. M., 1, 10
  and aggregates, 220, 221n
  and alien individuals, 54–5, 58n, 69
  and colours, 80n
  and conjunctive properties, 85–6
  and determinables, 100n, 116n, 119,
    120n
  and formal distinction, 131–4
  and identity of indiscernibles, 254–6
  and individuation, 251
  and instantiation requirement, 43–5,
    48
  and laws of nature, 149, 196, 199
  and meaning, 41
  and nominalism, 148
  and numbers, 216n
  and particularism, 4
  and Platonism, 71–2
  and proportion relations, 139
  and sets, 168n, 217
  and singularist causality, 163
  and structural universals, 87n
  and temporal parts, 249n
atomic properties, 86
atomic sentences, 15, 53, 60, 62, 66

atomism
  logical, 36, 62
  metaphysical, 86–7, 131
attributes
  basic, 7, 8, 28–35, 74, 82–4, 98, 131,
    136, 149, 171, 184, 189–97, 207,
    228, 248, 252
  conjunctions of, 74, 80–7, 93
  determinate, 29–32, 64–5, 75–6, 81–
    3, 93, 100–2
  hierarchies of, 81, see also universals,
    hierarchies of
  higher-level, 80–1, 100, 110–15,
    121–3, 127–32
  shape, 129–31, 194, 237
Ayer, A. J., 11n
Ayers, Michael, 165, 232n

B-series, 44
Bealer, George, 130n, 211, 220, 225,
  227n
Bedau, Mark, 162n
Bell, David, 42n, 95n
Bell, J. S. 76n
Benacerraf, P., 31, 83n
Bennett, Jonathan, 188, 236n
Bigelow, John, 39–40, 87n, 124–7,
  139, 170n, 214–15
Black, Max
  and ontological determinacy, 79
  and sets, 208–11, 215
  and Tractatus, 35–6, 60, 62n, 65
Bohm, David, 76n, 183
Boolos, George, 220n
Born, Max, 179, 182
Bradley, F. H., 19, 38, 109n, 187
Brillouin, L., 151n
bundle theory of particulars, 38, 55,
  239, 243–56

Burge, Tyler, 220n, 227n
Butler, Ronald J., 131n

Campbell, Keith, 5n
and causality, 239–42
and determinables, 108
and parts of tropes, 147n
and relations, 137, 140–2
and structural universals, 87, 88n, 89n, 93
Carruthers, Peter, 62n
Cartwright, Helen, 218n
Cartwright, Nancy, 151–4, 207
Cartwright, Richard, 231n
Casimir effect, 78, 151
Casullo, Albert, 85n, 86n, 243–5, 247, 250
categories, 64–5, 67
causal chains, 179, 185
casual cords, 181
casual powers, 86, 154, 168, 189–94, 207
causal relations, 83, 147–9, 183–4, 195, 207, 239–43
as energy flow, 150, 157–9, 179, 198
between events, 176, 179–81, 183–9, 191–2, 249n
as grounded relations, 118, 127
in laws of nature, 197–8, 200
between physical objects, 226, 231–6
between tropes, 241–3
types of, 149–64
see also forces, as causal relations
causal statements, 185–8, 203n
cause precedes effect, 195
Chappell, V. C., 218n
Chisholm, Roderick M., 84n, 230n
classes, see sets
collisions, 173–4
colours, 80n, 102–5, 107–16, 118–20
chromatic, 103–4, 110–16, 118, 134
and hierarchies of colour attributes, 103–6, 110–16
and higher-level colour attributes, 103–6, 110–16
perception of, 79–80
spectral chromatic, 110–12, 115–16
concept and object, 12–15, 18–20, 28–9, 35n, 36–7, 62
"concept horse", 22
concepts, 134–5, 213–14
formal, 2
conceptualism, 165

conditionals, 199–207
conjunctions
of attributes, 74, 80–87, 93
of determinables, 94
of states of affairs, 217
of universals, 88, 92, 94, 101, 192, 215
conjunctive properties, 84–7
conjunctive universals, 42n, 50
connnected parcels, 222–4, 252
context principle, 19–20, 129
contiguity, 178–83
Coplestone, F., 131n
copula, 25
correspondence principle, 77, 238n
counterfactual conditionals, 199–207
Creary, Lewis, G., 152–4
criterion of identity, 7, 8, 28–35, 228, 248n, 252
for basic attributes, 83
for bundles of properties, 244
for bundles of universals, 255
for complexes of co-instantiated properties, 250, 252, 254
for connected parcels, 222
for enduring particulars, 247
for events, 169, 173
for momentary particulars, 247
for numbers, 83
for parcels of matter, 219, 221–2, 224
for physical objects, 234
for sets, 167, 208, 213
for spatial collections, 209–11
for time slices, 247–8
for unified particulars, 249

Davidson, Donald, 168–9, 175, 186, 234
definite descriptions, 20, 106–7, 112, 118–19, 124, 127
determinables, 75, 94, 100–2, 108, 123, 128, 140
absolute, 64–5, 123
second-level theory of, 100–2, 109, 116, 124, 127–8
second-order theory of, 100–2, 118–21, 124
see also determinates and determinables
determinacy, ontological, 74–80, 121
determinate exclusion principle, 65, 102, 128

266

determinates and determinables
  entailment patterns for, 102, 128
  problem of, 100–2
  similarities and differences for, 102,
    116–21, 124–5, 128
differentiae, 35, 101–4, 116, 128, 130–1
Dirac, P. A. M., 183
distinction
  formal, 114, 131–2, 227
  real, 30, 131
  of reason, 130
Donagan, Alan, 2, 6n
Dummett, Michael, 13, 165n

Earman, John, 124n, 200n, 202
Ellis, Brian, 154
energy, 156–61, 164, 184, 194, 200,
    232–4
  in particularism, 240–1
Escher staircase, 47, 49, 57, 70
essence
  individual, 54, 132, 215n
  sortal, 68n
Euclid, 52
events, 7–8, 168–80, 185–9, 203, 241
  bare, 7, 177–8
  and causal relations, 176, 179–81,
    183–9, 191–2, 249n
  complex, 174
  and energy, 157, 164, 184
  interval, 171–2, 174, 178, 180, 246
  maximal, 172
  point, 171, 178
  reference to, 175
  separated, 173
  simple, 171–2
extension, 23, 95–6, 101, 113, 213–14
external properties, 51, 64

facts, 59–62, 170–1
Fair, David, 157–8, 194n, 195
Feyerabend, Paul, 77n, 238n
Field, Hartry, 124n
fields, 154–5, 182, 218, 223
Fine, Arthur, 124n
flocks, 209–10
forces
  as causal relations, 150–6, 185–9,
    195–7, 200, 228–33
  components, 151–4
  measurement of, 78
  and momentum flow, 158
  and particularism, 242

and supervenience, 238
form, logical, *see* logical form
formal concepts, 2
Forms, 4, 10, 17–18, 23, 71–2
Forrest, Peter, 69n
foundationism, *see* relations, founda-
    tionism about
fragment 1, 14–15, 36
fragment 2, 15–22, 36
Franklin, James, 47
free-will, 162
Frege, Gottlob, 33, 40, 60n
  and aggregates, 221
  and concept–object distinction, 12,
    18–20
  and definitions, 1, 43, 52
  and Fregean Platonism, 13, 18, 20,
    37
  and functions, 105–6
  and sets, 213–14, 215n
  and subordination, 110n, 113n
  and subsistence, 16, 19
  and third realm, 19, 20
functions, 18–19, 40, 105–12, 127

gas, 226–7, 230, 233–4
Geach, Peter, 3n, 75, 79, 103–9, 134–5,
    220n
genetic homoeostasis, 97
genetic inertia, 97
group theory, 40

haecceitism, 54
Hamlyn, D. W., 12, 37–9, 170, 172n
Hardin, C. L., 66n, 80n, 103n, 116n
Hart, H. L. A., 162n
Hart, W. D., 47, 157n
Heller, Mark, 229
Hertz, H., 156n
hidden variables, 76n, 183
Hilbert, David, 43, 49, 52
Hirsch, Eli, 224–5
Hume, David, 80, 130–1, 143, 148,
    179

identity
  of indiscernibles, 251–6
  qualitative, 9, 10
identity conditions, *see* criterion of
    identity
identity sentences for universals, 35n
indeterministic machines, 204–5
indistinguishability, 219n

267

individuation, 28, 145, 180, 203, 244, 250–5
inertia, 122–3
inertial frames, 174, 194
information trigger, 160–1
inherence, 17, 92, 109, 253–5
instantiation requirement, 43–50
internal properties, 36, 43, 51, 54, 59, 63–8, 140n
  categorial, 64–6
  logical, 64–7
internal relations, 35n, 127–8, 145n, 199, 248
  order relations as, 117–18, 140, 194
  and subordination, 114
inus condition, 203n
"is" of constitution, 218
Ishiguro, Hidé, 62n
island universes, 70

Jackson, Frank, 114n
Jammer, Max, 76n
Johnson, W. E., 100n

Kant, Immanuel, 156n, 159n
Kim, Jaegwon, 173n, 207, 235–6
kinds, 93–9
Klein bottle, 47, 57
Koyré, Alexandre, 77n
Kripke, Saul, 203, 204

laws
  of causal action, 153
  of causal influence, 153
  of motion, 151–3, 181
  of nature, 149, 194–200, 241, 243
Leibniz, Gottfried, 62, 82, 180–1
  and individuation, 253n, 254
  and order relations, 137–8, 141
Lemmon, E. J., 66n
Lewis, David, 50–2, 70, 87n, 90, 200, 216–17
library at Alexandria, 212
Linsky, Leonard, 35
Locke, John, 8n, 218n, 253n
logical atomism, 36, 62
logical form, 13–14, 62, 64–5, 107, 111, 185–8
logical grammar, 79
Long, Peter, 46
Longhurst, R. S., 230n
Loux, Michael J., 4n
Lowe, E. J.

and criteria of identity, 30, 33–4, 169, 248n, 249–51
and kinds, 96
and mereology, 221n
Lucas, J. R., 181–2
Lycan, William, 69n, 70n, 72

McGinn, Colin, 162n
Mackie, J. L., 200–6
McPherran, Mark, L., 4n, 10n, 17n
McTaggart, J. M. E., 44, 75
Martin, Gottfried, 136–8
Martin, J. L., 170n
mass, 81, 117–18, 121–7, 197–9, 227n, 236–7
mass terms, 27n
material objects, 218–19, 224, 227–9, 234, 236–8
material points, 180, 221
matter
  atomic, 219, 221–2, 225–6, 252
  classical, 77, 78
  continuously divisible, 219, 221–3, 225–6, 236–8, 252
  parcels of, see parcels of matter
Mayr, Ernst, 97
meaning, 41
mechanical trigger, 158–60
mental capacity, 104n, 134
mereology, 88, 133, 216–17, 221, 225n, 226
metaphysical atomism, 86–7, 131
Miller, Richard, 70n
mixtures, 222–3
modal primitives, 70, 72
Moore, G. E., 1, 2, 5n, 140n, 141, 143–5
Morris, Thomas V., 10
multiple occurrence, 9–11, 21, 41, 51, 68, 73, 141

naive combinatorialism, 43, 53–9, 67
natural kind sortals, 97
natural kinds, 93–9
Newton, Issac, 145–6, 183, 232
Newton-Smith, W. H., 68n, 77n
Newtonian mechanics, 122, 151, 156n, 181–2, 193
  Hamiltonian formulation of, 182
  Lagrangian formulation of, 182
Newton's cradle, 179
Newton's laws of motion, 151–3, 181
nominalism, 3, 5, 9, 142, 148

resemblance, 5, 131, 143
numbers, 19, 20, 27, 32, 83, 216n
real, *see* real numbers

object and concept, *see* concept and
object
objects, *see* material objects; particulars, arbitrary; particulars, unified;
physical objects; scattered objects
Ockham, William of, 84, 109n, 136n,
137–8, 141, 162
Ockham's blade, 82–4
ontological determinacy, 74–80, 121
overdetermination, 202
Owens, Joseph, 99n

paradox of heap, 75n
parcels of matter, 7–8, 27, 32, 55–8,
68, 218–27
connected, 222–4, 252
Pargetter, Robert, 39–40, 87n, 124–7,
139, 170n
part–whole relation, 90–3, 133, 221,
226, 236–8
participation, 5, 17, 71
particularism, 4–5, 84, 109
and causality, 239–43
and relations, 137, 253n
and resemblance, 108, 119–20
and similarities and differences, 142
and structural universals, 89n, 92–3
particulars
arbitrary, 165–8, 173, 175, 211–16,
228, 233–4
bare, 96
enduring, 245–50
momentary, 245, 247, 249
notion of, 1, 5–11, 17
possible, 58, 61
structured unified, 233–4
topological unified, 233–4
unified, 39, 165–8, 189–92, 228,
232, 248, 249
see also bundle theory of particulars
perception, 120
of colours, 79–80
perceptual determinacy, 79, 103
persistence conditions, 219, 224–5,
228, 234, 250
Peterson, Donald, 60n, 64n
phase of wave function, 183, 193
physical objects, 27, 32, 226–36
Plantinga, Alvin, 70

Platonism (*see also* Forms), 2–5, 10, 13,
17–18, 20, 23, 37, 71–2
Platts, Mark, 177n, 188
plural reference, 208, 215–16
points, material, 180, 221
possibility
established by actuality, 46
nature of, 58–68
possible names, 56
possible worlds, 43, 48–50, 62, 69–72,
123
predicate calculus, 14–15, 36–7, 53–4,
111
predicates
higher-level, 112–13, 121
and property names, 22–5
see also reference, of a predicate
proper names, 13–21, 32, 39–40, 63,
106, 112, 129
property names and predicates, 22–5
Putnam, Hilary, 42, 77, 96n
Pythagoreanism, 71

qualitative identity, 9, 10
quantification, 24, 26–37, 115–16
quantities, 76, 117, 121–6, 128, 132–4,
139–40
quantum mechanics, 76–8, 156, 170,
219n, 238n
Quine, W. V., 26–35, 179, 199n

range properties, 94
Rayleigh criterion, 230n
real numbers, 29–31, 39, 117, 140, 146
realism, transcendent, 72
reference, 216
of predicate, 41, 50, 95–6, 213n
of proper name, 32
Reichenbach, H., 77n
relational structural properties, 132
relational structural universals, 133
relations
arrangement, 237–8
basic, 197, 248
determinable, 101, 103
determinate, 125
distance, 190, 193–4, 199
formal, 253n
foundationism about, 137–41, 146–7
grounded, 117–18, 127
order, 117–18, 138–41, 193, 194
proportion, 117, 122–6, 139–41,
193–4, 196, 198

269

real, 136–8
Russell and, 136n, 140–2
second-order, 139, 196
spatial, 138, 141, 143–7, 233, 237
ungrounded, 126
see also causal relations; internal relations
relativity, 77, 122, 182, 194, 213
resemblance, 5, 71, 80, 108, 118–20, 131, 137, 141–3
Richardson, R. C., 162n
Robinson, Denis, 224–5
Russell, Bertrand
and causality, 179–81, 185
and relations, 136n, 140–2
and syntactic priority thesis, 12
and universals, 2, 6, 11n, 42, 95

saturatedness, 16–20, 28, 63–4
scales
interval, 123n
ratio, 122
scattered objects, 133–4, 231
Schrödinger's equation, 93
Searle, John R., 64n, 65n, 100n
secondary qualities, 80
set membership, 120, 213–14
sets, 7–8, 27–33, 40, 166–8, 208–18, 220, 226–7
ordered, 167, 173
as universals, 214–15
shape, see attributes, shape; universals, shape
Sharvy, Richard, 222n
Sheldon, Neil A., 154, 223n
Shoemaker, Sydney, 83n
Simons, Peter, 215n, 221n, 225n
situations, 46n, 52–4, 57–9, 61–2, 67–8
possible, 54–6, 58, 61, 72
Sober, Elliot, 27n
sortals, 33–4, 54, 97, 249
space, absolutism, about, 144–6
space-time, 45
Sparnaay, M. J., 78n
spatial collections, 209–12, 227, 233–4
species–genus relation, 101, 124, 128
spectral chromatic colours, see colours, spectral chromatic
Spinoza, Benedict de, 136n
states of affairs, 53n, 59–62, 170–1, 183n, 217
Stenius, Erik, 60, 208n
Strawson, P. F., 7, 17, 25, 74, 177

Suárez, Francisco, 131n, 253n
subordination, 20, 65, 74, 100–2, 110–16, 120
subsistence, 16, 19, 20
substance, 84, 137
substratum, 225, 251
supervenience, 137, 141, 149, 188, 234–39
Swoyer, Chris, 3n
syntactic priority thesis, 12, 28, 62

tables, 229–31, 234
Teichman, Roger, 22n
temperature, 122–3
temporal parts, 245, 249n
thing of reason, 141
third realm, 18, 19, 20, 22, 39, 213
Thomas Aquinas, Saint, 82, 136, 159n, 250n, 254
Tiles, J. E., 169n, 171n
time slices, 27, 32, 246–8, 249n
tropes, see particularism

universals
arrangement, 91
basic, 32, 73–4, 81–4, 192–3, 248
bundles of, 255
conjunctions of, see conjunctions, of universals
conjunctive, 43n, 50
hierarchies of, 65, 73–4, 102, 110–13, 143
higher-level, 64, 67, 99
modal nature of, 51–2
mode of composition of, 87–92
non-existing vs. existing, 45
notion of, 1, 5–11, 17
Russell and, 2, 6, 11n, 42, 95
and second-order arrangement, 91
sets as, 214–15
shape, 101, 103, 119, 132
structural, 87–93, 101, 132
uninstantiated, 4, 6, 51
universes, island, 70
unsaturatedness, 16–20, 28, 62, 64

vacuum state, 78, 151
Van Cleve, James, 244–5, 249–50
variables
first-order, 32
hidden, 76n, 183
second-order, 32
vectors, 143–5, 147, 151

270

components of, 151–4
velocity, 152, 170, 193–4
   components of, 152
verificationism, 79

Watling, John, 168n
Weinberg, Julius, 137n
whole, *see* part–whole relation
Wiggins, David, 24–5, 97n, 165n,
   218n, 248n

Wilder, Raymond L., 139n
Wiley, E. O., 98n
Williams, D. C., 240
Wittgenstein, Ludwig, 22
   and internal properties, 43, 54, 140n
   and ontological determinacy, 75n
   and quantification, 35–7
   and states of affairs, 59–62
   and theory of possiblity, 59–67
Wright, Crispin, 12, 37, 69n, 75, 80n